The Periodical Essayists of the Eighteenth Century

With illustrative extracts
From the rarer periodicals

George S. Marr

Alpha Editions

This edition published in 2020

ISBN : 9789354043345

Design and Setting By
Alpha Editions
www.alphaedis.com
email - alphaedis@gmail.com

As per information held with us this book is in Public Domain. This book is a reproduction of an important historical work. Alpha Editions uses the best technology to reproduce historical work in the same manner it was first published to preserve its original nature. Any marks or number seen are left intentionally to preserve its true form.

THE
PERIODICAL ESSAYISTS
OF THE
EIGHTEENTH CENTURY

WITH ILLUSTRATIVE EXTRACTS
FROM THE RARER PERIODICALS

BY

GEORGE S. MARR

M.A. (Hons.), B.D., D.Litt. (Edin.)

LONDON
JAMES CLARKE & CO., LIMITED
13 AND 14 FLEET STREET, E.C.4

PREFACE

THE present work is an endeavour to give an approximately complete and detailed survey of the periodical essay of the eighteenth century and its writers. In the preparation of the work, the author has seen and examined over one hundred and fifty periodicals. Many of these are now exceedingly rare, and full use has been made of the valuable collections in the great libraries: The British Museum Library, London; the Bodleian Library, Oxford; the Advocates', the Signet, and the University Libraries, Edinburgh. In addition the author has been privileged to see a number of periodicals in private collections.

The question of arrangement presented difficulties. The simplest solution was to adopt as far as possible a chronological plan. The advantages of this scheme outweighed the disadvantage of a certain "catalogue-y" effect which was almost inevitable when so many periodicals were being passed under review. A number of illustrative extracts support the critical statements made.

Up to the present time no work has appeared devoted exclusively to this subject and limited to this period. The work of Nathan Drake, carried out over a century ago, is only a partial exception to this statement. Accordingly it is hoped that this endeavour to deal with the whole field of the periodical essay in the eighteenth century may be found to be a contribution, however small, to the elucidation of the subject under review.

1 ALBYN PLACE, QUEEN STREET,
EDINBURGH, *September* 1923.   G. S. M.

CONTENTS

CHAP.		PAGE
I.	ORIGINS	9
II.	THE TATLER AND SPECTATOR, AND OTHER PERIODICAL ESSAY WORK OF ADDISON AND STEELE	21
III.	THE PERIODICAL ESSAY BETWEEN THE GUARDIAN AND THE RAMBLER	64
IV.	DEVELOPMENTS IN JOURNALISM OF THE PERIOD, AND THE WORK OF HENRY FIELDING	83
V.	JOHNSON'S PERIODICAL ESSAY WORK	116
VI.	THE ADVENTURER, WORLD, CONNOISSEUR, AND OTHERS .	132
VII.	THE PERIODICAL ESSAY WORK OF GOLDSMITH . . .	172
VIII.	EDINBURGH PUBLICATIONS, INCLUDING THE MIRROR AND LOUNGER	192
IX.	THE OBSERVER AND LOOKER-ON AND OTHERS . . .	216
X.	THE PASSING OF THE EIGHTEENTH-CENTURY PERIODICAL ESSAY	245
INDEX:	CHRONOLOGICAL LIST OF PERIODICALS	256
	ALPHABETICAL LIST OF PERIODICALS	260

THE PERIODICAL ESSAYISTS OF THE EIGHTEENTH CENTURY

CHAPTER I

ORIGINS

THE eighteenth century has come into its own. Its literary production is now valued at its true worth, and that is far higher than, in the past, was commonly supposed. Even in verse we have only to think of one name, Robert Burns, to make us realise that the eighteenth century gave us *some* poetry at least of the very first class; but it was in the realm of prose-writing that the best work was accomplished. The achievements of the eighteenth century in at least two departments of prose were really great—essay-writing and the novel. It is with the former of these that we wish to deal, and more particularly with the periodical essay, which had its rise in the first decade of the century and continued to flourish till wellnigh its close.

With regard to the origin of the essay as a distinct *kind* in literature it is not easy to speak with certainty. Within the last fifty years questions regarding the *origins* of literature and of literary kinds have indeed been much discussed, but usually with negative results, for the most important of these forms are ultimately the expression, the artistic expression, of elements which are part and parcel of human nature itself. One of the most fruitful results of comparative criticism in recent years has been to show that as no civilisation nor epoch is absolutely unique or stands isolated from others, so the literary forms of a people, though they may show striking differences, indicate their relationship with the common stock of humanity. This is especially true of the essay. It is as wide as the poles asunder from such a comparatively fixed and definite type as the sonnet, where a purely literary impulse seems to find its own expression independently of extra-literary influence. The essay, on the other hand, is easily moulded according to circumstances. Think of any country you please, and it would be rash to assert that the literature of its people, after it has reached a certain stage of development, does not possess a form bearing some resemblance to that of the essay. In Greece, for example, we find a group of ardent disciples listening to Socrates as he discourses upon the eternal questions of life and death. One of his hearers thinks that such " gold dew-drops of speech " might well be conveyed to a wider public than the few who gather round the person of Socrates; and so, directly or indirectly, we get literary form put to the words of the oracle, and Plato's immortal dialogues come into being. Only a part of the wisdom of the philosopher will be preserved, but at least the endeavour is made. Coleridge, again, gathered round him at Highgate a great group of men, and the stimulus and inspiration of his conversation were immense, but much of his wisdom, thus communicated to a few, never reached the outside public. And Shelley could keep a group entranced around him till the hours of the night sped quickly past, and sunrise came unobserved, but little record of these fascinating talks have come down to us. There have been periods when almost a whole nation's *forte* was talking, and it was so at the beginning of the period we are to consider—the eighteenth century. Taine has sketched the conditions in France in *Les origines de la France Contemporaine*. In describing the *ancien régime* he emphasises what he calls *la vie du Salon*, when apparently man's chief end was to concoct witty sayings or discuss with *finesse* any subject from Plato downwards. But it was only through the essay that the general public got a glimpse of the brilliant coteries at London or Versailles. Where, as in France, exclusive attention was given to this drawing-room life, literary production was correspondingly scanty. One outlet, no doubt, was in letter-writing; and we find Swift, in his bulky *Journal to Stella*, doing practically nothing else but reproduce the conversation and small talk of each day. His letters are really essays—periodical essays—to one person. Thus the periodical essay was largely suggested by Defoe and modelled from the social conditions of Queen Anne times. It might easily occur to Addison that the audience who listened to his conversation could be greatly enlarged, and his influence correspondingly extended, if he put pen to paper, and gave on a single sheet (which could be scattered broadcast) the wise thoughts and humorous reflections which would otherwise be only communicated to a few. Such a project, working on the literary form as it existed at the time, may well have done something to form the periodical essay. That it *was* in a most intimate way connected with the somewhat artificial society of the time is seen by the constant reference to the beau and the coquette, and to all the little occurrences at the coffee-house or in my lady's chamber. Such being the case, the reflection it gives of this society's life and manners is simply invaluable. It was to these periodicals that Thackeray went when he wished to enter into the very breath and life of the time; and it is by perusing them and their later fellows that the whole panorama of these phases of eighteenth-century town life is brought before our eyes. The life of the street, the coffee-house, and the theatre are all there, and the countless moral observations to which these things give rise; and the little periodical essay answered the needs of that somewhat artificial society so well; it was discussed in the drawing-rooms and in the coffee-houses with such a feeling of satisfaction for its daily contribution to the little round of their life, that the form remained unquestioned for wellnigh a century. There is nothing to be compared to it in any other branch of our literature, not even in the vogue of the sonnet in the Elizabethan age. We will find, in our detailed examination of the minor periodicals of the century, that literally scores of them look back to Addison and Steele as their standard of perfection, and maintain, to the last minutiæ, the arrangements and devices of the *Tatler* and *Spectator*. It was not till the last decade or so of the eighteenth century, when new forces were being brought to bear on society and stirring it to its depths, that men were no longer satisfied with the little moral essay, the little didactic tale, the evergreen Eastern allegory, and the imaginary "characters" drawn for their improvement, but called for a stronger and more varied literary diet. And then that particular form of the essay became extinct.

The essay periodical as a *kind* lived and died therefore in the eighteenth century. But it is necessary for us to consider some earlier developments; the tree, though visible to all, has its roots far underground. It was Bacon who was the first in England to give the essay its place and name. But Bacon's essays were not of a *periodical* nature; and he was no doubt under the influence of Montaigne, whose popularity in translation was great. The latter justifies our statement regarding the relationship between writing and conversation when he says in the preface to his *Essays*, "In contriving the same, I have proposed unto myselfe no other than a familiar and private end—gentle Reader, myselfe am the groundworke of my booke" (Florio's translation). He is giving us in print what he might have told us in conversation.

The Elizabethan and Jacobean Pamphleteers supply a faint adumbration of "periodicity." Their work came out at irregular intervals as controversy waxed and waned, and Greene, Dekker, and Nash give us not only controversy, but papers on the morals and manners of the times and general disquisitions which bear a distinct resemblance to one section, at least, of the papers of Addison and Steele. The actual title *Essays*, introduced by Bacon, was not at first popular. There were many "character" writers (some two hundred collections in the seventeenth century have been catalogued): Jonson calls his notes *Timber* or *Discoveries*: Earle gives to his interesting paragraphs (they are little more) a generic title *Microcosmographie*: Selden has his *Table Talk*: Howell his *Familiar Letters*: and Owen Felltham his *Resolves*. It was with Cowley that the name was revived in the title-page of his most readable collection. None of these mentioned can be termed periodical essayists, though some of them are excellent in their kind. The essays of all these writers did not appear first in periodicals, but each batch was published at one time in collected form. There was little connection in these days between journalism and literature. The news-letters of the period gave intelligence regarding current events and news abroad, but nothing in the nature of literary articles. Once the connection was established it is easy to recognise the stimulus given to essay production. For there is no direct incentive to write short essays and lay them past till they "make a book." Exceptional men, as the ever-youthful and buoyant Pepys, will continue writing in this way, finding sufficient pleasure in the secret diary; the majority will soon tire of a literary labour which has no immediate outlet. The periodical was a most convenient vehicle for communicating essays to the outer world; and the regular flow of such work coincides with the appearance of the weekly or bi-weekly paper. The first of such papers to appear was the *Mercurius Librarius, or A Faithful Account of all Books and Pamphlets* in 1680, but this was little more than a catalogue of literary production. It is to Sir Roger L'Estrange that the credit is due for the first step to something more than a catalogue. In the following year (1681) he published the *Observator in Dialogue, Question and Answer*. The actual dialogue is carried on in very short questions and answers. There is no extended literary treatment of a subject, various though the subjects are. The *Observator* is only the embryo of the Queen Anne periodical. An advance was made by Tom Brown in his *Amusements: Serious and Comical*. Brown had undoubted literary talent, and this guided him to adopt the right tone for such essays. An essay (as the name suggests) has as its endeavour merely an "attempt" at a subject; extended or exhaustive treatment is not desiderated, and in these papers of Brown's serious subjects are not treated heavily, but are interspersed with many lighter sallies. Take his *Essay on London*; it is the first in a vein fruitful of good result, culminating in Goldsmith's *Citizen of the World*. "Imagine, then," he says, "what an Indian would think of such a motley herd of people, and what a diverting amusement it would be to him, to examine with a traveller's eye all the remarkable things of this mighty city." This imaginary visitor from the East is taken to the tavern, to the meeting-house, and elsewhere, the idea being developed further in later papers. But Tom Brown has not the credit of establishing the essay periodical. With all his talent, he lacked the necessary sober perseverance for such an undertaking. It required a more regular production to give the start to the eighteenth-century periodical, and this was supplied by the *Athenian Gazette*, afterwards altered to the *Athenian Mercury*, the title being suggested by St Paul's statement regarding the Athenians, who delighted " to hear or to tell some new thing." Such was to be the purpose of this paper. It was begun on Tuesday, 17th March 1691, by John Dunton (popularly known as the father of journalism), aided by Wesley (father of the great evangelical preacher) and Sault. But it was the first-named of the three who wrote practically the whole paper. The usual columns of news were supplemented by answers to correspondents. It is obvious that many of the questions are simply pegs upon which to hang his views, and Dunton writes upon almost every conceivable subject which could interest the people. The popularity of the *Athenian Mercury* was great; and the paper ran for six years. Without doubt it gave hints to Steele and Addison when they inaugurated their work in the reign of Anne. These *Answers to Correspondents* range from a few lines to quite a long essay, and cover many subjects: Love, and Natural History, Superstitions, Folklore, and Religion. Dunton had been asked, for example, the old question, What is love ? And his answer is: " 'Tis very much like light,—a thing that everybody knows and yet none can tell what to make of it. 'Tis not money, fortune, jointure, raving, stabbing, hanging, romancing, flouncing, swearing, ramping, desiring, fighting, dying—though all these have been, are, and still will be mistaken and miscalled for it. What shall we say of it ? 'Tis a pretty little soft thing that plays about the heart; and those who have it will know it well enough by this description. 'Tis extremely like a sigh, and could we find a painter could draw one, you'd easily mistake it for the other. 'Tis all over eyes, so far is it from being blind, as some old dotards have described it, who certainly were blind themselves. It has a mouth, too, and a pair of pretty hands, but yet the hands speak, and you may feel at a distance every word that comes out of the mouth gently stealing through your very soul. But we dare not make any further inquiries, lest we should raise a spirit too powerful for all our art to lay again." Such a passage is a great advance on anything that had gone before. It approaches a style which the essay periodical demands—a style light, simple, and with more than a touch of humour. Dunton has been often discredited as little better than a madman because of his *Life and Errors*, which he afterwards wrote. We cannot wholly subscribe to such a view. However much his mind may have become affected in later years (influenced, it is said, by a disastrous second marriage), we see Dunton here at his best.

There is another periodical which comes, in time, before the *Tatler* and is deserving of our close examination. We refer to the *Review*, published by a relation of Dunton's, but one who has a much higher position than the worthy bookseller on the roll of fame. Daniel Defoe was Dunton's brother-in-law, but few know him from this relationship; it is as the author of *Robinson Crusoe* that he is famous the wide world over. Defoe was a most remarkable man and had a most remarkable career, but no achievement of his (outside his great masterpiece in fiction) is more noteworthy than his periodical production, the *Review*. Its full title is: *A Review of the Affairs of France and of all Europe as influenced by that nation, being historical observations on the publick transactions of the world, purged from the errors and partiality of news-writers and petty statesmen of all sides, with an entertaining part in every sheet, being advice from the Scandal Club, to the curious enquirers; in answer to letters sent for that purpose.* Defoe commenced this paper in 1704 and continued it with certain interruptions (he was in prison part of the time) till the year 1713, issuing it at first weekly, then bi-weekly, and finally three times a week. It would be almost incredible, if we did not remember Defoe's remarkable fecundity (the list of his works occupies several columns in the British Museum catalogue), to believe that he wrote it all himself, and yet such seems to have been the case. It means that in less than ten years he wrote about five thousand pages of material covering almost every conceivable subject. But it is the *Advice from the Scandal Club* which specially calls for attention. There is little doubt that he framed this latter part of the *Review* to attract a more general audience, some of whom might not find the earlier part of the paper so entertaining. The *Scandal Club* usually takes up about half of each issue, and so popular did it become that, in December 1704 and January 1705, he published an additional sheet called *A Supplementary Journal to the Advice from the Scandal Club*. This was a substantial issue for these days, the December part containing twenty-two pages of material. Later on Defoe separated the *Scandal Club* from the *Review* altogether, and issued it as the *Little Review, or an Inquisition of Scandal; consisting in answers to questions and doubts, remarks, observations, and reflections*. The Club itself was started as early as the second number of the *Review*, and Defoe, with his incorrigible and consistent method of pretence, solemnly asserts that such a Club exists in Paris, and that he merely translates the transactions of the *Mercure Scandale* of that city. The title must not be permitted to mislead us. Defoe is not endeavouring to relate "scandalous" stories in the modern acceptation of the term, for he is strictly, as always, on the side of morality. All vices and little indiscretions come under review and are reproved. The Club idea gave him the opportunity of introducing a diversity of experience which otherwise it might reasonably be thought no single man could be supposed to have realised for himself. The Club idea satisfies that sense of verisimilitude to which as the first of our "realists" he thought necessary to pay heed, and in this Addison and Steele agreed with him. Taking in all probability the "question and answer" idea from his brother-in-law, he certainly handed on the Club idea to Steele; and it was developed to perfection in the hands of Addison himself. It is only as we read Defoe's series of talks in these *Scandal Club* columns that we come to realise the close connection which the opening papers of the *Tatler* bear to them. Defoe's *Scandal Club* papers are the true "usher in" of the Queen Anne essay periodical. The idea may be realised in a crude form, but it is there. Aristotle gets the credit of being the first to say that " a play should have a beginning, a middle, and an end"; so to Defoe belongs great praise for the plan of his *Scandal Club*. These *Scandal Club* papers have a wonderful variety. A letter, for example, is sent by a tradesman, who finds he has to work for a few hours on the Sunday morning. He has to do it, or he will lose his business, and yet the words of the fourth commandment have been troubling his conscience. Defoe's reply is a little moral essay, with the addition of delicate, humorous touches. He questions the exact literalness of some of the commands of the Bible, but adds, " In your case, you own it is against your conscience, and that alone, above all other arguments, is directly against you." In another paper he presents a feature which became common in later periodicals, a mock trial, going into its minutest details. Defoe distinguishes himself by his downright common sense. Some one had asked him whether there was a material fire in hell; and his answer is, " It is as hard to bear the reflections of an accusing conscience as flames ; ask these poor wretches who carry about them a Hell on earth, whether they would not willingly exchange their bitter thoughts for burnings, to the greatest height you can raise the notion." Again, some of Addison's and Steele's *Vision* devices have been forestalled by Defoe in these papers. And his style is well-suited to this way of writing. It is simple and straightforward, as his novels *Moll Flanders* and *Roxana* and *Robinson Crusoe* afterwards showed. And Defoe was gifted with a faculty for vivid and realistic presentation, proved supremely in his *True Relation of the Apparition of one Mrs Veal*. This was just the style to suit the periodical essay. We give as an example of the *Advice from the Scandal Club*, the issue for 8th August 1704 (the first year of the issue of the *Review*).

" There was a young lady brought before the Society this week, in a very strange condition, the mob took her up for a mad-woman, but it soon appeared she was not a lunatick ; she was so thin she looked like a spectre, that some people were afraid she was a ghost ; by her mien she appeared well-bred, and something of quality was to be discerned by her very outside ; she had very good clothes on, but all out of fashion, and she would by no means let her face be seen ; she had been taken up, sitting all alone upon a bench by *Rosamund's* pond, in the park, sighing as if she would break her heart, and people fancied she waited an opportunity to drown herself.

"The Club were strangely put to it what to do with her, they began to be rough to her, but the handsomeness of her behaviour told them presently she did not deserve it, so they intreated her to let them see her face. The whole Society were amazed when they saw her, the extraordinary sweetness and majesty of her countenance astonished them ; and not expecting to find such a face, under such a dress, they asked her if she would please to give any account of herself. She spoke low, but freely enough, and told them she would. First she told them she was born not far off from ———, that her father took a disgust at her, because she affronted a drunken gentleman who offered her some incivilities, and keeping an ill woman in the house, he turned her out of doors.

"She came up to London, and would have waited upon a certain Duchess, but as soon as she hear'd her name, her Grace told her she was not fit for her service ; she applied herself after that to abundance of ladies of quality, but none would entertain her ; so she took lodgings in the city and lived by herself.

"As soon as she appeared abroad a little, she wondered what was the matter, none of the city ladies would keep her company ; she went to the exchange, none of the shopkeepers would say, 'What d'ye lack madam' ; if she went to a church, or meeting-house, nobody would open a pew to her, or ask her to sit down.

"She met with affronts at the corner of every street, but especially from those of her own sex ; at last she came to the park, and then she found it was the same thing, the ladies kept all on the other side of the mall, and would not be seen so much as near her. Some few incivilities she met with in the park from the men, which disordered her not a little. My L—— M—— of —— assaulted her, but as soon as he knew her, he begged her pardon, and told her, he never meddled with any of her name, and so left her.

"And thus she went on, till tired and disconsolate, she sat down to rest herself on the bench, where she was taken, by the pond.

"This discourse put the Society upon longing to know who she was. She told them she was of an ancient family, in the North, but all her relations were extinct, now she was the last of her house, and afraid she should be the last in the nation, and her name was *modesty*. The Society immediately rose up at the mention of her name, and all of them paid her the respect due to her quality, offered to send a guard with her to her lodgings, and told her, they were sorry her ladyship was grown so much *out of fashion*."

This paper follows so closely what were to become the popular features of the *Tatler* essays, and the style is so appropriate to the subject, there are so few words wasted, and the effect is produced in such a simple and direct fashion that it may be questioned very much if the majority of people would detect the difference between it and a *Tatler* issue, if they read it as one of the numbers of the *Tatler*. Multiply this paper by many others similar to it in subject and style, and it will be realised that in any estimate of the eighteenth-century periodicals which professes to be strictly historical in its judgment, we must give a high place to these papers of *Advice from the Scandal Club* with their amazing and almost inexhaustible fertility, written as they are in a style so simple, direct, and suitable to work of that kind.

Two or three minor periodicals deserve passing notice because of the fact that they appeared before the year of issue of the *Tatler*, and so have interest as precursors. The *Gentleman's Journal, or the Monthly Miscellany by way of a Letter* was published in 1692, and ran for nearly a year. This early magazine has for its staple interest general news, but, in addition, stories and allegories, poetry, and even music appear. It had a more noteworthy successor in the *Monthly Miscellany by several hands*, which, appearing in 1707, continued till the year the *Tatler* was begun. Essays on many subjects are given, the first being on Divinity. The paper opens in the vein of the eighteenth-century "moderates": "We met at Clito's, who had invited us to a Platonic Supper, a moderate and sound entertainment of diet and discourse. For such was the ancient way of feasting, when the body and the mind were equally treated with a suitable satisfaction." The actual treatment of the subject is rather heavy, but the essay is interesting because it points forward to Addison's *Saturday* papers on Religion in the *Spectator*. As a whole the periodical traverses a field extra-literary in character. When we are given in the issue for June 1708 an account of several libraries in and about London, "for the satisfaction of the curious, both natives and foreigners," we may be reading about literature but are far from the literary essay itself.

The British Apollo (1708) is another periodical published before the *Tatler*, but possessing little more than historical interest. Its full title, *The British Apollo, or Curious Amusements for the Ingenious, by a Society of Gentlemen*, is reminiscent of the productions of Tom Brown and Dunton the bookseller. An examination of the contents corroborates this impression. The questions asked are frequently of a most curious nature, and since the replies extend to a column or a column and a half they suggest the longer miscellaneous periodical essay which was to come. One issue, which contained the *Oracle's* opinion on Charity Schools, created so much interest that the writer enlarged it a little and published it as a separate paper of the length of a *Tatler* or *Spectator* number. But this was only an individual instance, and does not represent the average issue. The *Tatler* itself, on its appearance soon after, quickly outstripped such a collection of misleading and often somewhat silly paragraphs of information. The human appeal and fine literary quality of the *Tatler* were not slow to become recognised. As Thackeray in his *Lectures on the English Humourists* justly remarks, "What a change it must have been—how *Apollo's* oracles must have been struck dumb, when the *Tatler* appeared, and scholars, gentlemen, men of the world, men of genius, began to speak!"

CHAPTER II

THE *TATLER* AND *SPECTATOR*—AND OTHER PERIODICAL ESSAY WORK OF ADDISON AND STEELE

THE *Tatler* and *Spectator* therefore were not sudden growths, they had roots in the seventeenth century. But this does not detract in the slightest from the actual achievements of Steele and Addison, because the earlier attempts were never developed nor specialised. The idea was there, but it had not been consistently carried into practice. The *Tatler* was the first real essay periodical, the first of a new literary kind, the earlier papers had been almost completely conveyers of "news," and only in a minor degree literary productions. The majority of our great writers from Shakespeare downwards have taken ideas from earlier writers—it is in the manner in which they have developed these ideas that their distinction comes. We do not think it is profitable to spend much time over the question whether Addison or Steele is the greater in the realm of the essay periodical. Recently one or two attempts have been made to exalt the latter. The highways and most of the byways of literature have been trodden by so many critics that there is a temptation on the part of the latest traveller to say something new by reversing accepted judgments. Certainly personal tastes are worth noting; Dr Johnson, Hazlitt, and Leigh Hunt all preferred the work of Steele to the work of Addison. Leigh Hunt, for example, said frankly, "I prefer open-hearted Steele with all his faults to Addison with all his essays"; but the accepted judgment must still stand that Addison's work, as it is greater in quantity, possesses also a truer balance and a better appreciation of the true *ethos* of the periodical essay. Steele, however, has, and must always continue to hold, the distinction of being before Addison in point of time. The greater

THE EIGHTEENTH-CENTURY ESSAYISTS

originality is his, the credit of inaugurating an essay kind which was to maintain its place for wellnigh a hundred years.

It was on Tuesday, 12th April 1709, that Steele published the first number of the *Tatler*, giving (in quite modern style) the impression away gratis. It is quite easy to trace in the early issues the descent from the then common news-sheet; for the section under the *St James Coffee-house* gives foreign and domestic intelligence. This latter department soon dropped into a very subordinate place, and we have in the *Tatler* the first paper to devote itself almost entirely to the social life of the time, with the special objects in view to reform and to instruct, to amuse and to ridicule. Defoe's *Review* had been nine-tenths political, but the very title (the *Tatler*) shows Steele's bent; there is to be something particularly devoted to the entertainment of the fair sex, and the paper is named in their honour. The *Tatler* was issued periodically three times a week until the appearance of the 271st number on 2nd January 1711, and no other paper, with the exception of the *Spectator* itself, which followed immediately, can vie with it for varied interest. Steele was assisted by his "powerful auxiliary" Addison, by Swift, Congreve, Hughes, Philips, and Harrison, but he cannot be denied the direct credit of its inception. In the paper Steele sets up a kind of *eidolon* in the person of *Isaac Bickerstaff*, a benevolent old bachelor, borrowing the title from Swift, whose famous counter-almanac against poor Partridge had been so successful and had created so much fun. The institution of sending "news" from the various coffee-houses—*Wills'*, the *Grecian* and *St James'*, and from *White's Chocolate House*—gave the opportunity of dealing with subjects of a very varied nature in the same issue. Steele soon supplemented his editorial "staff" with the introduction of the charming *Jenny*, a half-sister of *Isaac Bickerstaff*. But the earlier dozen or so papers are rather short, are made up of two or three sections, and can scarcely be called *individual*. Gradually, however, after the eleventh number, when Addison first appeared, the single issue contained only two small papers, and later still only one. This gave scope for more extended literary treatment, and the lively papers this produced give a representative picture of the varied life of the time. Steele's *forte* is certainly the treatment of questions relating to the fair sex, and naturally a large number of the papers contain discussions covering almost every possible domestic topic, marriages and match-making and etiquette. Various characters about town are also depicted in the coquette, the beau and the profligate, the scholar and the politician. Combined with all this there was another interest—an extraneous one. A number of the characters depicted were supposed to be represented in real life, and part of the interest was to find out who the personage represented actually was in Society. For example, in the paper No. 52, *Delamira resigns her Fan*, it is probable that the Hon. Lord Archibald Hamilton of Motherwell was the *Archibald* referred to, and *Delamira* the youngest daughter of James, Earl of Abercorn. Gradually, however, this wholly extraneous interest disappeared. An example of the light *persiflage* which Steele indulged in when he dealt with the weaknesses and little foibles of " the sex " may be exemplified by giving a passage from the sixtieth number of the *Tatler*, where he argues that " women are to be gained by nonsense."

"There is not anything in nature so extravagant, but that you will find one man or other that shall practise or maintain it; otherwise *Harry Spondee* could not have made so long an harangue as he did here this evening, concerning the force and efficacy of well-applied nonsense. Among ladies, he positively averred, it was the most prevailing part of eloquence: and had so little complaisance as to say, ' a woman is never taken by her reason, but always by her passion.' He proceeded to assert, ' the way to move that, was only to astonish her. I know,' continued he, ' a very late instance of this ; for being by accident in the room next to *Strephon*, I could not help overhearing him, as he made love to a certain great lady's woman. The true method in your application to one of this second rank of understanding, is not to elevate and surprise, but rather to elevate and amaze. *Strephon* is a perfect master in this kind of persuasion : his way is to run over with a soft air a multitude of words, without meaning or connexion ; but such as do each of them apart give a pleasing idea, though they have nothing to do with each other as he assembles them. After the common phrases of salutation, and making his entry into the room, I perceived he had taken the fair nymph's hand, and kissing it, said :

THE EIGHTEENTH-CENTURY ESSAYISTS

'Witness to my happiness, ye groves! be still ye rivulets! Oh! woods, caves, fountains, trees, dales, mountains, hills, and streams! Oh! fairest! could you love me?' To which I overheard her answer, with a very pretty lisp: 'Oh! *Strephon*, you are a dangerous creature: why do you talk these tender things to me? but you men of wit.'.... 'Is it then possible,' said the enamoured *Strephon*, 'that she regards my sorrows! Oh! pity, thou balmy cure to a heart over-loaded! if rapture, solicitation, soft desire, and pleasing anxiety.... But still I live in the most afflicting of all circumstances, doubt. Cannot my charmer name the place and moment?

"There all those joys insatiably to prove,
With which rich beauty feeds the glutton love."

Forgive me, madam; it is not that my heart is weary of its chain, but——' This incoherent stuff was answered by a tender sigh, 'Why do you put your wit to a weak woman?' *Strephon* saw he had made some progress in her heart, and pursued it, by saying that, 'He would certainly wait upon her at such an hour near Rosamond's pond; and then—the sylvan deities, and rural powers of the place, sacred and inviolable to love, love the mover of all noble arts, should hear his vows repeated by the streams and echoes.' The assignation was accordingly made. This style he calls the unintelligible method of speaking his mind; and I will engage, had this gallant spoken plain English, she had never understood him half so readily: for we may take it for granted, that he will be esteemed as a very cold lover, who discovers to his mistress that he is in his senses."

Steele's most generous helper was Addison. The latter wrote parts of thirty-four numbers of the *Tatler*, and forty-one are wholly by him. Some of these papers by Addison are very fine indeed and are scarcely surpassed by the *Spectator* papers themselves. They include the character sketches of the *Political Upholsterer* (who appears several times); *Tom Folio* the broker in learning, and the *Ned Softly* paper. Steele gives practically nothing by way of literary criticism, his character and temperament seemed to exclude him from that sphere, but Addison later on in the *Spectator* was to make a serious contribution to literary criticism of the time. In the two last-mentioned papers Addison used the weapon of literary criticism in a light, half-amused fashion, in a manner which is wholly delightful. We give the *Ned Softly* paper as an outstanding example of Addison's style. It is light and perfectly adapted to the subject.

"I yesterday came hither about two hours before the company generally make their appearance, with a design to read over all the news-papers; but, upon my sitting down, I was accosted by Ned Softly, who saw me from a corner in the other end of the room, where I found he had been writing something. 'Mr Bickerstaff,' says he, 'I observe by a late Paper of yours, that you and I are just of a humour; for you must know, of all impertinences, there is nothing which I so much hate as news. I never read a Gazette in my life; and never trouble my head about our armies, whether they win or lose, or in what part of the world they lie encamped.' Without giving me time to reply, he drew a paper of verses out of his pocket, telling me, 'That he had something which would entertain me more agreeably; and that he would desire my judgment upon every line, for that we had time enough before us until the company came in.'

"Ned Softly is a very pretty poet, and a great admirer of easy lines. Waller is his favourite: and as that admirable writer has the best and worst verses of any among our great English poets, Ned Softly has got all the bad ones without book; which he repeats upon occasion, to show his reading, and garnish his conversation. Ned is indeed a true English reader, incapable of relishing the great and masterly strokes of this art; but wonderfully pleased with the little Gothic ornaments of epigrammatical conceits, turns, points, and quibbles; which are so frequent in the most admired of our English poets, and practised by those who want genius and strength to represent, after the manner of the ancients, simplicity in its natural beauty and perfection.

"Finding myself unavoidably engaged in such a conversation, I was resolved to turn my pain into a pleasure, and to divert myself as well as I could with so very odd a fellow. 'You must understand,' says Ned, 'that the sonnet I am going to read to you was written upon a lady, who showed me some verses of her own making, and is perhaps the best poet of our age. But you shall hear it.'

"Upon which he began to read as follows :—

"To Mira, on her Incomparable Poems.

I

"'When dress'd in laurel wreaths you shine,
 And tune your soft melodious notes,
You seem a sister of the Nine,
 Or Phœbus' self in petticoats.

THE EIGHTEENTH-CENTURY ESSAYISTS

II

'I fancy when your song you sing
  (Your song you sing with so much art),
Your pen was pluck'd from Cupid's wing;
  For, ah! it wounds me like his dart.'

"'Why,' says I, 'this is a little nosegay of conceits, a very lump of salt: every verse has something in it that piques; and then the dart in the last line is certainly as pretty a sting in the tail of an epigram, for so I think you critics call it, as ever entered into the thought of a poet.' 'Dear Mr Bickerstaff,' says he, shaking me by the hand, 'everybody knows you to be a judge of these things; and to tell you truly, I read over Roscommon's translation of "Horace's *Art of Poetry*" three several times, before I sat down to write the sonnet which I have shown you. But you shall hear it again, and pray observe every line of it; for not one of them shall pass without your approbation—

"'When dress'd in laurel wreaths you shine.'

"'That is,' says he, 'when you have your garland on; when you are writing verses.' To which I replied, 'I know your meaning: a *metaphor!*' 'The same,' said he, and went on—

"'And tune your soft melodious notes.'

"'Pray observe the gliding of that verse; there is scarce a consonant in it: I took care to make it run upon liquids. Give me your opinion of it.' 'Truly,' said I, 'I think it as good as the former.' 'I am very glad to hear you say so,' says he; 'but mind the next—

"'You seem a sister of the Nine.'

"'That is,' says he, 'you seem a sister of the Muses; for if you look into ancient authors, you will find it was their opinion, that there were nine of them.' 'I remember it very well,' said I; 'but pray proceed.'

"'Or Phœbus' self in petticoats.'

"'Phœbus,' says he, 'was the god of Poetry. These little instances, Mr Bickerstaff, show a gentleman's reading. Then to take off from the air of learning, which Phœbus and the Muses had given to this first stanza, you may observe, how it falls all of a sudden into the familiar: "in petticoats!"'

"'Or Phœbus' self in petticoats.'

THE ESSAYS OF ADDISON AND STEELE

"'Let us now,' says I, 'enter upon the second stanza; I find the first line is still a continuation of the metaphor.'

"'I fancy when your song you sing.'

"'It is very right,' says he; 'but pray observe the turn of words in those two lines. I was a whole hour in adjusting of them, and have still a doubt upon me, whether in the second line it should be, "Your song you sing; or, You sing your song?" You shall hear them both:

"'I fancy, when your song you sing
    (Your song you sing with so much art),'

"Or

"'I fancy, when your song you sing
    (You sing your song with so much art).'

"'Truly,' said I, 'the turn is so natural either way, that you have made me almost giddy with it.' 'Dear sir,' said he, grasping me by the hand, 'you have a great deal of patience; but pray what do you think of the next verse?'

"'Your pen was pluck'd from Cupid's wing.'

"'Think!' says I; 'I think you have made Cupid look like a little goose.' 'That was my meaning,' says he; 'I think the ridicule is well enough hit off. But we come now to the last, which sums up the whole matter.'

"'For, ah! it wounds me like his dart.'

"'Pray, how do you like that "Ah!" doth it not make a pretty figure in that place? *Ah!* . . . it looks as if I felt the dart, and cried out as being pricked with it.'

"'For, ah! it wounds me like his dart.'

"'My friend Dick Easy,' continued he, 'assured me, he would rather have written that Ah! than to have been the author of the Æneid. He indeed objected, that I made Mira's pen like a quill in one of the lines, and like a dart in the other. But as to that . . .' 'Oh! as to that,' says I, 'it is but supposing Cupid to be like a porcupine, and his quills and darts will be the same thing.' He was going to embrace me for the hint; but half a dozen critics coming into the room, whose faces he did not like, he conveyed the sonnet into his pocket, and whispered me in the ear, 'he would show it me again as soon as his man had written it over fair.'"

THE EIGHTEENTH-CENTURY ESSAYISTS

Swift did not contribute much to the *Tatler*, though suggestions made to Steele may have borne fruit. We have seen how his *Isaac Bickerstaff* was taken at the very commencement by Steele. This adoption may have been only after a number of conversations with Swift, and thus indirectly the latter may have exercised considerable influence in the structure of the new paper. The small quantity of work which Swift *did* contribute to the *Tatler* does not make us particularly anxious for more. The taste shown is doubtful, and by reflection Steele's work only shines the more bright. As far as the periodical essay is concerned, both Addison and Steele understood much better the " style " required than did Swift.

Thomas Hughes contributed five or six numbers in whole or part to the *Tatler*, and they are of moderate worth ; William Harrison sent in an undistinguished paper called *Medicine, A Tale*. Heneage Twisden contributed a humorous genealogy of the *Bickerstaff* family in one of the early numbers ; and no less a personage than Congreve the *Character of Aspasia* (the Lady Elizabeth Hastings). This last-mentioned sketch is light and does not show Congreve at his best. It is in his *Comedies* that Congreve excels. Single papers by a Mr Fuller and Mr James Greenwood complete the list. It will be seen how completely the *Tatler* was Steele's own, outside of the forty or fifty numbers contributed by his " powerful Auxiliary " ; and the strain began to tell. Steele's nature was not like Addison's. He found it difficult to continue persistently in one line of work. It may have been, too, that Steele allowed his violent feeling for party politics to appear too frequently to please his readers, perhaps because of a temporary exhaustion of literary fertility, at any rate he brought the *Tatler* to an end with the ingenious plea that his identity had been discovered. " I never designed in it to give any man any secret wound by my concealment, but spoke in the character of an old man, a philosopher, a humorist, an astrologer, and a censor, to allure my reader with the variety of my subjects, and insinuate, if I could, the weight of reason with the agreeableness of wit. The general purpose of the whole has been to recommend truth, innocence, honour, and virtue, as the chief ornaments of life; but I considered that severity of manners were absolutely necessary to him who would censure others, and for *that reason, and that only,* chose to talk in a mask. I shall not carry my humility so far as to call myself a vicious man, but at the same time must confess my life is at best but pardonable. And with no greater character than this, a man would make but an indifferent progress in attacking prevailing and fashionable vices, which Mr Bickerstaff has done with a freedom of spirit, that would have lost both its beauty and efficacy, had it been pretended to by Mr Steele."

So much interest was taken in the *Tatler* that it was re-issued in Edinburgh by James Watson "opposite the Luckenbooths." He seems to have started with the issue of Steele's No. 130, and numbered it No. 1; at least the British Museum copy No. 31 corresponds with Steele's No. 160. It is an almost exact reprint of the *Tatler*, with the exception that the Edinburgh issue introduced local advertisements. Just a fortnight after Steele's last *Tatler* appeared in London, Watson's re-issue also came to an end, and he now started a direct imitation—the *Tatler, by Donald Macstaff of the North.* The first number was published on Wednesday, 13th January 1711. The old *eidola* are kept in a slightly different form. For example, *Jenny, Isaac's* half-sister, is replaced by *Mary Macstaff, Donald Macstaff's* sister. The essays are an imitation of Steele's, pure and simple. One (No. 4) treats of the severity of parents to their children, and is a good article warning parents of the results likely to ensue by being over-severe and strict in the treatment of their children. He illustrates his remarks by reference to Terence's comedy of *The Brothers,* Demea and Micio. In No. 10 he says, "The design of this paper is to ridicule folly and affectation, not to expose misfortunes and imperfections which are natural and unavoidable." But, on the other hand, he seems to have written against characters whose personal identity he only thinly veiled, for he once says, "I have lately received private intimations that there are such things as swords and pistols to be feared if I continue to be as particular as I have been hitherto." How closely he followed Steele's general scheme may be seen from the fact that he writes from *MacClurg's Coffee-house* reflections on wits and politicians; from the *Jew's Chocolate House* remarks on the beaux and the ladies; from the *Exchange Coffee-house* observations on citizens, would-be wits and would-be politicians; and from his own apartment all sorts of miscellaneous subjects. It is interesting to see so vigorous a publication of so early a date emanating from Edinburgh. But we must remember that Edinburgh had long been famous as a publishing centre. As far back as 1508 Walter Chepman and Andrew Myllar had issued their precious prints of Scots poems and prose-pieces, and we shall have to note many other publications from Edinburgh later on. It is notable that in 1710 Defoe got license to start the *Edinburgh Courant* in that city, and it has been suggested that the kindness he received from the Scotch contrasted with the ungrateful rewards of all his toil in England, which Defoe more than once speaks of in prefaces to the volumes of his *Review*.

The *Female Tatler* also followed closely on the appearance of Steele's *Tatler*. This work was written by Mr Thomas Baker, and commenced its circulation in 1709. It extended to many numbers, most of which are now no longer extant. Its gross personalities obtained its author a sound cudgelling from an offended family in the city; and in the month of October 1709, it was presented as a nuisance by the grand jury at the Old Bailey. Mr Baker, whose general style of writing was ironical, took every opportunity of recording the singularities of Steele, whether personal or moral. In No. 72, for instance, he has ridiculed Sir Richard's absence of mind and peculiarity of attitude in walking the streets. " I saw Mr Bickerstaff going to the corner of St James, in the beginning of December. It was a great fog, yet the squire wore his hat under his left arm, and, as if that side had been lame, all the stress of his gait was laid upon the other; he stooped very much forward, and whenever his right foot came to the ground, which was always set down with a more than ordinary and affected force, his cane, with a great vibration of the arm, struck the stones, whilst a violent jerk of his head kept time with the latter. I observed several besides

THE ESSAYS OF ADDISON AND STEELE

myself that took notice of this strange singularity, which nobody could imagine to proceed from less than either madness or despair. It is not to be conceived how any wise man alive, that had been such an implacable enemy to all singularities and mimic postures, and writ so learnedly concerning the use of the cane, could make such a ridiculous figure of himself in the street, at the very moment that his 'os homini sublime, etc.,' was a-printing." The allusion in the Latin quotation is to the motto of the *Tatler* in No. 108. Steele is supposed to have ridiculed Mr Baker under the character of *Nick Doubt* in No. 91 of the *Tatler*.

Only two months after the rather sudden close of the *Tatler* by Steele, there appeared on Thurdsay, 1st March 1711, the most widely famous, as it is the longest and best of the eighteenth-century periodicals, the *Spectator*—a title which is inseparably connected with the name of Joseph Addison. And with the completion of this work the high-water mark is reached. Dr Johnson complained in the *Rambler* that Addison had come first in time, and so had the advantage in choice of subject for his paper. We feel a certain sympathy for this position. But the field being a fresh and untrodden one, does not explain Addison's success; questions of style and treatment must also be considered, and with the exception of one or two essays by the doctor himself; the inimitable creations of Goldsmith, his *Beau Tibbs* and his *Man in Black*; and some of the *World* articles of Chesterfield and Walpole, there is no reading in the whole eighteenth-century periodicals at once so varied and so pleasant as is to be found within the pages of the *Spectator*. Addison was the right man in the right place. Steele had been accustomed in the course of his rather irregular late-hour existence to dash off his articles: his paper still had the continental news-section, and notions often jostled one another in a single essay. With Addison at the head, things went differently. Addison was the very soul of order, and his essays are usually longer than those of Steele, one paper as a rule filling up each issue. There is something in the easy grace and polish of his clear limpid style, touched as it is with gentle irony, which tells of long practice and a nice exercise of judgment. Though it is often the case that Addison wrote his essays " straight off," it must be remembered that he also used up old material on hand, especially for his literary and critical papers. He had studied for nearly ten years at Oxford, where he used to walk under the elms by the Cherwell, reading his favourite Latin authors. He had travelled far with eyes open and observant; and he had been a keen, if silent, spectator of almost all the phases of human life. He had now reached the " age of wisdom," and was thus fully prepared for the task he had undertaken. And in this task he was aided by the fact that the time and atmosphere were suitable for such an undertaking. The troublous period of the previous half-century (including a civil war and a revolution) had passed, and the people were settling down in Queen Anne's reign to that steady pursuit of commerce which was to be the source of England's greatness for the future. The best days of the drama were fading far in the distance, and the novel had not yet arisen to take its place; and though the " topsy-turvification " in morals and much else of Charles II.'s reign had passed away, there remained not only lesser evils to purge from men's habits and lives, but a positive work of reform, in the shape of supplying subjects for conversation, rules for good manners, and for the observance of the lesser morals, which both Addison and Steele could and did present in an attractive manner. The people were apparently delighted with the new departure, and as time went on almost the whole gamut of human emotion was touched in allegory, vision, letter, or direct conversational style, in the pages of the *Spectator*.

The general scheme of the *Spectator* shows less artificiality than the *Tatler*. It was published daily, and the *eidolon* reappeared in the first number where the *Spectator* himself is introduced. But note how chary of detail is the account given. No individual name is applied to the *Spectator*, he has only general characteristics which are vague and impersonal—he is " a silent man," goes everywhere and talks little, and thus he is not tied down to any particular line of conduct. In any case the *Spectator* is never really obtruded—he is only *nominis umbra*. And the idea of a club which Defoe had originated, and which Steele had exemplified at least once in his humorous description of the *Trumpet Club*, is carried on. The second number of the *Spectator* gives a draft of the characters by Steele, but practically the only one which is developed is that of Sir Roger de Coverley, and the credit is due here almost wholly to Addison; otherwise the Club in no way dominates the paper or restricts free action. The *Spectator* had a very long run, ending 6th December 1712 with the five hundred and fifty-fifth number. There was another set, issued by Addison himself about two years afterwards; and still later a volume, bearing the same name, but really a spurious issue, since neither Addison nor Steele had any hand in it. The success of the *Spectator* was due, first of all, to its balance and restraint, for it never gave offence by savage Swiftian attacks. The didactic papers are moderate in tone, and Addison's ironic humour is so finely pitched that he persuades almost unconsciously while seeming to assent to that which he is really trying to reform. This is the triumph of consummate art. He never over-indulges the public in any one line, whether it be narrative, social talk, or homily, and so monotony is prevented. The first six or seven papers give an idea of the quality and variety set forth. After the *Spectator* has been introduced and the Club mentioned in the initial two papers, the third gives one of these visions in the method which Addison was so fond of—this time the vision of *Public Credit*. The next by Steele is a complete change, and turns attention to the subject which had drawn down Swift's ire in his *Journal to Stella* as to the "fair-sexing way" Steele had. The fifth issue strikes at fashionable crazes and gives a humorous account by Addison of Italian Opera, recently introduced into London. The next again illustrates one of the most important aspects of the paper—the moral and didactic side,—for one of the chief purposes of the *Spectator* had been given "to enliven morality with wit, and to temper wit with morality." Though this particular paper is by Steele, it was the "Saturday" papers of Addison's which particularly emphasised this aspect, and though a good deal of his work savours to us now of platitude and commonplace, it was fresh and pertinent then. The *Spectator* was afterwards bound in volume form and sold largely—for the next half-century at least,—becoming the standard reference for minor manners and morals. Even in Sir Walter Scott's day and later (for it will be remembered what Dickens has given of his early experiences in *David Copperfield*) the *Spectator*, along with the other chief eighteenth-century periodicals, formed a regular prescribed course of reading for the young. The seventh number gives an excellent example of the way little foibles are treated with the lightest possible touch of ridicule; here Addison deals with *Omens* and the disturbance caused in the home circle of a hypersensitive and superstitious lady. And so the ball, once started rolling, goes on almost by itself—letters, stories, morals, apologues, and humorous hits at the foibles of the times. The stories make a prominent and important section. Addison seems to have had a real genius for tale-telling, and if he had lived in our own day, or even a generation after his own, he might have been a successful novelist. Mention need only be made of the *Vision of Marraton* (No. 56), the *Story of Eudoxus and Leontine* (No. 123), the *Vision of Mirza* (No. 159), the *Story of Theodosius and Constantia* (No. 164), of *Hilpa and Shalum* (No. 584), and, much the best of all, the *Sir Roger de Coverley* series. The character of *Sir Roger* had originated with Steele, but was never developed, and we owe to Addison almost the whole of the thirty papers which deal with the various aspects of *Sir Roger's* character, and more particularly with his life in the country. We are told how he manages his family, and chooses a chaplain; his fox-hunting; his Tory politics; his adventure with gypsies round his country-seat; his dispute with *Sir Andrew Freeport*; his return to London and his conversation in Gray's Inn walks; his reflections on the tombs in Westminster Abbey, and his remarks at the playhouse, are all related to us with perfection of style and humour, and finally an account is given of his death and legacies. We give a passage from one of these papers as an illustration of Addison's style. Here is *Sir Roger's* account (No. 106) of his choice of a chaplain.

THE ESSAYS OF ADDISON AND STEELE

"My chief companion, when Sir Roger is diverting himself in the woods or the fields, is a very venerable man who is ever with Sir Roger, and has lived at his house in the nature of a chaplain above thirty years. This gentleman is a person of good sense and some learning, of a very regular life and obliging conversation: he heartily loves Sir Roger, and knows that he is very much in the old knight's esteem, so that he lives in the family rather as a relation than a dependent.

"I have observed in several of my papers, that my friend Sir Roger, amidst all his good qualities, is something of a humorist; and that his virtues, as well as imperfections, are as it were tinged by a certain extravagance, which makes them particularly his, and distinguishes them from those of other men. This cast of mind, as it is generally very innocent in itself, so it renders his conversation highly agreeable, and more delightful than the same degree of sense and virtue would appear in their common and ordinary colours. As I was walking with him last night, he asked me how I liked the good man whom I have just now mentioned? and without staying for my answer told me, that he was afraid of being insulted with Latin and Greek at his own table; for which reason he desired a particular friend of his at the university to find him out a clergyman rather of plain sense than much learning, of a good aspect, a clear voice, a sociable temper, and, if possible, a man that understood a little of back-gammon. 'My friend,' says Sir Roger, 'found me out this gentleman, who, besides the endowments required of him, is, they tell me, a good scholar, though he does not show it. I have given him the parsonage of the parish; and because I know his value, have settled upon him a good annuity for life. If he outlives me, he shall find that he was higher in my esteem than perhaps he thinks he is. He has now been with me thirty years; and though he does not know I have taken notice of it, has never in all that time asked anything of me for himself, though he is every day soliciting me for something in behalf of one or other of my tenants his parishioners. There has not been a lawsuit in the parish since he has lived among them; if any dispute arises they apply themselves to him for the decision; if they do not acquiesce in his judgment, which I think never happened above once or twice at most, they appeal to me. At his first settling with me, I made him a present of all the good sermons which have been printed in English, and only begged of him that every Sunday he would pronounce one of them in the pulpit. Accordingly he has digested them into such a series, that they follow one another naturally, and make a continued system of practical divinity.'

THE EIGHTEENTH-CENTURY ESSAYISTS

"As Sir Roger was going on in his story, the gentleman we were talking of came up to us; and upon the knight's asking him who preached to-morrow (for it was Saturday night) told us, the bishop of St Asaph in the morning, and Dr South in the afternoon. He then showed us his list of preachers for the whole year, where I saw with a great deal of pleasure Archbishop Tillotson, Bishop Saunderson, Dr Barrow, Dr Calamy, with several living authors who have published discourses of practical divinity. I no sooner saw this venerable man in the pulpit but I very much approved of my friend's insisting upon the qualifications of a good aspect and a clear voice; for I was so charmed with the gracefulness of his figure and delivery, as well as with the discourses he pronounced, that I think I never passed any time more to my satisfaction. A sermon repeated after this manner, is like the composition of a poet in the mouth of a graceful actor.

"I could heartily wish that more of our country clergy would follow this example; and instead of wasting their spirits in laborious compositions of their own, would endeavour after a handsome elocution, and all those other talents that are proper to enforce what has been penned by great masters. This would not only be more easy to themselves, but more edifying to the people."

There is a certain unity and completeness about this latter set as developed by Addison which show his superiority over his friend Steele in this respect. The two papers of this series written by Steele are more scrappy, and the one by Tickell, though humorous, is perhaps ill-advised, and neither displays the same sure grasp of *Sir Roger's* character. Grouped together, fused and expanded a little, the whole series would have made a decent novel, and points the way to Richardson and the rest. Fielding in *Tom Jones* (perhaps the greatest single novel we possess) still reflects the influence of the periodical in his prefixing short papers discussing sundry matters of passion and principle at the beginning of each "book" of his story. Thus we can trace a sequence. Following on the decline of the drama at the close of the Elizabethan age, and the deservedly severe strictures of Jeremy Collier, there grew up the periodical essay, and out of the essay a new kind, the novel, which was soon to sever itself from the parent stock.

Another general feature of the *Spectator* which we must take account of are the papers on literary criticism. More

THE ESSAYS OF ADDISON AND STEELE

than a taste in a lighter and more inconsequential kind had been given in the *Ned Softly* paper, in the *Tatler*, but it was not till the *Spectator* was well under way that Addison, in pursuance of his idea of bringing new subjects under the observation of the many, designed to attract the general reader to literary subjects, so often neglected; and contributed papers on *Chevy Chase*, *The Children of the Wood* ballad, on *True and False Wit*, on Milton's poem *Paradise Lost*, and on the *Pleasures of the Imagination*. The worth of these papers has been very variously estimated, but that variation in value has arisen very largely from the different standpoints adopted. Here our viewpoint is the historical one, and we rank these papers as of no mean merit. Addison by this time had left far behind the almost schoolboy standard of literary criticism revealed in the *Account of the greatest English Poets*. He had now arrived at maturity, and the amount of his reading had surely considerably increased from the almost negligible quantity shown in the early verse production. It may be that the essays on *True and False Wit* seem to us now dull and artificial, with a marked ethical bias. But they suited the time and had a wide influence. It may be that some critics have, in the nineteenth century, read many connotations into Addison's use of the term "imagination" in his papers on the *Pleasures of the Imagination*, and thus give them a meaning which the writer certainly did not give. But for fifty or more years they were read with respect and often with admiration, and the way in which Addison has shown how sight as a pleasure of the sense aids the imagination commands our admiration of a finished product of his limited point of view. It may be that the papers on *Paradise Lost* are superfluous *now*, when, from our romantic standpoint, we can readjust the value of Milton's great work, but at the time and for the time they were excellent. Addison's work as a literary critic cannot be neglected, and from our historical standpoint his papers are worthy of a high place in the lists of our periodical essays. We give as an example of Addison's work the following passage from one of his papers on the *Pleasures of the Imagination*. The style is Addison's own, and in it he sets forth an idea which, familiar to us, was new to the readers whom he was addressing.

"But among this set of writers there are none who more gratify and enlarge the imagination than the authors of the new philosophy, whether we consider their theories of the earth or heavens, the discoveries they have made by glasses, or any other of their contemplations on nature. We are not a little pleased to find every green leaf swarm with millions of animals, that at their largest growth are not visible to the naked eye. There is something very engaging to the fancy, as well as to our reason, in the treatises of metals, minerals, plants, and meteors. But when we survey the whole earth at once, and the several planets that lie within its neighbourhood, we are filled with a pleasing astonishment, to see so many worlds, hanging one above another, and sliding round their axles in such an amazing pomp and solemnity. If, after this, we contemplate those wild fields of æther, that reach in height as far as from Saturn to the fixed stars, and run abroad almost to an infinitude, our imagination finds its capacity filled with so immense a prospect, and puts itself upon the stretch to comprehend it. But if we yet arise higher, and consider the fixed stars as so many vast oceans of flame, that are each of them attended with a different set of planets, and still discover new firmaments and new lights that are sunk farther in those unfathomable depths of æther, so as not to be seen by the strongest of our telescopes, we are lost in such a labyrinth of suns and worlds, and confounded with the immensity and magnificence of Nature.

"Nothing is more pleasant to the fancy, than to enlarge itself by degrees, in its contemplation of the various proportions which its several objects bear to each other, when it compares the body of man to the bulk of the whole earth, the earth to the circle it describes round the sun, that circle to the sphere of the fixed stars, the sphere of the fixed stars to the circuit of the whole creation, the whole creation itself to the infinite space that is everywhere diffused about it; or when the imagination works downward, and considers the bulk of a human body in respect of an animal a hundred times less than a mite, the particular limbs of such an animal, the different springs that actuate the limbs, the spirits which set the springs a-going, and the proportionable minuteness of these several parts, before they have arrived at their full growth and perfection; but if, after all this, we take the least particle of these animal spirits, and consider its capacity of being wrought into a world that shall contain within those narrow dimensions a heaven and earth, stars and planets, and every different species of living creatures, in the same analogy and proportion they bear to each other in our own universe; such a speculation, by reason of its nicety, appears ridiculous to those who have not turned their thoughts that way, though at the same time it is founded on no less than the evidence of demonstration. Nay, we may yet carry it farther, and discover in the smallest particle of this little world a new inexhausted fund of matter, capable of being spun out into another universe."

And finally there come hundreds of miscellaneous articles which refuse any general classification—*Street Cries, Diaries of a Citizen* and of a *Fashionable Lady*, account of a *Lady's Library, Journeys of Stage Coaches, Clubs*, including in their membership all sorts and conditions of men, Letters on all subjects under the sun, various characterisations, adventures, fables, and even poetry, for Addison has inserted several of his hymns or paraphrases which show his religious creed in its best aspect of simple faith and adoration. Such are the general features of the *Spectator*. We shall see how far they were maintained or modified in subsequent essay periodicals.

It was just three months after the rather sudden and unexpected stoppage of the *Spectator* proper, and before the extra volume published by Addison had appeared, that Steele with his characteristic restlessness and energy started another paper on Thursday, 12th March 1713, called the *Guardian*. It had apparently been projected before the close of the *Spectator*, for he makes mention of it in a letter to Pope, dated 12th November 1712, and seems to have entered upon the scheme without the help of Addison, who does not appear till No. 67. In his letter to Pope he had said, " I desire you would let me know whether you are at leisure or not ? I have a design which I shall open a month or two hence, with the assistance of a few like yourself. If your thoughts are unengaged I shall explain myself farther." Addison, however, contributed not a little to the success of the periodical, giving in all over fifty papers, including an excellent consecutive " run " of no less than twenty-seven numbers. As for the general features of the publication, the title would seem to suggest a more serious set of papers, but it is in effect a continuation of the older paper with a slight loss of freshness, which is scarcely to be wondered at. It was continued till 1st October 1713, after one hundred and seventy-five daily issues had been published, closing rather abruptly, due it is said, to a quarrel Steele had with Jacob Tonson. In the first number, Steele says (speaking as the *Guardian*), " The main purpose of the work shall be to protect the modest, the industrious ; to celebrate the wise, the valiant ; to encourage the good, the pious ; to confront the impudent, the idle ; to contemn the vain, the cowardly ; and to disappoint the wicked and profane " ; and in the second number, *Nestor Ironside* (as he calls himself) proceeds to explain his position and title and how he came to be *Guardian* to the *Lizard* family.

Thus Steele still keeps up the idea he had in the *Tatler*, only extending *Isaac Bickerstaff*, and his half-sister *Jenny Distaff*, to a larger circle. The discussion of news from the tea-table of *Lady Lizard* is disappointing in results, and a live interest in the family is never developed. But in the *Guardian* we have important new contributors in Pope and Bishop Berkeley. The famous philosopher's papers, which number some dozen or more, are directed mainly in support of Christianity and against Freethinkers. Bishop Berkeley has a very clear trenchant style, eminently suitable for periodical essay work, and we have here a lighter and most interesting side to his character. There are more than mere traces of humour in the author of *Alciphron's* accounts of the pineal gland in man as the *Seat of the Soul*, his investigation of several, and especially his examination of that of the Freethinkers. Here is an excellent passage (No. 39) showing Berkeley at his best. He writes in a fine spirit of irony.

" On the eleventh day of October, in the year 1712, having left my body locked up safe in my study, I repaired to the *Grecian* coffee-house, where, entering into the pineal gland of a certain eminent free-thinker, I made directly to the highest part of it, which is the seat of the understanding, expecting to find there a comprehensive knowledge of all things human and divine ; but to my no small astonishment, I found the place narrower than ordinary, insomuch that there was not any room for a miracle, prophecy, or separate spirit.

" This obliged me to descend a story lower, into the imagination, which I found larger, indeed, but cold and comfortless. I discovered Prejudice, in the figure of a woman, standing in a corner, with her eyes close shut, and her forefingers stuck in her ears ; many words in a confused order, but spoken with great emphasis, issued from her mouth. These, being condensed by the coldness of the place, formed a sort of mist, through which me-thought I saw a great castle with a fortification cast round it, and a tower adjoining to it that through the windows appeared to be filled with racks and halters. Beneath the castle I could discern vast dungeons, and all about it lay scattered the bones of men. It seemed to be garrisoned by certain men in black, of a gigantic size, and most terrible forms. But, as I drew near, the terror of the appearance vanished ; and the castle I found to be only a church, whose steeple with its clock and bell-ropes was mistaken for a tower filled with racks and halters. The terrible giants in black shrunk into a few innocent clergymen. The dungeons were turned into vaults designed only for the habitation of the dead ; and the fortifications proved to be a churchyard, with some scattered bones in it, and a plain stone-wall round it.

"I had not been long here before my curiosity was raised by a loud noise that I heard in the inferior region. Descending thither I found a mob of the Passions assembled in a riotous manner. Their tumultuary proceedings soon convinced me, that they affected a democracy. After much noise and wrangle, they at length all hearkened to Vanity, who proposed the raising of a great army of notions, which she offered to lead against those dreadful phantoms in the imagination that had occasioned all this uproar.

"Away posted Vanity, and I after her, to the storehouse of ideas ; when I beheld a great number of lifeless notions confusedly thrown together, but upon the approach of Vanity they began to crawl. Here were to be seen, among other odd things, sleeping deities, corporeal spirits, and worlds formed by chance ; with an endless variety of heathen notions, the most irregular and grotesque imaginable. And with these were jumbled several of Christian extraction ; but such was the dress and light they were put in, and their features were so distorted, that they looked little better than heathens. There was likewise assembled no small number of phantoms in strange habits, who proved to be idolatrous priests of different nations. Vanity gave the word, and straightway the Talapoins, Faquirs, Bramines, and Bonzes drew up in a body. The right wing consisted of ancient heathen notions, and the left of Christians naturalised. All these together, for numbers, composed a very formidable army ; but the precipitation of Vanity was so great, and such was their own inbred aversion to the tyranny of rules and discipline, that they seemed rather a confused rabble than a regular army. I could, nevertheless, observe, that they all agreed in a squinting look, or cast of their eyes towards a certain person in a mask, who was placed in the centre, and whom by sure signs and tokens I discovered to be Atheism.

"Vanity had no sooner led her forces into the imagination, but she resolved upon storming the castle, and giving no quarter. They began the assault with loud outcry and great confusion. I, for my part, made the best of my way, and re-entered my own lodging. Sometime after, inquiring at a bookseller's for a *Discourse on Freethinking*, which had made some noise, I met with the representatives of all those notions drawn up in the same confused order upon paper."

It is a curious characteristic of the period that at a time when deistical speculation was rife all the deists are mentioned only to be condemned and ridiculed by Addison and Berkeley to Dr Johnson himself. This is put very well by the late Sir Leslie Stephen, in his *English Thought in the Eighteenth Century*: "The deists are almost uniformly mentioned with a mixture of contempt and dislike. Addison dislikes them as much as he can dislike anyone. Swift dislikes them also, as much as he can dislike anyone; and the phrase in his case represents, perhaps, the greatest intensity of aversion of which the human soul is capable. With the whole body of essayists, from Steele downwards, a deist is a futile coxcomb to be ridiculed like the 'Virtuoso' and the fine gentleman. The novelists are equally clear."

Pope, again, who had replied to Steele's letter that he would be glad to assist, gives no less than eight contributions. No. 40 on the *Pastorals of Pope and Philips* is a little masterpiece in irony, and pitched so fine, that even Steele did not at first see beneath its seeming simplicity, much to the chagrin of the author. Again, his paper (No. 78) on the *Recipe for making an Epic Poem* contains not a little fine satire on the "imitation" of the times, and even turns the attack upon himself. It describes, in grave detail, how to imitate the ancients with regard to the fable, the manners, the machines, the description, and the language, in a style not unlike Vida's famous advice to the youth of his day to

THE ESSAYS OF ADDISON AND STEELE

" come and steal " !   The following passage will sufficiently illustrate Pope's *Pastorals of Pope and Philips.* It is an excellent example of the cleverness, if not actual genius, of Pope in a department of literature in which he wrote with distinction.   Had he only written more of the class of work given in the *Guardian* we are safe in saying that he would have become famed for a certain light ironic type of essay, hardly to be excelled by any of the periodical writers throughout the whole of the eighteenth century.

" Having now shown some parts, in which these two writers may be compared, it is a justice I owe to Mr Philips, to discover those in which no man can compare with him.   First, that beautiful rusticity, of which I shall only produce two instances out of a hundred not yet quoted :

> " ' O woful day ! O day of woe, quoth he,
>   And woful I, who live the day to see ? '

That simplicity of diction, the melancholy flowing of the numbers, the solemnity of this sound, and the easy turn of the words, in this dirge (to make use of our author's expression) are extremely elegant.

" In another of his pastorals a shepherd utters a dirge not much inferior to the former, in the following lines :

> " ' Ah me the while ! ah me, the luckless day !
>   Ah luckless lad, the rather might I say ;
>   Ah silly I ! more silly than my sheep,
>   Which on the flow'ry plains I once did keep.'

How he still charms the ear with these artful repetitions of the epithets ; and how significant is the last verse ! I defy the most common reader to repeat them without feeling some motions of compassion.

" In the next place I shall rank his proverbs, in which I formerly observed he excels.   For example :

> " ' A rolling stone is ever bare of moss ;
>   And, to their cost, green years old proverbs cross.
>   He that late lies down, as late will rise,
>   And, Sluggard like, till noon-day snoring lies.
>   Against ill-luck all cunning foresight fails ;
>   Whether we sleep or wake it nought avails,
>   Nor fear, from upright sentence, " wrong." ' '

THE EIGHTEENTH-CENTURY ESSAYISTS

" Lastly, his elegant dialect, which alone might prove him the eldest born of Spenser, and our only true Arcadian ; I should think it proper for the several writers of pastoral to confine themselves to their several counties : Spenser seems to have been of this opinion ; for he hath laid the scene of one of his pastorals in Wales, where, with all the simplicity natural to that part of our island, one shepherd bids the other good-morrow in an unusual and elegant manner.

"'Diggon, Davey, I bid hur God-day ;
Or Diggon hur is, or I mis-say.'

" Diggon answers,

"'Hur was hur while it was day-light :
But now hur is a most wretched wight,' etc.

" But the most beautiful example of this kind that I ever met with, is a very valuable piece which I chanced to find among some old manuscripts, entitled, *A Pastoral Ballad*; which, I think, for its nature and simplicity, may (notwithstanding the modesty of the title) be allowed a perfect pastoral. It is composed in the Somersetshire dialect, and the names such as are proper to the country people. It may be observed, as a farther beauty of this Pastoral, the words Nymph, Dryad, Naiad, Faun, Cupid, or Satyr, are not once mentioned through the whole. I shall make no apology for inserting some few lines of this excellent piece. Cicily breaks thus into the subject, as she is going a-milking :

"'*Cicily.*—Rager, go vetch tha kee, or else tha zun
  Will quite be go, bevore c'have half a don.

Roger.—Thou shouldst not ax ma tweece, but I've a be
  To dreave our bull to bull tha parson's kee.'

" It is to be observed, that this whole dialogue is formed upon the passion of jealousy ; and his mentioning the parson's kine naturally revives the jealousy of the shepherdess Cicily, which she expresses as follows :

"'*Cicily.*—Ah Rager, Rager, chez was zore avraid
  When in yond vield you kiss'd tha parson's maid :
  Is this the love that once to me you zed
  When from tha wake thou broughtst me gingerbread ?

Roger.—Cicily, thou charg'st me false—i'll zwear to thee,
  Tha parson's maid is still a maid for me.'

THE ESSAYS OF ADDISON AND STEELE

In which answer of his are expressed at once that 'spirit of religion' and that 'innocence of the golden age,' so necessary to be observed by all writers of pastoral.

"As to the conclusion of this piece, the author reconciles the lovers, and ends the eclogue the most simply in the world:

"'So Rager parted vor to vetch tha kee,
And vor her bucket in went Cicily.'

"I am loth to show my fondness for antiquity so far as to prefer this ancient British author to our present English writers of pastoral; but I cannot avoid making this obvious remark, that both Spenser and Philips have hit into the same road with this old west country bard of ours.

"After all that hath been said I hope none can think it any injustice to Mr Pope, that I forbore to mention him as a pastoral writer; since upon the whole he is of the same class with Moschus and Bion, whom we have excluded that rank; and of whose eclogues, as well as some of Virgil's, it may be said, that according to the description we have given of this sort of poetry, they are by no means pastorals, but 'something better.'"

But outside the work of Pope and Berkeley, we have little to add to the normal papers of Addison and Steele. There is nothing notable in Budgell's contributions. One new feature, which created not a little fun and mild excitement, was the establishment of a Lion's Head at the office door, and readers were invited to pop in contributions, which they could do, as Addison gently insinuates, in the quietness of the night, if they were frightened to be recognised by day—and no doubt some of the papers were made use of.

The institution of the *Lion's Head* is described in No. 114 with Addison's usual touches of humour: " I think myself obliged to acquaint the public that the lion's head is now erected at Button's Coffee-house, Covent Garden, where it opens its mouth at all hours for the reception of such intelligence as shall be thrown into it. It is reckoned an excellent piece of workmanship. The features are strong and well furrowed. The whiskers are admired by all that have seen them. It is planted on the western side of the coffee-house, holding its paws under the chin upon a box, which contains everything that he swallows. He is, indeed, a proper emblem of *knowledge* and *action*, being all head and paws." Addison also keeps up the fun by several references later on to the " Roarings of the Lion," and how it was treated by the town.

Addison's other contributions to the *Guardian* are very much the same as his *Spectator* articles, a great deal of advice to the ladies about their use or non-use of the tucker, and other articles of dress, visions and stories, criticism in the shape of a discussion of Strada's *Prolusion*, and moral papers on how to bear calumny, and on the proper employment of time. The general impression derived from a reading of the *Guardian* is that it is very much a reproduction of the *Spectator* both in style and tone, weaker as a whole, smaller in bulk, and with the almost inevitable suggestion of staleness. It contains, however, much interesting and readable matter, and deserves to rank along with the *Tatler* and *Spectator* as giving a wonderful picture of the life of the times worked up in essays of no mean merit.

But Steele, with his strong party passions, could not keep out political references; the famous Dunkirk letter (No. 128) being a case in point; and this was to prove disastrous. In the *Englishman*, which was practically a continuation of the *Guardian*, his outspokenness caused his expulsion from the House of Commons. It is chiefly memorable for its twenty-sixth number, which contains the article on Alexander Selkirk, and which is supposed to have suggested the central idea to Defoe for the world-famous *Robinson Crusoe*. The article is a plain straightforward account of Selkirk's adventures on Juan Fernandez, and it is curious to compare the account of the island with that given in the romance. Selkirk makes mention of sea-lions on the island, but these are omitted by Defoe in his narrative, probably because people at that time would think he was romancing in his description of them.

This paper, the *Englishman*, was first issued in October 1713, and ran for fifty-six numbers to February 1714. In the first number Steele claims to succeed the *Guardian*. " For valuable considerations," he says, " I have purchased the Lion, Desk, Ink, and Paper, and all other goods of *Nestor*

THE ESSAYS OF ADDISON AND STEELE

Ironside, Esquire, who has thought fit to write no more himself, but has given me full liberty to report any sage expressions or manners which may tend to the instruction of mankind, and the service of the country." But the *Englishman* compared with the *Guardian,* which it so professedly succeeds, shows a decided falling-off. In the latter journal Addison had played a prominent part and had more than one excellent series of papers; but in the *Englishman* his fine touch and gentle irony are absent. And the political bias of Steele is evident more than ever; many papers show decided Whig leanings. But Steele fortunately still retains his old charm when he deals with subjects for the ladies. The ninth number on *Female Liberty* is excellent, and the seventeenth number on the *History of Dresses* is both interesting and amusing. The last-mentioned number is a typical example of the kind of paper in which Steele particularly excelled. At the commencement of the *Tatler* he had announced his special province to be that which concerned the fair sex, and he continued to write in the same strain to the last.

"Mr Ironside was yesterday in the evening in the back room at *Button's* with some of his favourite acquaintance, and the discourse which started amongst them happened to be upon Dress: when the sage had heard the different opinions of the company upon this subject, which were delivered very freely (for there is something so familiar or comick in the old gentleman, that the superiority of his years, wisdom, and experience, give no manner of check to younger people), after having made some observations upon the same subject, he proceeded to talk his own way, with a little of the singularity of his age.

"I have often (said Nestor) reflected that the history of dresses would be a matter of much entertainment, and not without instruction. The female world, as being the more ornamental part of mankind, are naturally addicted to innovation and invention of this kind. I had an acquaintance once with a lady, who professed to me that she made it her study; but instead of laying on upon her face different colours, and daubing herself with an artificial complexion, her manner was, in the beginning of the year, to have her face drawn in a little oval, extremely like, and without flattery. She had many dresses painted on a kind of isinglass, which she could clap upon the face of this oval, and observe what colours or subdivisions of colours, best became her complexion. I have seen her make the same face bear a becoming sadness, a downcast innocence, an heedless gaiety, or a respectful attention, according to the different lights and shades that were thrown upon it by the application of the several dresses round the head and neck. This gave my friend the reputation of the most careless, unaffected creature in the world; and yet, said they, how everything becomes her? Nothing at all artful, yet surpassing all the art in the world. The truth of it was, that she never attempted to disguise nature, but to adorn it; and she easily surpassed those who studied to be what they were not, by endeavouring only to appear to the utmost advantage what she was. She would indeed triumph in this judicious manner of dressing, upon occasion, not without some insolence.

"I remember, on the fourth night on which *Alexander the Great* was acted at the Duke's Theatre, it was known the court would be at the play, and jewels were at that time extremely much wore; she resolved upon a desperate experiment to try her skill, and entertain the eyes of the King in opposition to the whole town, who dressed for his observation. She contrived to have a place kept in the front row for her, and to come in after the whole audience was seated, and the King himself in his Box. It naturally created a good deal of bustle to get to her place, and she arrived at it with a kinswoman of no consequence by her side, the common trick of celebrated beauties. When all around her were blazing in jewels, that made their faces appear blank, and drew the eyes of the spectators to the gems about their ears and hair, my beautiful friend stood open to the view of the whole court, dressed only in her hair, and in a white sarcenet hood negligently pinned on it. The novelty of her appearance, the lowly obeisance with which she met the eyes of the King, and the graceful recovery of herself from the disturbance she had given the company in coming so late, fixed the admiration of the court and whole assembly on that object. The King pronounced her the best dressed woman in the company; and pointing to a Foreign Ambassador that sat near him;—Behold, says he, yonder is an *English* lady! You will easily imagine how spitefully the fans worked thro' the whole house; and I overheard several, upon enquiry who she was, answer, some kept hussy I warrant her. This judicious young woman was longer young than any I have ever known; and by following nature, was never out of fashion to her dying-day. She ever led her own year of life; and by never endeavouring to appear as young as those of fewer years, appeared always much younger than those of her own."

THE ESSAYS OF ADDISON AND STEELE

But there are only too few papers of the kind which we have given. A great deal of space is devoted to Swift's delinquencies in the *Examiner*: more and more does the political bias make itself felt; but that the paper was popular enough is shown by its comparatively long run of about sixty numbers.

The *Examiner*, which we have mentioned as having aroused the ire of Steele, had at the time great political importance, but considered from a purely literary point of view it does not possess the same value. It was established by the Tory side, and had the support of the ministry. It was begun in 1710, and continued for four years under the successive editing (if we may call it so) of Dr William King, Swift, St John, Dr Atterbury, Prior, Dr Friend, Mr Oldisworth, and the rather notorious authoress of the *New Atlantis*, Mrs Manley. Commencing in the month of August, it was published weekly on Thursdays, in professed opposition to the *Tatler*. Some articles by Steele in the latter periodical had offended "the other party." The design of the *Examiner* was different from that of the *Tatler*, but the connection of Swift with the magazine makes it interesting, and we are desirous of discovering what use he made in it of his trenchant pen. Swift's attempts reveal the fact that his style did not suit that of the periodical essay. His manner of writing was too bitter, too severe, too unrelenting and savage to deal fitly with the subjects which Addison and Steele loved to touch upon, and his essays are on the whole disappointing. They are usually strongly worded remarks and criticisms upon politics and politicians. Even when an essay by Swift introduces a general subject, as satire or jealousy, it usually quickly particularises into a direct attack on some personage whose identity it is not difficult (or rather would not be difficult at the time) to determine. It has been said that the "purpose mania" often mars a novel; it also endangers the permanent worth of periodical essays. But here and there we come across some papers of value from the purely literary point of view. For example, in the issue for 7th December 1713, there is an essay with the motto *Scribendi principium et fons* which in directness of style and finished sarcasm is equal

THE EIGHTEENTH-CENTURY ESSAYISTS

to many of the papers appearing in the better known periodicals.

"When I have nothing else to do, I often divert myself with looking over the pamphlets and papers, the books and ballads of the week or the month, according as the tide of the press brings in these transitory amusements to us, by due and regular returns. It is observed by naturalists, upon the *Bill of Christenings*, that Providence is extremely generous to mankind, in supplying the world with a pretty even number of males and females, so that nature can be at no great loss in making matches, and may go on, in good order, to chuse out of one sex, a sufficient stock of pleasures and conveniences for the other. The same just distribution holds good in the learned world; the commonwealth of Letters seems to be split and divided into two very equal partitions; not out of a design to create quarrels and animosities, but for promoting mutual comfort and edification; and I believe, in a little time I may be able to affirm, that the numbers are pretty near upon a balance on both sides; and that the world may more properly be divided into writer and reader, by way of exact cantonment, than if we were to slice it down the equator, or set it out in halves, by any other partition, however minute and circumstantial.

"In my perusal of the Labours of my fellow-moderns, I often skip from page to page; dip here and there, and taste a little of one author, and a little of another, according as the grave, the merry, the splenetic or the sleepy fit comes on me. I would have the whole man employed in reading, and as much regard paid to the health of the body, as the improvement of the mind, in that noble exercise. Thanks to my contemporaries, they do not stint our constitutions: let poor, barbarous, illiterate nations number their *authors*, as they do their *Kings*; with us the state of learning is perfectly anarchical; our wits and writers make a people of themselves, a vast innumerable multitude, we have more pens worn than swords. We go cased in Quills, after the manner of some Indian princes, and carry about us the same natural armour that Claudian speaks of, in his fine description of a porcupine. There are, I know, some sour critics who often advance a very odd sort of notion; that none ought to be suffered to write, but only those who can; but this restriction is a manifest breach of our most autocrat and established liberties. Give me, as Horace expresses it, the pleasure of dipping into a large heap."

(Then he discusses the production of pamphlets, so common in his day.)

THE ESSAYS OF ADDISON AND STEELE

"A pamphlet, like a theatrical or dramatic action, must consist of a beginning, a middle, and an end. An author's usual exordium is the danger of his country. A State must be in danger every time these people of importance write; this opens their mouths, as it did the dumb prince's, when his father was about to be murdered. Their fellow-subjects are to be made tame intelligent creatures, whom they are sent to warn and admonish. An author is to express his aversion to writing, and deference to abler pens; but then the call of his country, the public good—and so forth. Here it may be proper to hint at what all good men fear, or all honest men apprehend; what some foresee, what others have at heart, and what the rest cannot chuse but express their concern for.

"Towards the middle of a pamphlet, when the author should fall directly upon his main business, he may support his facts by some such expressions as these: There were good grounds to believe; men were left to judge; 'twas not improbable; a report then ran; many did not stick to believe; we saw clearly through that affair—and the like. If there be occasion for a Greek or Latin fragment, the loosest and most general scraps ought to be hauled in, in form; whose universality leaves them at the mercy of every schoolboy. (While) the least attempt to speak to the purpose, empowers a pamphleteer to give out: Thus have I fully proved; I have now demonstrated beyond all contradiction; They can never answer it; and so hastens to a conclusion. Before he takes his leave, an author should not forget to say: He has discharged his conscience as a good subject; something should be added, too, about opening of eyes and alarming the nation. Just as FINIS comes in sight, it is not amiss to commit a cause or country to the protection of some abler power than his humble pen; which, however, is perpetually devoted—and so forth. By such strange discoveries and improvements every poor obscure Pamphlet comes to give a splendid shilling for part of its frontispiece."

But such papers are few and far between. Steele, in the *Tatler*, had been giving occasional papers or part of papers on political subjects, but in the *Examiner* it is the other way round; only occasionally do we get papers of a purely literary nature. It is politics pure and undiluted; thus the value of the paper is vitiated so far as its relation to the *Tatler* and *Spectator* literary kind is concerned.

A second paper which appeared side by side with the *Spectator*, but as a very minor luminary, and one which makes a curious contrast to the *Spectator*, is *Delights for the*

THE EIGHTEENTH-CENTURY ESSAYISTS

Ingenious, a "monthly entertainment for the Curious of both Sexes." It was published monthly during 1711 at the price of threepence, and shows at how early a date miscellaneous magazines commenced to appear. It is written by John Tipper, author of the *Lady's Diary*, with assistance from readers, and he takes as his motto what seems to be a free translation of the Latin motto, "Omne tulit punctum, etc."

> "He certainly doth hit the white
> Who joins instruction to delight."

The contents of his magazine are various, and include verses and enigmas, but each month there is usually a short story and an essay of the *Spectator* pattern. The essay in the first number is *Of neat and elegant behaviour*, and collects together a great deal of excellent advice as to walking, talking, eating, and manners generally. The short story is called *Gratitude in Perfection*, and gives an account of how a benefit conferred on a Turk by an Englishman in Italy was gratefully repaid by the former, when he had an opportunity to do so, when the Englishman was in trouble in the East. The story in the next number is nearer Addison's *genre*. It is called the *Whimsical Fop*, and tells humorously of a beau who cannot make up his mind to a profession but turns monk at last. Then replies to correspondents are given, and these often take up a page or two, and are really short papers, *e.g.* on health, the comparative happiness of rich and poor, and so on. Thus, while retaining so much of the *Spectator* features, the author, Mr Tipper, has rather striven to give an *Olla-podrida* for the tea-table or the club-room.

Steele's paper *The Lover* followed in the year 1714. It professes to be written in imitation of the *Tatler* by *Marmaduke Myrtle, Gent.* (*i.e.* Steele), and appeared three times a week, the first number being that for Thursday, 25th February 1714. In his first essay, Steele refers to the title he has chosen and says that in all the periodicals that had hitherto been published insufficient attention had been paid to "the softer affections of the mind, which, being properly raised and awakened, make way for the operation of all good arts." He clings to the *Club* idea, for he introduces and describes several characters who are to assist him : *Mr Severn*, a young man, twenty-five years of age ; *Mr Oswald*, a widower ; *Mr Mullet*, a gentleman of fortune ; *Mr Johnson*, a married man ; *Mr Wildgoose*, an old bachelor ; and lastly himself, *Mr Marmaduke Myrtle*. This makes quite a formidable array of characters to make use of, but the majority are really never at all developed. In the second number he discusses his fondness for one of his lady friends, *Mrs Ann Page* ; and so he proceeds, giving in the forty essays of *The Lover* a wonderful store of love affairs and advice in love. It is, of its kind, a most successful periodical, and displays Steele in a style of paper which he made his own.

Of the forty numbers published, three were by his great ally Addison. The first of these (No. 10) comments on the extravagant fondness (then prevalent) for china-ware : " There are no inclinations in women," he says, " which more surprise me than their passions for chalk and china. The first of these maladies wears out in a little time, but when a woman is visited with the second, it generally takes possession of her for life. China vessels are playthings for women of all ages. An old lady of fourscore shall be as busy in cleaning an Indian Mandarin, as her great-granddaughter is in dressing her baby. The common way of purchasing such trifles, if I may believe my female informers, is by exchanging old suits of clothes for this brittle ware. I have known an old petticoat metamorphosed into a punch-bowl, and a pair of breeches into a tea-pot." Then he moralises on the uselessness of the craze, and advises the ladies rather to heap up piles of earthen platters and brown jugs ; " but there is an objection to these which cannot be overcome," namely, that they would be of some use, and might be taken down on all occasions to be employed in the services of the family, besides that " they are intolerably cheap, and most shamefully durable and lasting." In the second he characteristically came forward to speak in favour of his friend Budgell, recommending his translation of *Theophrastus*, just as he had done with regard to Tom D'Urfey in the *Guardian* (No. 67) when D'Urfey had fallen upon evil days. His third contribution, No. 39, dated May of the same year (1714), is a directly didactic paper, and reproves *Will. Wormwood*, " who is related to me by my mother's side," for possessing a discontented temper and for his general slovenliness of disposition.

The *Reader*, also by Steele, ran practically side by side with the *Lover*; at least it was begun a month before the latter was finished, and is indicative of Steele's restlessness and changeful energy. He introduces himself this time as a man who has almost read himself blind; he is constantly frequenting coffee-houses and devouring all the papers. But the *Reader* is much more political in tone than the *Lover*; it is in fact more like the *Englishman*, and constantly, like the latter periodical, makes animadversions against Swift's *Examiner*. Then there are moanings as to the perilous state of the Church and the country generally. But No. 8 still keeps up the *Club* idea. This time it is a party " who are never quite drunk or sober, but go to bed mellow every night." This was a feature quite characteristic of Steele's time, and even Addison was charged with too great a love for a bottle of wine; but it was a characteristic still present at the end of the century; Sir Walter Scott had the same charge levelled against him, and Peacock in his novels laments the earlier and more social times. But the *Reader* soon came to an end, nine papers only being published.

In the following few months there appeared another short-lived paper by Steele, *Town-Talk, in a Series of Letters to a Lady in the Country*. The first number was published on Saturday, 17th December 1715. It was a weekly paper, and, like the *Reader*, only nine numbers were published. The essays are all written in the form of letters, but really differ very little from *Tatler* papers. Steele discusses, literally, as the title suggests, the talk of the town, and if it is true it is not very elevating. The first number gives a much criticised account of the affairs of the *Blind Gallant*. It is only just to state that Steele at once apologised for it. In the second number he also relates the conversation he had on a visit to a lady friend, and these accounts are often as vivid as Swift's *Polite Conversation*, but without the terrible satire which the latter has infused, with a special purpose, into his work. The fifth is political and relates to the fears entertained with regard to the Pretender (it was, of course, the time of the '15 Rebellion), and he continues the discussion in Nos. 8 and 9. The sixth contains an interesting reference to Selden's *Table Talk*, which Steele apparently knew well.

With this periodical we may also group two others—*Chitchat* and the *Tea-Table*, both by Steele. *Chitchat* continues *Town-Talk*, but it only ran for three numbers, during March 1716; and so also the *Tea-Table* only appeared three times. It is to be noted that a number of these titles were used again and again for periodicals, and some are in use at the present day.

There were also papers published about the same time of an increasingly political character. For example, the *Whig-Examiner* was started by Addison and his party to correct the views of the *Examiner* run by Swift and the Tories. The first number was published on Thursday, 14th September 1710, and it continued to appear on Thursday of each week, but it had only a short life. "The design of this work," writes Addison, " is to censure the writings of others, and to give all persons a re-hearing who have suffered under any unjust sentence of the *Examiner*. As that author has hitherto proceeded, his paper would have been more properly entitled the *Executioner*."

After such a " fighting " commencement, we are scarcely surprised to find a considerable political bias throughout the papers, but most of them still retain the humorous touches which betray Addison's hand. The first number has some humorous discussions on different forms of the old puzzle: "What animal is it

> "Which has four feet at morning bright?
> Has two at noon, and three at night?"

The second gives another criticism of an *Examiner* paper; while the next gives a version of a speech by Alcibiades; the fourth a clever panegyric on nonsense, with special satiric references to the kind displayed by the *Examiner*; and the fifth is almost purely political.

But amongst papers of this type the *Freeholder* is outstanding. Addison wrote in it, it is true, for special party defence purposes; but amongst its fifty-five numbers are to be found papers by him of the true *Spectator* type; manners, dress, wit, and humorous characterisation being found. Chief among the latter are his pictures of the *Tory Foxhunter* (Nos. 44 and 47), which make very pleasant reading, and show Addison's hand had not lost its cunning. In the first number, dated 23rd December 1715, he puts forward the title and design of his work. "I shall in the course of this paper (to be published every Monday and Friday) endeavour to open the eyes of my countrymen to their own interest, to show them the privileges of an English freeholder which they enjoy in common with myself, and to make them sensible how these blessings are secured to us by His Majesty's title, his administration, and his personal character." A rather remarkable paper is the twenty-seventh, which gives the vision of a Highland seer, *Second-sighted Sawney*, "Transmitted to me by a student in Glasgow, who took the whole relation from him." Sawney was descended of an ancient family, very much renowned for their skill in prognostics. Most of his ancestors were second-sighted, and his mother but narrowly escaped being burnt for a witch. As he was going out one morning very early to steal a sheep, he was seized on the sudden with a fit of second-sight. The face of the whole country about him was changed in the twinkling of an eye and presented him with a wide prospect of new scenes and objects, which he had never seen till that day." This seems a most promising beginning, but it turns out the usual class of vision, this time the Temple of Rebellion with Sedition, Ambition, Envy, Disgrace, Poverty, and Disappointment all appearing. Thus there is a decided political shade over nearly all the pages of the *Freeholder*.

Steele thought the humour of the *Freeholder* too nice and gentle for such noisy times, and that "the ministry made use of a lute, when they should have called for a trumpet."

But all the papers were not written by Addison and Steele; all apparently did not realise the true meaning and spirit of the essay periodical, or had not the powers to attain to them—for this was the period which called forth Theo-

THE ESSAYS OF ADDISON AND STEELE

bald's remark, " It may well be called the age of Counsellors, when every Blockhead who could write his own name, attempted to inform and amuse the publick." There is at least one essay periodical which does not lie under this sweeping condemnation. The *Freethinker*, published a little before Steele's *Theatre*, was undertaken by no less a person than Ambrose Philips. In all one hundred and fifty-nine numbers were issued. Philips was assisted by not a few learned men, including the Archbishop of Armagh, Stubbs, and Dr Pearce. The *Freethinker* was afterwards reprinted in a three-volume edition. Fielding thought it nearly as good as the *Tatler* or *Spectator*. We cannot subscribe to this opinion, but it is a periodical which certainly deserves attention. The paper was issued on Mondays and Fridays, and first appeared on 24th March 1718. The motto is a good Horatian one, *Sapere aude*. The scheme followed is closely akin to that of the *Tatler* and *Spectator*. But the title is apt to be misleading. The periodical is not atheistical in tone but rather the opposite, for in the first number Philips discusses the degradation into which the term *Freethinking* has fallen. He hopes to restore it, and make it a name of praise and reputation. In the third number he enters more fully into his designs. He does not want " to appear a strange, heathenish creature to the Ladies," rather he wishes " to embellish their understanding and give their minds a beautiful turn," and he strongly incites them to a love of letters by citing the example of Queen Elizabeth. The next essay is a stock one *On Curiosity*, but the fifth supplies a variation. It is an account given by a chaplain of a journey made from Aleppo to Jerusalem in the year 1697. The eighth number presents an amusing account of how Jack Shepherd has ended his career at Tyburn just a short while before, and gives an account of some of his adventures. Poetry appears in the ninth, and in the next essay Philips returns to the purpose of his title, and discusses the importance of the free use of our reason. Then again comes the important principle of variation, and No. 11 devotes itself to lighter talk on love and vanity. The fifteenth issue deals with duelling and its dangers to society, and gives an affecting story of a duel. The story ends thus, "The moral of this story does not intimate to us that we should renounce our Christianity to preserve an imaginary honour, but that we should lay aside duelling rather than forfeit our title to Christianity." The advice was unfortunately not taken till about the middle of the following century. The seventeenth gives advice to a Cambridge student in love: "Go, like a good boy, to mind your studies; a cooling dyet (*sic*) and a course of mathematics may restore you to yourself." Philips, like Addison, manages to maintain an admirable balance between the serious and the gay. The actual style of the paper will best be shown by an extract. The one we give is from the seventh number. It has maintained the true spirit of the periodical essay. The style is simple and nervous, the humour has that light touch which Addison and Steele had made popular, and the subject is a favourite one.

"To this piece of history, I shall subjoin a matrimonial story in low-life, as it was told me by a gentleman, whose curiosity led him to be present at it. I remember (said he) in my youth, I happened to ramble, with a friend, on Easter Monday, into St Pancras Church in the fields; where a great many, whose necessity puts them upon frugality, are married at under-rates and save the expense of a license. We found the little Church crowded with Lovers. No discontent appeared amongst them, but what proceeded from an impatience, that one couple only could be married at a time. We observed, among the rest, a plump, black-eyed damsel, who tugged after her a bashful young fellow. She bustled with him through the crowd, and gained the rails of the communion-table, in spite of opposition. There is it seems a bye-law peculiar to this Church, by which every couple before the ceremony begins, are required to lay down half the fees on the Book, and are allowed credit for the remainder till the service is half over. The bridegroom accordingly deposited one moiety; and the Doctor read away. When now, coming to his usual resting place, he made a full stop. Whereupon the Clerk hinted to the young man 'that this was the time to pay down the remainder of the dues.' The poor fellow was heavily dismayed at this demand, and searched his pockets for what he knew was not to be found. At last he whispered to the bride, and she answered him only with a dejected countenance. There was a profound silence for some minutes, till they were told nothing further could be done unless the residue was forthcoming.

THE ESSAYS OF ADDISON AND STEELE

What could they do in these neutral circumstances, half-married and half-unmarried ? The woman, who first recovered her confusion, said, 'Pray, sir, marry us as much as you can afford for that money,' to which he replied, he had gone to the utmost syllable. Upon this, after a little pause, she untied her shoe, and pulled out three shillings and ninepence (a hidden reserve for pin-money), and with a deep sigh laid it upon the book; and so the suspended nuptials were perfected. A few more lines will serve to dispatch another little marriage incident, and to disengage me from my promise. When the Lady Betty Modish was to be married to Sir Thomas Truby, she came to Church with a kind of non-juring sample upon her conscience. This appeared, when she was to repeat the word obey. Here her voice failed on a sudden. The minister insisted upon her speaking out; but she continued mute; and all was at a stand. Hereupon Sir Thomas with great presence of mind, whispered the minister to go on, saying, 'Leave that punctilio to me, I pass my word for the lady's orthodoxy.' And accordingly the Knight made her sensible, upon every dispute, that his honour was engaged for her obedience."

In the twenty-third number there is an admirable discussion of the *ethos* of the periodical itself. Philips calls it " the throwing out short lectures from the press, upon stated days," and he dilates upon the widespread nature of the periodical essay, and its application to all the needs of both sexes; and he " wishes his own modicum of praise, for he has made philosophy the amusement of the coffee-houses." It is instructive to trace a development, as the magazine proceeds, in the introduction of features not always so appropriate. For example, from the fifty-fifth number onwards, Philips gives a set of discourses regarding which he himself says that they will be easier to read when they are published in collected form. He thus condemns them as they are, for in the essay periodical each number should be complete in itself.

Though Philips posed as a *Freethinker*, he was not against religion. He came to its rescue in papers on atheism, superstition, and enthusiasm. On the whole his treatment of these themes tends to the heavy side. The lighter discourses on love and allied subjects are thrown in between political lectures about the duties of government, as if they were merely there to sweeten the political pill. The opening sentence of one of these lectures is sufficient to frighten the reader away. For example, the hundredth number commences, "I shall now speak to the second general head of my eighty-first lecture, wherein I have observed that a Minister of State should have a more distinct knowledge of transactions." It would seem that Philips is safe only so long as he keeps close to the Addisonian pattern of essay. Examples of this latter type are, *On the Art of Grinning* (No. 28) and *On Omens and Superstitions* (No. 66). They are both good, though reminiscent of Addison. The latter essay was an answer to idle fears occasioned by an eclipse of the moon. Stories help to give variety. For example, Nos. 80 and 84 form what Philips calls "two winter evening tales," and others (Nos. 92, 109, and 110) are "To entice young ladies to delight in reading, and to lead them insensibly into the paths of philosophy." These are fairy stories with a moral designed to keep one contented with one's lot. A gipsy girl sacrifices her youth to become a queen, and the toothless old sovereign becomes the blooming gipsy, but they both regret the exchange, and are retransformed by the obliging fairy godmother in attendance. There is a pretty and fanciful application of sight through coloured glasses, contrasted with the distorted views of man in his pursuit after illusory objects (No. 125). Frequently there is a lament that the good advice of the author is being thrown away; and a letter (No. 108) says that the animadversions of the *Freethinker* upon masquerades have done nothing to put a stop to the follies and vices attendant on these popular assemblies. But optimism dies hard, and in No. 147 Philips is still hoping against hope that "if our lovely spinsters, who have so much leisure, and as good eyes for reading as our youths have, did but know the pleasures of sound knowledge they would find the fictions of novels and romances to be insipid amusements, compared to the realities of philosophy"; and "by the time that the *Freethinker* grows as voluminous as the *Grand Cyrus*" he does not question but "he shall be honoured with a shelf in every virgin's closet, and be thought a more entertaining author." Vain hope; the novel as a new literary kind was only at the commencement of a most vigorous life, while Philips's *Freethinker* was fast hastening to a close.

The fault of the *Freethinker* is, that, though it contains a large number of excellent essays, it gives too many papers of a serious type, somewhat akin to those of Dr Johnson in his *Rambler*, but lacking the genius which the latter combined with his rather melancholy outlook on life. Often they are merely dull, but in the whole bulk of essays which the *Freethinker* contains there are compensations. We have both variety and excellence, and a wide and general appeal, and the periodical remains a notable production.

To show the variety of papers which were being published at the same time as the *Freethinker*, we instance the *Delphick Oracle* (1719-20). It came out monthly, at a shilling, the first number in September, and continued the older seventeenth-century manner of L'Estrange and Dunton rather than that of the *Tatler* or *Spectator*. Questions are put and answers given, and some of the latter, ranging to nearly three or four pages, come under the heading of essays. All subjects are touched upon, poetry and religion and matrimony, just as the *Athenian Oracle* had in an earlier reign attempted to do.

The *Old Whig* and *Plebeian* again, both of which appeared at the same time, are of a different nature, almost wholly political in tone. They had a short-lived existence, but make interesting reading, for they contain the documents which record the regrettable split between Addison and Steele. No. 1 of the *Old Whig* is "On the state of the Peerage, with remarks upon the *Plebeian*." Addison's attack is written in a surprisingly vigorous manner, and the way in which he carries it out is quite methodical. He quotes a paragraph from the article in Steele's *Plebeian*, examines it caustically and disposes of it; takes up another paragraph, treats it in the same manner, and so on to the end. Dr Johnson, in his life of Addison, gives a full account of this dispute. As regards papers of a purely social or general nature there are none.

In the following year we have the penultimate periodical of Steele's. This was the *Theatre*, written in the character of *Sir John Edgar*. The first number appeared at the beginning of the year 1720, and the paper appeared twice a week for fourteen weeks. No doubt this periodical came as a surprise. For several years before Steele had been in quasi-retirement in Wales. In the first number *Sir John* introduces himself as a man sixty-one years of age. He has a son *Harry* and a dear lady friend, *Sophronia*, with whom they often talk about the theatre, because she has always believed in and encouraged theatrical diversions. And it is at the tea-table of *Sophronia* that *Sir John* says he gathers up much of the material to work into his essays. This scheme closely resembles that of *Lady Lizard* and her tea-table as described in the *Guardian*. The fourth and fifth papers adopt a favourite device; they record and comment on opinions overheard at different places about his own periodical the *Theatre*. In the seventh number Steele goes on to mention and criticise several plays. A new feature is introduced in the ninth and the succeeding numbers. *Sir John* enters the complaints and remarks in general of " the injured Knight," as he calls him, " Sir Richard Steele " ! Thus Steele openly airs his own grievances. In the fifteenth number he returns again to criticism of the drama, and two numbers later Steele even criticises his own work. There is more than a hint of literary exhaustion in the procedure.

There followed a continuation of the *Theatre* in the *Anti-Theatre*, fifteen numbers of which were published. This time Steele is *Sir John Falstaffe*. It was the last appearance of Steele as a periodical essayist; his last effort in a literary kind of which he had practically been the founder, and in which he had laboured so long and so successfully. A paper which may by a chance be his is *Pasquin*, which appeared in 1723 (Steele did not die until the year 1729). This paper is similar in kind to the *Theatre*, but is more political in tone, and is constantly making sarcastic references to the *True Briton*, a paper which was vigorously carried on by Wharton, but which is almost entirely political in its purpose and in its execution.

Thus ended the literary production of Steele. He died in 1729, ten years after the death of Addison. They had been born in the same year, 1672, and the closeness in time of their birth had been realised in the closeness of their literary connection in their lives, though it was regrettable that they were partially estranged at the time of Addison's death by the stupid political quarrel in the *Plebeian* and *Old Whig*. The natures of Addison and Steele were very different, and it has become almost a habit now to exalt the wayward and impulsive Steele over the quieter and more sedate Addison. And certain incidents are quoted to support the case for Steele to the discredit of Addison. But the story, for example, which relates how Addison rigorously exacted the repayment of a small loan from Steele, is, if true, best represented as a stern lesson and rebuke. Steele's habit of running into debt cannot be condoned. The other stories, which more than hint at a discreditable reason for Addison's comparatively early death, have never been authenticated. And the work of the two men justifies the older view that Addison was indeed the more balanced in literary style as well as in life. But the very differences in the natures of the two men made them all the more powerful in conjunction. Addison with his clear and simple style, almost perfect in its own way, unerringly touched upon the foibles of the beau and the man of fashion; while Steele made an equally effective, if more emotional, appeal to the fair sex. The *Tatler* and *Spectator* had been written for a certain section of society. The lower classes could not read at all; the middle classes (or at least the lower middle class) were immersed in business. It was the upper class, the court circle and leisured people of society, to whom the appeal of Addison and Steele was specially made. It was the class who by reason of their very leisure needed guidance, and it was to this somewhat artificial society that the *Tatler* and *Spectator* had come as a tonic, producing a marked effect in a thousand ways, in manners and morals and life. The critic of literature who preserves the strictly historical standpoint will always give a high place to the work of Addison and Steele.

CHAPTER III

THE PERIODICAL ESSAY BETWEEN THE *GUARDIAN* AND THE *RAMBLER*

In many histories of English Literature the work of Johnson in the *Rambler* is considered immediately after the *Tatler*, *Spectator*, and *Guardian* of Addison and Steele. Even in the *British Essayists*, the collection of periodical essays which still remains the classical one, that is the order of sequence. But the last number of the *Guardian* appeared in October 1713, the first number of the *Rambler* in March 1750. There is a " gap " here of nearly forty years, and it is the history of this " gap " which we now endeavour to give. Many of the periodicals which were issued were extremely short-lived, and quickly vanished from the eye of the public. Nathan Drake in his work on the periodical essayists names titles of several periodicals which cannot now be traced. They seem to have been swallowed up in oblivion, and others of the periodical essays are so scarce that only one or two copies exist to-day, and these copies are often in an imperfect condition. But in a history of the periodical essay of the eighteenth century which professes to be at all complete, they cannot be neglected. Many of these minor periodicals had an influence at the time; they did something to continue the stream of periodical essay life, and therefore cannot be omitted, however mediocre we may feel them to be.

It had been expected that the *Stamp Act*, which came into force and exacted a tax of a halfpenny on every half-sheet, would suppress altogether many papers and periodicals. For a time it may have had some result in this direction, but soon the numbers, instead of decreasing, began to increase. Take newspapers, for example. The *Flying*

FROM THE GUARDIAN TO THE RAMBLER

Post and *Post Bag* of 1715 gave interesting details of the progress of the Earl of Mar to Edinburgh during the Jacobite Rising of that year: the *Dublin Gazette* and *Dublin Courant* a somewhat highly coloured account of a massacre carried through by soldiers in Switzerland. Such events gave practice in descriptive writing. The *St James' Evening Post* and the *Daily Courant* are representative papers of the London press. But these newspapers yielded little fruit at the time so far as periodical essays are concerned. Defoe was perhaps the only prominent man of letters who wrote to papers about this period. Later Fielding took up the succession, and still later some of the best work of Johnson and Goldsmith was published in the first instance in newspapers. These papers were largely retailers of news; and the literary value of the majority of the papers is almost negligible. But two may be singled out as exceptions to this rule. They were Applebee's *Original Weekly Journal* (1714) and Mist's *Weekly Journal* (1715). To both of these Defoe contributed. The former, Applebee's *Journal*, was issued on Saturdays and was made up of three leaves in small folio. It was a Tory publication, though moderate in tone. It was not until June 1720 that Defoe began to contribute. He had promised to write what were called the *letters introductory*, containing a short essay frequently on a political subject of interest at the time, sometimes an article of a more purely literary character. Defoe wrote under the character of *Oliver Oldway*. To this latter paper, Mist's *Journal*, Defoe also contributed a few papers, but not nearly so many as to Applebee's. It is surprising to find Defoe writing to Mist's *Journal* at all, because it was founded to support the claims of the Pretender, and Defoe was supporting at the same time the ruling government, if not actually in their pay. It is not always easy to say with certainty which of the articles were written by Defoe. In a collection of them published by Lee a number of years ago, there are not many which show an improvement in style or treatment upon the *Scandal Club* papers in the *Review*. Yet it was at this later period that Defoe's novel production was at its best. *Robinson Crusoe* and *Captain Singleton* appeared in 1720, and two years later

THE EIGHTEENTH-CENTURY ESSAYISTS

Moll Flanders. The explanation probably is that Defoe wrote them hurriedly. With so many literary irons in the fire, all that he wrote could not be equally good.

But in Mist's *Journal* there also appeared a series of essays much after the style of the *Spectator* papers, written mainly by Theobald. They were afterwards bound up separately, as Johnson's *Idler* papers and Goldsmith's *Citizen of the World* papers later on. The first of these " insert " essays appeared on Monday, 11th April 1715, in Mist's *Journal* and they were continued three times a week for ninety-six numbers. Theobald has an excellent preface to the collected edition (1717, 3 volumes) of these periodical essays. He says: " It was a hard task to come after the *Spectator* and avoid striking into paths he had trod, and still a harder to invent new subjects, and work upon them with any degree of the same genius and delicacy. Another disadvantage was the vast multitude of papers that pretended to give an equal diversion to the Town which, though they died soon, and have left no memory behind them, yet found readers heavy enough to sympathise with their dullness. That period of time may be well called the age of counsellors, when every blockhead who could write his name attempted to inform and amuse the publick."

In the first number Theobald humorously represents himself as being " lineally descended from *Benjamin Johnson* of surly memory," and describes how he came up to town, went about " the clubs, publick meetings, and mixed assemblies of all kinds." He has determined to make " a strict inquisition into the licens'd vanities of both sexes." " In short I reserve to myself the uncontrollable privilege of being gay or grave, at my own pleasure," but he " refuses to recognise the names of Whig and Tory." Theobald thus understood the two important features—the one positive, the other negative—taught by Addison for the success of a magazine of this nature—variety and abstention from party politics. And it is surprising how well he maintains these features in his paper. In Nos. 7 and 10 he deals with Shakespeare's *Lear*, and after recounting the foundation of the story in history, he adds, " I intend not to charge it with these errors, which all this author's

FROM THE GUARDIAN TO THE RAMBLER

plays lie under, through his being unacquainted with the rules of Aristotle, and the tragedies of the Ancients." Such a sentence reveals the critical position of the period. Again, *Mr Johnson* tells of his aunt, who, for ten years, has made him read for an hour each week, to her, out of some Greek author. She knows no Greek, and yet *Mr Johnson* finds that " she was flushed with anger and indignation, melted and died away with a languishing softness as the subject required." He explains this by saying " that Homer commonly conveys the images he represents to the soul in words that bear a near similitude to the ideas, which help to impress them more forcibly to the mind." This might be a forecast of criticism actually applied to Tennyson's poetry, but more probably it is just a variant of the then common idea, " the sound is but the echo of the sense," expressed by Pope himself in the *Essay on Criticism.* In the thirty-third number ill-natured critics come in for condemnation ; *Othello* is criticised in the thirty-sixth, and Theobald again refers to Aristotle and the views on Drama held by the Ancients. He writes also on *Julius Cæsar* (No. 70) ; is inclined to put it first among Shakespeare's plays ; and gives a list of the best passages, including Mark Antony's speech. This frequency of critical papers on Shakespeare by Theobald need not surprise us, when we remember that he edited Shakespeare himself and made some famous, and (whether consciously or not) often happy emendations. His " and a' babbled of green fields " of Falstaff's death in *Henry V.* is famous. He recommends (No. 36) the story of *Œdipus Tyrannus* as eminently suitable for tragedy, and gives praise to " Mr Pope's *Homer*." He finds that " the spirit of Homer breathes through all the translation." We would not echo this remark to-day ; but this critical series of papers by Theobald has historical interest for literary criticism. In the other essays many of the usual subjects of morals and manners are discussed : on the Giving and Taking of Advice (No. 26) ; on Flattery (No. 17) ; on Jealousy (No. 16) ; on Pride and its Folly in all Men (No. 27) ; on Superstition and its Effects (No. 11) ; on Gallantry (No. 92) ; on Hope (No. 83) ; on the Blessings of the Married State (No. 87) ; on Dreams (Nos. 38

and 84); on Love (No. 49); and on Modesty (No. 52). All these subjects are treated in much the same way as they were handled by Addison and Steele in the *Tatler* and *Spectator*. A more serious group of essays are reminiscent of Addison's " Saturday " papers in the *Spectator*. Examples of these are an essay on *The Immortality of the Soul* (No. 78) and another on *Self-examination* (No. 95). As an illustration of Theobald's style, perhaps no better example could be given than the thirty-eighth number, which follows out the " vision " method.

" I am so far of opinion that our common dreams proceed from reflection and indigestion, that, to prevent this fantastic disturbance of my slumbers, I have for some years accustomed myself to go supperless to bed. Fancy, however, I am convinced, will sometimes operate on an empty stomach, and strange images be presented to us in our sleep, even when we live most physically, and endeavour to keep the noxious humours in subjection. Tertullian, I remember, has from some certain dreams attempted to prove the excellence of our souls. There are others, I believe, which at best but evidence the vigour of the animal spirits, and the strange power of that mimic fancy, as Dryden stiles her, over sleeping reason.

" The reverie into which I so lately slipt has given me assurance of this notion, by furnishing out a vision of such extravagance as no trace of thought or reason can account for.

" Methought, I was situated in the midst of a wide and pleasant field, that looked gay and delightful as the poet's Elysium; the deliciousness of the clime, and the balmy breezes that blew with such fragrancy, persuaded me that I was transplanted to the Asian Continent; and the buildings and towers, that I beheld on the distant skirts of the plain, seemed such as I was only acquainted with from a knowledge of antiquity. On my left hand, I saw a grove of myrtles, whose walks were chequered with frequent arbours blooming with jessamine and woodbine. On the right, I beheld a fountain which diffused its waters in great plenty from a rising ground, and which were received in a spacious vale beneath. The streams that arose from it were of so faint and sickly a scent, that I thought they checked the austerity of my nature, and tainted me with thoughts of unusual softness and effeminacy.

" My curiosity was not a little prompted to discover the mystery of this sudden alteration, when approaching the vale I saw a concourse of people, some naked, others dressing, and who had all

FROM THE GUARDIAN TO THE RAMBLER

been bathing in the fountain. Their countenances were, for the most part, wan and consumptive; and those, who looked with most bloom and colour, had their features tempered with a maidenly blush, and lines which seemed peculiar to the softer sex. On the remote bank I beheld swarms of creatures of a more rugged disposition; their arms and habits confessed them natives of old Greece and Rome, nor were there a few with painted skins, such as we are told the sons of Britain formerly were. These all looked down with contempt on the generation of bathers, and some with such glances of indignation as showed 'em resolved to launch down their spears, and transfix them on the spot.

"Whilst I stood gazing with some wonder, and longing to be informed what this odd mixture should intend, I was accosted by an old fellow, whom I should easily have mistaken for Diogenes, had he communicated his sentiments from a Tub. Friend, says he, I perceive by the earnestness of your looks, you are a stranger to this place. Know then that those waters, in which such numbers continually bathe, flow from the celebrated fountain of Salmacis. They still retain a quality, for which they have been in all ages noted, of enervating the souls of those who wash in them; the most martial spirits are not secured from their infection; and the heroes who have ventured their limbs in that stream, have afterwards exchanged the javelin for the distaff. If you want further proofs of their emasculating property, than from the mien and complexions of those animals you have seen, follow me to yon grove, and I'll show you in what employments the frequenters of this spring spend their lazy hours.

"My old guide, without giving me leave to reply, led the way to the grove, and I followed him with pleasure and expectation of the novelty. In the first arbour we came to, I saw a spruce ruddy-looking youth, who was chaffering with an old hag, about curious teeth-powder, and paste for the hands. We proceeded not much further e'er we started a second, who was mighty busie in pickling of cucumbers. Where we made the third stand we found the passage embarrassed with French tailors and peruke-makers, and perceived they were attending on a man of mode, and waiting for improvements in dress and fashions.

"As we struck into another walk, we were alarmed with the sound of affected harmony; and, approaching, surprised a beau playing with a fan, and practising airs out of an opera. The next remove presented us with a pale-faced animal, receiving visits in a damask bed, and diverting himself with a favourite cat, with a red ribbon about its neck.

THE EIGHTEENTH-CENTURY ESSAYISTS

"The next object was a creature of gallantry and intrigue adjusting his cravat and peruke in the glass; and on his table lay several billets of gilt paper and inscribed to Clelia and Amarillis; and by them a catalogue of appointments made, and visits in arrear. From another arbour, at no great distance, we heard a mighty tittering as from some females; and discovered a tall young fellow in scarlet, at Blind-man's-buff with his mother's chambermaids.

"At several stations we could perceive them dressing out for the masquerade; at others, practising Boreas and Minuets; nor failed we of some who were diverting themselves with the needle, and exercising their fancies with the disposition of colours in patchwork. The variety of objects could not but furnish out a diversity of amusement; and I was not a little pleased at a spark and his ladies, who in an Indian nightgown and brocaded waistcoat, was frothing up the chocolate.

"What most surprised me in this antick dream, was, that many of the faces I met with in the grove were such as I remember to have seen at the theatres, drawing-rooms, and coffee-houses.

"Soon as I waked, I began to recall the circumstances and particulars of my vision; and to discant on the moral of so chimerical a medley. How often, thought I, have affluence of fortune, and a vice of education, made our sons as effeminate as the waters of Salmacis are reported to have done? How many have been sunk in luxury to a degree of womanhood, who owed the service of their sword or brain to their country?"

It will be seen from this paper that Theobald has caught the true manner and style of the Addisonian vision. And Steele is imitated in lighter articles. The petition of *Martha Twistroll* (No. 25) concerns the new fashion in head dresses, and Theobald says he has sent a specimen "into the country to my good cousin, with direction for her to fix it on a pole in the orchard, to serve for a scarecrow." Letters from correspondents complete the list of the features of the earlier periodicals reproduced. Some of these letters are genuine, most of them are obviously "made up" from *Emilia, Sarah, Clarinda, Diana Doubtful,* and *Timothy Dry-eyes*. Their main themes are love and marriage, and they are often very amusing. Theobald has, to the smallest details, made his paper a model of the *Spectator*, and he has succeeded uncommonly well. In the last number he sums up the aim of his labour. He has endeavoured " to make his essays as little dependent on time and circumstances as possible, so that they should be the same amusement whenever taken in hand," and he emphasises the care he has taken in such a difficult design. Posterity has not fallen in with his views; even the *British Essayists* know not the *Censor*, but there is not a little bright and interesting reading within its pages.

We group along with Theobald's *Censor* papers a number of minor periodicals. There is no classification of them so convenient as the chronological one. If the enumeration of them is apt to become somewhat tedious, it is simply because no star rose in the literary firmament until Fielding began to write in the *Champion*.

Occasional Papers (1716-1718) were issued at threepence a number. The writers of these are given by Drake to be J. Barnes, B. Avery, B. Grosvenor, S. Wright, and J. Evans. None of them has become widely known. The papers are largely political, but there are discussions of a literary character, as, for example, those on orthodoxy, on the pride of authors, on plays and masquerades, and on genius. Each issue contains only a single essay, while these essays are reminiscent of the *Spectator* models. They are, as a rule, longer and a little heavier in tone. An essay on *Plays and Masquerades* deals with them from the moral point of view, and quotes with relish some stinging remarks of Jeremy Collier. Then Letters to the Editor also occur. We may group along with this periodical another which is also rather political in tone, the *Entertainer*. Published weekly on Wednesdays, the first number appeared on 6th November 1717. The *Entertainer* gives short accounts of men of different characters and dispositions, but is much more political in tone than its attractive title would lead us to expect.

The *Wanderer*, which appeared in the same year, is of more interest. Its author was Mr Fox, and twenty-six numbers were issued, the first of which appeared on Saturday, 9th February. After the first number, it was issued weekly on Thursdays. In the introductory essay Fox refers to the difficulties he will meet in writing after an author

(Addison) who has carried all before him both in matter and in style. But he intends to eschew Whig and Tory politics. He proceeds in the usual fashion to give an imaginary description of himself: "My complexion is neither fair nor black; but a little fretted with that enemy to beauty, the small-pox." In the second number there is a vision of some of the mighty dead. It closely follows Addison's scheme, as its opening serves to show: "Running over a various multitude of little passages in my thoughts, I, at last, fell into a profound contemplation of the uncertainty of things in this life." The fourth essay is on religion; the fifth gives advice on the choice of a husband; and the sixth is a letter from a gentleman in love. Fox gives several papers on the sacrament, reflections on the mutability of life, and on despair itself. These last papers are scarcely to be expected from a *Wanderer*, but the titles of the periodicals cannot be pressed too closely, as instance the case of Johnson's *Rambler* itself. We are much struck by the artificial attitude to Nature in all these earlier periodicals. Take this extract from an article on *Spring* in the tenth number: "The crystal streams, which lately mourned in silence, are now relieved from the cold embraces of the frigid mass, and slide softly down, or wanton through their little channels in pleasing murmurs. Grass is produced, flowers bloom, trees bud, the groves are gay, and songs of amorous birds are echoed from bough to bough; and thus, while the world seems to rejoice in a perfect palingenesis, the soul of man grows more susceptible to every pleasing object." Such phrases as "crystal streams" and "songs of amorous birds" are stock material, and are reproduced in all the minor eighteenth-century poets who looked at Nature from Piccadilly and Cheapside. In the last number Fox deigns to explain his title. He has *wandered* over many subjects, but concludes: "If I have been so happy as to encourage virtue, and to detect and put vice out of countenance; to instruct the ignorant, or to entertain the learned, my studies have answered my design, so far as they concern others "—the same moral design which Addison had in view.

We noted earlier that a portion of the *Tatler* had been

issued in Edinburgh, and a few years later another *Tatler* was issued in the same town. From time to time we will have to review periodicals issued in the capital of Scotland. Later in the century they increased in number and in importance—for Edinburgh became the centre of a brilliant literary coterie. The paper to which we presently refer was the *Mercury* or the *Northern Tatler* (1717), *by Duncan Tatler, Esq.* The first number appeared on the first day of the New Year. In his general introduction the author says: "When a new paper comes abroad in the world, the readers of it are naturally curious to know the author, and the ends of that publication," and, as the sub-title indicates, he professed to draw inspiration direct from Steele and the *Tatler*. "I am come," he says, "of the ancient and honourable *Tatlers* of the North. I am now the only *Tatler* alive, and there is not another of the whole race existing, in so much that both our name and family are like to terminate with myself." In the manner which had become customary, this *Issac Bickerstaff* of Scotland proceeds to describe himself. Of superior talent, he had gone through a university course, and travelled widely. He has seen much in the world requiring correction, and thus his aim is suggested. "The end and purpose of this paper is to instruct, rectify, and reform the north country. It is designed for the use of all men, especially for the witty and political fellows who have time to peruse and need to be reformed by it. This paper will also be serviceable to the fair sex." He will treat of love, gallantry, and pleasure; poetry, music, physic, and painting; learning and conversation; breeding and behaviour. Closely following Steele, he dates his various sections from the *Chocolate House*; the *Royal Coffee-house*; the *Caledonia Coffee-house*; the *Holyrood Coffee-house*; and *my own apartment*. In the first number he discusses some general news from his own apartment, and he has also some remarks on conversation, emanating from the *Caledonia Coffee-house*. In the second number he expatiates on the advantages of a life of rest and retirement, far from the madding crowd; and in the section headed from *Holyrood House* he discusses that much-discussed character, the beau. He is not afraid to speak out;

he remarks he will not be browbeaten into silence: " by way of warning," he says, " to the wits, critics, and blockheads in town, they may beware of exercising their talents on me or my performances." This interesting Edinburgh periodical shows that in the transfer from the one capital to the other the essay periodical had not lost its true aim and purpose.

Four years later, 1721, there was published a paper termed *Terræ Filius* (1721), *or The Secret History of the University of Oxford in several essays*. Drake has termed it " a witty, but intemperate work," and the phrase aptly describes it. It was written by Nicholas Amherst. Amherst had been expelled from Oxford for some misdemeanour, and it is probable that it was from this event that the paper arose. For the resentment of Amherst to the treatment meted out to him is clearly revealed in the essays of which this periodical is composed. It was published twice a week, and the first number appeared on Wednesday, 11th January 1721. There were fifty numbers in all, the last being dated 6th July of the same year. In the second number Amherst declares that he will not confine himself to any particular method, " but shall be grave or whimsical, serious or ludicrous, prosaical or poetical, philosophical or satirical, argue or tell stories, weep over his subject or laugh over it, be in humour or out of humour, according to whatever passion is uppermost in his breast."

It must be conceded that the character which he chose was not ill-supported. The papers are vigorously written, and there is much wit and humour in the work. One great object he had in writing was to reprobate the attachment of the University to the Stuarts, and to prove that his own persecution and expulsion originated from his zeal in support of the House of Hanover.

The *Tea-Table*, which appeared in the year 1724, is of considerable interest. Steele, it will be remembered, had already made use of this title for an extremely short-lived attempt of his, but this successor to the name was longer lived. The *Tea-Table* was published twice a week, and the first number appeared on Friday, 21st February 1724. In this first essay, the author sketches the gay state of the town, and doubts that " *two guineas* will be thought better bestowed on a masquerade ticket, than *twopence* for the *Tea-Table*. Such a paper as this is intended to be, ought indeed to be considered as a common good, and the authors, after their death, deserve to have statues erected to their memory. I do not doubt but the plainness, freedom, and sincerity with which it will be writ, will gain it abundance of enemies among those whose lives and actions cannot bear examining into; but all the good and virtuous will praise it, and read no other." This beginning promises well, and shows some considerable appreciation of the true aim and object of the essay periodical. The second number gives a short paper on recreation; the third recounts some of the foolish practices the author is going to attack. And they had better beware of the result. " Can beaus and ladies and lap-dogs be in such eminent danger, as they are at present threatened with, from the *Tea-Table*, and nature suffer no convulsion, and the air and the elements be at peace, and give them no notice of it ! "

The seventh number is a cleverly drawn satiric picture of the times into which he has fallen : " But, thank Heaven ! the empire of this horrid tyranness, Reason, is now almost at an end. Few there are, very few, but have eased themselves of her chains, and thrown off a burden that was too heavy for them to bear ! " A series of papers didactic, satiric, and humorous follows. There is some small attempt at literary criticism. In the twentieth number a discussion on poetry is given, but there are no signs of unrest yet against the neo-classic *régime*. The end of poetry is still " either to please or to instruct," and further in the same paper he sets forth an argument for the reading of poetry. " I am persuaded we are very frequently so much at a loss how to spend our time agreeably and elegantly, that at least it deserves as much encouragement and regard as most other of the arts and sciences which do not answer to this near so well." After such a statement little more need be said. The writer is still deep in Cimmerian darkness— the dawn of Romanticism is still far off. He lacks all appreciation of the true poetic spirit.

One feature (a negative one it is true) calls for praise. Until the thirty-sixth number, when the author closes his periodical, he succeeds in keeping clear of politics. The closing essay is rather neatly and effectively written. The author remarks that the *Season* is so far advanced that the frequenters of the *Tea-Table* are setting out every day for the country, so he has determined to conclude, but with this hope (apparently unfulfilled) that next winter he may promise himself to see the *Tea-Table* revived again and with more glory and splendour than ever.

The style itself of many of these papers is clear and good. A standard eighteenth-century style had been generally adopted since Addison had given the perfect examples he did in the *Spectator*. Others had carefully modelled themselves upon him.

In the same year there was issued another periodical, the *Plain Dealer*. Like others of its kind, it came out twice a week, appearing first on Monday, 23rd March 1724. In nearly all the periodicals of the class, the first number is occupied with a description of the character " behind the scenes." The *Plain Dealer* introduces himself as a talkative old bachelor. This paper is so typical of many others of the same or similar nature that we quote it entire. The Latin motto at the head of the paper is from Martial : " Est vivere bis, vita posse priori frui."

"When a stranger comes into company, the whisper goes round, who is he ? and the face each man wears, is the effect of his information. You ought, therefore, to know who I am, that you may regard what I say ; and then it is to be hoped, we shall converse without jealousy.

" I am a talkative old bachelor, in my grand climacteric, of a sanguine complexion ; well-limbed, strong and hearty : in stature more than middling ; my face is round and smooth, my forehead high and open, my eyebrows are widely arched ; my teeth sound and white ; I have a nose a little aquiline ; eyes black and sprightly ; my hair is brown and short, but somewhat of the thinnest, with a silvering of grey among it : I wear my clothes plain, am a great lover of walking, and go commonly alone ; I carry a pair of mouse-coloured gloves in one hand, and my oaken stick in the other, instead of a cane : for I am naturally partial to the manufactures of my country, and an irreconcilable enemy to the East India Company.

" My father, who was one of the cavaliers of the last century, had a dash in his temper of what his mistress called surly, but he

FROM THE GUARDIAN TO THE RAMBLER

was of frank heart and simple manners. There was an unlucky kind of contrast in his disposition, for he was amorous but unpolished. He seems to have been rather serious than witty, but to have loved wit in others, and was particularly charmed with the wantonness of Mrs Behn. That arch baggage has made bold, in her comedy, called the *Rover*, both with his name and his character. Whoever has seen Ned Blunt, has seen, not the copy, but the very life of my father.

"He left me an estate, rather moderate than plentiful; which I have neither improved nor diminished. I was naturally disposed to quiet and affected to think calmly. For this reason I have obstinately resisted marriage. I pass my summers at Blunthall, the ancient seat of our family, in the dirtiest part of Sussex; my winters I enjoy in town, where I am the oldest member now alive of an assembly of both sexes, very numerous and diversified. We meet, twice a week, at the house of a sober widow, whom we placed there on purpose. But, because I delight in study and am an enemy to the faction and flutter of the polite end of the town, I have my lodgings in a low-built, silent house in the city, which has a large shady garden, and covers the very spot where, of old, as Stow tells me, stood the watch tower of Barbican.

"It has always been my custom to keep a daily account in writing, of my actions and observations, even to particulars of no seeming importance. By help of these notes I live over again my past time, and learn wisdom from my follies.

"I have lately been reflecting, and taken it strongly into my fancy, that, wanting children of my own, I should be everybody's father. I have so many things to say, and am so fond of teaching, that I promise to myself no small fame, from the success of my weekly counsel. The subject of my paper gave me little or no pain; my propensity to talking required that it should be general, and undoubtedly copious; but the name was a difficulty, that I could not easily get over, that large part of mankind, which consists of superficialists, judging everything by appearance, taste but coldly of a meaning which is not dressed to their relish; and the will, that is too stubborn to bend to the fancy, shall hardly be able to work upon the understanding.

"This doubt was so knotty, that I submitted it to the assembly, where a learned clergyman spoke first, and was for calling it the *Inquisitor*. He was honestly proceeding to give his reasons for that name, but was shortly interrupted by an alderman's wife, who, with eye of fire, and face as red as her ribands, told him, that however the Inquisition might agree with his principles, it would never go down with honest people and Protestants. If you desire, said she to me, that your paper should be read by the friends of the Government, you should give it a sober name, and call it the *Truthteller.*

"A pert coquette, who sat next her, a toast, and a great fortune, burst into a loud laugh. 'Oh! Heavens,' cried the gipsy, 'I shall faint at the odious formality of that title. Ah, madam, how could you be so unreasonably mistaken. The *Truthteller.* Lord, deliver us; why, the Court can never bear it, and all the gay world will despise and abhor it—no, no, if you wish your paper to spread and grow public, you have nothing to do but call it the *Secret.*'

"'For my part,' answered a grave virgin, about fifty, 'I think they would do well to entitle it the *Coquette*; there's scarce a fop in town but would be fond of that name; for he would consider the paper as his property.'

"A famous critic interposing, remarked, that the taste of the age was vitiated, that no name could be acceptable, unless it were musical; and the wind, says he, of modern arguments, being an overmatch for their weight, I am for calling it the *Bagpipe.* 'Oh, much rather the *Flute,*' replied the coquette; 'the bagpipe is so filthy, so horrible an instrument! that 'twould be impossible to bear the sound of it unless 'twere introduced in an opera.'

"A justice of the quorum, my next neighbour in the country, and an eminent fox-hunter, maintained with invincible strength, both of voice and authority, that it ought, by all means, since it was intended for society, to be called the *Goodfellow.* But he bowed, and changed his mind, when our alderman's young daughter, who sate at her mother's elbow, blushed and whispered in his ear that for her part, she could think of no name, that would be so pretty as the *Sweetheart.*

"An old maid of the widow's, to whom, for pleasantry sake, we indulge the familiarity, and privilege of impertinence, had been standing all this while behind her mistress's chair, and broke out, on a sudden, with an air of amazement. 'Hey-day, if you must whip it about thus, and keep it constantly spinning, the best thing you can do is to call it the *Whirligig.*' All the company laughed at this wench's conceit, till the critic, assuming a surprised and decisive air, assured us, positively, it must take; for that nobody could fail to expect as much wit, at least, in the *Whirligig,* as in the *What-d'ye-call-it.*

"I was unsatisfied with all this, and having a natural partiality to my own character, I bethought myself of the *Plain Dealer.* The whole assembly agreed in approbation of that name, and gave it as their joint-opinion, that, whether it would be generally liked or no, it was never more generally wanted.

"The ladies, when they hear that my design is plain-dealing, will consider me, perhaps, an old-fashioned fellow, who can have nothing to do with them; yet I know they will be frequently kind enough to furnish me with business, and I shall handle them, as often as they allow me opportunity. The Church and the State I have no great genius for meddling with, they are either well as they are, or will never be the better for anything I can say to them. But the passions, the humours, the follies, the disquiets, the pleasures, and the graces of human life, all these I claim a right to consider as my subjects; and shall treat on them, without prejudice, in the most frank and open manner; so that the watch tower of Barbican shall again resume its use, and overlook this ancient city, for her service and her safety."

The style in this paper approaches very close to that which we desiderate in the periodical essay. It is simple, direct, and colloquial without being in the least vulgar.

In the second number the author commences his *plain-dealing* in an attack on what he terms the great abuses of the time: masquerades, gaming and stock-jobbing; and stories and papers on love, life, and happiness appear. Many of the didactic essays are specially well written. The *Plain Dealer* continued to appear until about the hundredth number, and the collection makes better reading than the majority of these minor periodicals. The author keeps close to the Addisonian scheme, and by avoiding party politics, steered clear of the rocks which had wrecked early in their course similar undertakings.

We have already dealt with the *Censor* papers of Theobald. They appeared in Mist's *Weekly Journal*, to which also Defoe contributed. This *Journal* appears to have come temporarily to a close in the year 1724. In the following year a fresh start was made with it. The first number of this new *Weekly Journal* of Nathaniel Mist, the printer of Great Carter Lane, was published on Saturday, 1st May 1725, towards the close of George I.'s reign. In this first number Mist says he will give news, accounts of trials, and so on, "and as I know it is in the nature of man to be greedy of knowledge, I shall conceal nothing from my readers which by good intelligence comes from my hands." The single issue is considerably larger than the *Spectator*, being a four-page sheet, and as one turns over the now discoloured and time-stained pages the whole life of the early Georgian era seems to come back with vividness and life. The feature of the paper is undoubtedly the essay which appears every week, occupying usually at least a page or a page and a half. But in addition to this, are columns of home and foreign intelligence; accounts of marriages; accidents and events; and fully a page devoted to advertisements. These last seem much the same every week: lotions for pimply skins, pills to cure bile, hair dyes infallible and safe; even the device of the *testimony* (sworn-in before a magistrate) to the cure effected on some erstwhile suffering patient appears.

But the essays claim our attention. Now the writer defends these same rather extensive advertisements as being both useful and necessary; now he gives a version of a fable, revised to suit the occasion; now an account of Jonathan Wild "of most ingenious and most roguish memory," who had but lately departed this life. Letters are also sent to him after the *Tatler* and *Spectator* pattern—some of them probably genuine. For example, there is a bitter complaint from a young man at the University who likes classics, and laments being forced to learn logic and mathematics. Poems appear, and essays in lighter vein to suit female readers. The art of kissing, for example, is discussed in several numbers. Individual papers are written in palpable imitation of the *Spectator*. A walk in Westminster Abbey is given, and attempts at literary criticism directly following Addison's lead. One is on poetry, in which Poetry is distinguished as being addressed to the imagination, etc., etc., in the usual style. There is, however, an interesting criticism of a new edition of Shakespeare, and Theobald's edition receives favourable notice. In all, there are a hundred and fifty-one numbers of this paper. Quite an interesting volume of selections could be made from it alone—a selection falling far below Addison's best, but giving much the same style and variety.

Mist's *Weekly Journal* passed into Fog's *Weekly Journal*

(1732) in a rather curious manner. The former journal had come to a rather abrupt conclusion when the Government, or at least those in " high quarters," commenced an action for libel against Nathaniel Mist, the publisher, and the latter fled for safety abroad. But in order that the views of Mist should be carried on at home in his absence a friend started Fog's *Weekly Journal*. He thus made such an obvious play upon the exiled publisher's name that every one understood his object in commencing the publication. This journal gives ample general news of the day, some of its articles upon home affairs are good, and advertisements abound, but there are no articles which would come under the heading of " periodical essays."

It is said that Chesterfield wrote one or two of these articles. It is not an easy matter to determine which. There are none of such outstanding merit that they would justify us in saying " these are Chesterfield's "; none possess that clarity and ease of style which render the letters of Lord Chesterfield inimitable.

In one of the numbers of Mist's *Journal* there had appeared an advertisement of the *Humorist*, a collection of anonymous essays. The volume seen is dated 1725, and contains thirty-three essays in all. A long dedication is humorously made to the " Man in the Moon," whom the author has often seen at a distance, though not possessing the honour of his acquaintance. He has ventured to address his august majesty since (and here he anticipates the experiences of Dr Johnson) he has become disgusted with the uncertainty and stinginess of patrons of earth. From the preface which follows it would appear that the essays had already been published separately and are now bound up together, so that they can fairly be classed as periodical essays. The length of the essays is about that of the usual *Spectator* article, and the subjects are very varied. The first concerns news-writers " who lodge high, and study nightly for the instruction of such as have the Christian charity to lay out a few farthings for their labour." The second discusses enthusiasm, and is against a religious delirium which outruns reason. The author describes at length a sect devoted to " The Art of Trembling " and ridicules their pretensions. "The Preacher on his part declared that he felt wondrous Joys and Raptures, which, he said, nobody else could feel, in these his holy shiverings, when the spirit took him by the Throat and shook his Bones and tossed him, as it were, in a Blanket." This paper is conceived and executed extremely well. The third turns to an old favourite, the seat of the various affections, and this time the spleen is discussed. It is the spleen which rules us by fancy. When the author, for example, hears a poet repeating his own verses, this never misses " to set his spirit and his teeth on edge." The next, which describes a Country Entertainment to which the author went, satirises the scandal-mongering that goes on even in the country. "Committees of twos and threes all over the dining-room" tore to pieces the reputations of their dearest friends. The *Humorist*, it will be observed, is the satirist so far. But love, ambition, pride, anger, avarice, death and grief are treated of with less keenness of satire and with much the manner of the earlier periodicals. There is an interesting article on *Criticism* in which the author laments its present degradation. "Bless me!" he says, "that the learned *Art of Criticism* should grow so cheap and common! Now-a-days Porters and 'Prentices examine Wit, and hold Sessions upon the stage. But all things are fallen from their first Dignity!—and so it has fared with the genteel and ancient calling of Criticism." He hears a haberdasher's boy say, with reference to the *Cato*, that he wished he could have had some *serious talk* with Mr Addison, as in some places he is either too copious or concise, and in others too careless or elaborate. He proceeds to draw out a "receipt" on how to write a criticism: "You must take so many terms from Aristotle, etc., etc.; you must tell the Reader you are the most learned man of the age for fear he should not find that secret out; neither can it be amiss to say your author is but just come from school, that people may not suspect you ought to be sent thither." There is just a trace of "making fun of the rules" which heralds the approaching reaction. Taken altogether the collection is a very fair specimen of a number of similar productions of the time.

CHAPTER IV

DEVELOPMENTS IN JOURNALISM OF THE PERIOD, AND THE WORK OF HENRY FIELDING

ALTHOUGH we have noted the slavish imitation of the *Tatler* and *Spectator* on almost every hand, it would be wrong to suppose that no farther developments took place in periodical literary work. A rather interesting development in journalism was a paper called *New Memoirs of Literature* (1722), which appeared monthly. It is not a regular essay periodical, but is occupied, as the title runs, " with accounts of new books printed both at home and abroad, with dissertations upon several subjects, miscellaneous observations, etc." Individual essays, such as *Thoughts on Friendship* and an essay on the *Georgics* of Virgil, bring us near to the usual periodical essay type. The *Memoirs* form an early example of a class of magazine which was to prove highly successful in the nineteenth century—the critical *Review*. Here, however, very little real critical faculty is exercised.

The mention of a new type of periodical introduces us to a group of magazines which differ also from the *Tatler* and *Spectator*, yet possess certain affinities with them. The tendency was to include a greater variety of material, general news, and so on, while Addison and Steele had limited themselves almost constantly to one or two little essays. Undoubtedly the most prominent of these new magazines was the *Gentleman's Magazine*. A large number of volumes of the *Gentleman's Magazine* accumulated as time went on; and the earlier volumes show that it was a species of historical chronicle. Letters to the " Editor," *Sylvanus Urban*, are frequent, and other main features are biographical memoirs, antiquities (accompanied in the later volumes by illustrative plates), accounts of books and pieces of verse. Information which we usually consider the special possession of the newspaper appears also in the *Gentleman's Magazine*. Births, marriages, and deaths are given and the prices of stocks. The magazine, in its own words, " contains more in quantity and greater variety than any book of its kind and price. All the Pieces of Wit, Humour or Intelligence daily offered to the Publick in the newspapers, and therewith some other matters of Use and Amusement that will be communicated to us." This brief summary of the contents of the *Gentleman's Magazine* is sufficient to show that it was a development quite distinctive from the periodical essays of the reign of Queen Anne.

Of other magazines which followed the *Gentleman's Magazine* (a long list of which might be given) we select only two or three for special mention, as they contain the best features of the rest. A full and detailed examination of these magazines lies outside the scope of our present inquiry. We are concerned with them only in so far as they contain periodical essay work or as they affected the life of the essay periodical.

The *London Magazine* or the *Gentleman's Monthly Intelligencer* was started a year after the *Gentleman's Magazine*. The *London Magazine* continued in existence between the years 1732 and 1779, or for the long period of nearly half a century. In the Preface the author says : " As the miscellaneous kind of writing is in its own nature peculiarly engaging, variety of subjects having a certain quality of unbending and entertaining the mind ; so this work may boast of a greater variety in less compass than any other kind of performance, and truly answers our motto, *multum* (we might say *plurima*) *in parvo*." The *London Magazine* collected into each monthly issue a number of papers from other periodicals, as well as original essays. For example, the first number (April 1732) contains a paper from the *Universal Spectator*, on Love and Generosity ; a paper from the *Weekly Register*, the subject being, Matches made by parents for their children, without their inclination, with comments on the unhappiness which usually ensued ; a paper from Fog's *Journal* (No. 178) on the subject of Religion; a paper from the *London Journal* (No. 666) criticising an issue of the *Craftsman*. The latter paper is also given. It is a criticism of the reign of King Charles I., and contains a review of the faults and failings of the king. These are succeeded by a paper from the *Free Briton* (No. 123) containing a proposal to erect a trophy in memory of the victory of the Boyne; a paper from the *Grub Street Journal* (No. 118) on Dr. Bentley's *Preface* to Milton's *Paradise Lost*; and a paper from the *Weekly Register* (No. 104), the story of an unhappy marriage. This list of individual papers is bound up with items of general intelligence, poetry, and a catalogue of books. Such is the first number of the *London Magazine*. It will be seen it is as much a collection of essays as an original production. Some of the supposed *extracts*, however, are not genuine, others are parodies of the papers they refer to. The difference between this magazine and the *Spectator* is at once apparent. Addison gave, as a rule, only one or two essays in each number and issued his periodical three times a week or even every day. In the *London Magazine* a whole batch of essays, original or copied, is bound up to form a monthly number, together with the more general features which have become traditionally associated with the magazine as distinct from the essay periodical. This particular magazine, the *London Magazine*, with its very long life, is sufficient to prove the popularity of a paper designed to give more varied literary material than the *Tatler* or *Spectator* had ever intended to provide. In the literary papers the old subjects, however, are still dealt with: love in all its manifestations; manners and the minor morals; and little stories and allegories. As the magazine proceeded an increasing number of articles appeared of a political nature. The position of England with regard to other nations is discussed, and the proportion of trade news bulks larger and larger as the country gradually increased its commercial enterprise. These extra-literary features may explain the long-lived nature of this magazine, as it would thereby appeal to a wider circle of readers.

The *Scots Magazine* (1739) again is an obvious imitation

of the *Gentleman's Magazine* and the *London Magazine*. Although both of these were known in Edinburgh, the authors of the *Scots Magazine* complain that they do not give adequate space to Scottish affairs. The *Scots Magazine* is published to supply this deficiency. This magazine had a long and varied career, and continued till the beginning of the second quarter of the nineteenth century (1826), when it became merged (for all practical purposes) into *Blackwood's Magazine*. The *Scots Magazine* was intended to give " a general view of the religion, politics, entertainments, etc., in Great Britain." It has a section in which political affairs are discussed by a Political Club, the members of which adopt classical names, but as the papers are purely political, they lie outside our province. The importance of the magazine for us is the publication of essays, some reprinted, some original. This " exchange system " (if it may be so called) with the London and other magazines was apparently getting common. In one of the later volumes, for example, we have an issue of the *Lounger* (itself an Edinburgh periodical) reprinted, and the whole of Young's *Night Thoughts*. The authors call themselves " the public bees of the literary world to extract from each fruit and flower some of the most mellifluous juices." The Letters to the Editor are very much in the *Spectator* manner. For example, in the first number occurs a letter from *Sophia* exposing the wiles of " young sparks about town." The papers from which extracts are made are the *Craftsman* and *Commonsense*, the *Universal Spectator* and the *Weekly Miscellany*. The papers from the *Universal Spectator* are well chosen. There is, for example, a dialogue between Charon and Mercury after the manner of Lucian, in which a number of ghosts present themselves at the ferry ; and a lawyer, *Mr Bribewell, Mistress Prudella*, a prude, and a Methodist (who comes in for a severe cross-examination about his religion) are all humorously and yet satirically described. But outside of this literary section, this magazine becomes merely a chronicle of the time ; valuable no doubt in its way, but not distinguished in literary style.

The only other magazine we need refer to in this section is the *Ladies' Magazine* (1749) or the *Universal Entertainer*.

DEVELOPMENTS IN JOURNALISM

It was published weekly on Saturdays (No. 1, Nov. 18). The title *Ladies' Magazine* was a novelty at the time, but an examination proves it to be misleading. There is little or nothing to show that the periodical was intended for ladies. *A history of England by question and answer continued in instalments throughout each issue* can scarcely be termed a theme specially attractive for ladies, no more than the extracts from Anson's *Voyage round the World*. A few sentimental stories are more relevant to the title, but the letters and poems and the chronological diary of home and foreign affairs are in no way exceptional. There is no feature to make it pre-eminently a *Ladies' Magazine*.

It is evident that in the reign of George I. and George II. both the newspaper and this new form of magazine were becoming increasingly important. The *Craftsman*, for example, is said to have attained a circulation of 10,000, and a writer in the opening number of the *Gentleman's Magazine* remarks: "Newspapers are of late so multiplied as to render it impossible, unless a man makes it his business, to consult them all. They are becoming the chief channels of amusement and intelligence." Lecky, in his *History of England in the Eighteenth Century*, gives ample details to support this statement. We can scarcely overestimate the work of the periodical essayists of the magazines and newspapers in popularising and diffusing knowledge, and in gradually enlarging the circle of intelligent readers.

The *Craftsman* referred to above, and credited with being a "thorn in the flesh" to Sir Robert Walpole's ministry, is so frequently mentioned by other papers, and seems to have had such an influence in its wide circulation, that it deserves fuller treatment. Commenced on Monday, 5th December 1726, it appeared twice a week under the editorship of Mr Amherst, who adopts the pseudonym of *Caleb D'Anvers*. In the introductory essay Caleb introduces himself and gives an account of his family. He had been educated under the famous Dr Busby at Westminster School, then at Christ Church College, and then passed to become a lawyer at Gray's Inn. He is now acting the part of a *Spectator* of mankind, but especially with regard to the manifest abuses which have crept into politics. "It shall therefore be my chief business to unravel the dark secrets of *Political Craft*, and trace it through all its various windings and intricate recesses." To this object Amherst, at first, closely adheres, but soon finds that variety will do his paper no harm. In the thirty-eighth number he gives a letter signed by *Brittanica* in which the writer spiritedly defends her own sex. She declaims against the insolent superiority of the male, and finishes up with characterisations of Queen Elizabeth, Queen Anne, and the Empress of Russia in order to show what women can accomplish. Other papers deal with prodigies, omens, and portents, and are reminiscent, once again, of the *Tatler* and *Spectator*.

In the forty-sixth number Amherst introduces a new feature. Referring to the *Lettres Persanes* published not long before in Paris, he invents a Persian correspondent. The epistles of the Persian to a friend in London he has accidentally found in what he calls " an escrutoire," and *Caleb D'Anvers* has had them translated. A " selection " from these letters is given in several numbers, but they are mostly political in import. But one is specially interesting. It is an account, supposed to be added by Captain Lemuel Gulliver, of his visit to the Island of Grimbagnia which Swift had forgotten to chronicle ! There is more than once spirited writing on abuses at elections, and the fifty-eighth number is very amusing. It takes the form of a dialogue between Sir Edward Courtly, Kt., the candidate for parliamentary honours, and R. Brieth, Cordwainer. We have all too little of this presentation of what might be *actual conversation* in these periodical essays, but such a paper supplies a link with the novel. Another feature worthy of note is extracts (rather frequently given) from Cicero's *Letters* and Pliny's *Letters*, and from others of the Latin classics.

Apart therefore from the great importance of Amherst's *Craftsman* in the political turmoil of the time, there is not a little excellent reading in the kind which Steele and Addison had exemplified in the reign of Queen Anne.

Another paper, even more directly political than the *Craftsman*, may simply be mentioned. This is the *Occasional Writer* (1727), issued at sixpence, only four copies of which are extant. The paper is addressed directly to His Majesty. "As I think it my unquestionable duty to give your Imperial Majesty all the light I am able into the posture of your affairs here, I am determined (notwithstanding the reluctance I feel to communicate any news ungrateful to your imperial ear) to let you know . . ."—then follows a long, rambling article running over the position of affairs. This is regarded as critical. The essays are purely political and polemical, and are only mentioned to show the specialisation in kind which was gradually taking place in the sphere of journalism. And the periodical essay was becoming affected by that tendency of the time.

The *Senator*, which appeared in the following year (1728), has good and bad elements about equally mixed. It was published twice a week at the price of twopence, and the "editor" takes the pseudonym of *A. Standfast, Esq.* It is a single sheet. *Caleb D'Anvers* of the *Craftsman* is strongly abused. "When dirt is to be thrown, he is the ablest man that hurls the most. Of this class seems Mr D'Anvers"—short certainly, but pungent. The fourth number is on the art of finding fault; the fifth returns to the familiar *vision* method, and in this dream Experience takes the sleeper to the Temple of Liberty. Five numbers further on a paper begins with general remarks on laughers and jesters, but resolves itself in the end into more derogatory remarks on *D'Anvers* and the *Craftsman*. But in the next number the *Senator* proceeds to give an account of himself. An interesting itinerary of his visits to the Parks, to Parliament House, and to the coffee-houses is given. The twenty-second is a curiously interesting number. It gives an account of a club or parliament of *footmen*, and reminds one strongly of a similar institution which Thackeray sketches in *Pendennis*. It is just possible that Thackeray had read the *Senator*, since in his wide reading in eighteenth-century literature (especially in the preparation for the writing of *Henry Esmond*) he was attracted towards these minor periodicals. They are highly important in any study of the social life of the century. They give scenes and contemporaneous descriptions of manner and mode of life, which nothing can better. We give the twenty-second number in full. It is conceived in a humorous vein, and the style is happily adapted to the spirit of the article.

"I have formerly heard of a Parliament of Women, and lately of a Parliament of Footmen; but I never imagined that it was really possible for so many idle fellows to agree to play the fool with so much solemnity, till the other day I happened to pick up in my chamber, a blotted scrawl very ill-spelt, which, after I had read over with some difficulty, and much astonishment, was owned to be the property of my servant, and purported to be a Journal of one day's proceedings in an assembly of which Jeffrey is a member. I own I was weak enough to grow a little peevish upon the first perusal of it; but upon the fellow representing to me that there was nothing new or secret in the Affair; that it was a very old jest, and most of the gentlemen about town had one time or other vouchsafed to be pleasant upon it, I e'en put my anger in my pocket, tho' the reader will see, I have as little reason to be pleased with it as anybody, and considering the present recess from all public affairs, I resolved to translate it into common English for the amusement of my holiday readers.

"'VOTES OF THE PARLIAMENT OF FOOTMEN, No. 1
"'*Tuesday, January* 23

"'Mr Speaker alone, and then the other members present drawls each a single mug of twopenny to Church and King.
"'A Bill for the better regulation of all lords, ladies, masters and mistresses, within the bills of mortality, and for the better payment of servants' wages, was read a first time, and ordered to be read a second time.
"'Ordered that the grand committee for vails and board wages do sit every morning in the little room up two pairs of stairs.
"'Ordered that the grand committee for all grievances from Stewards, housekeepers, and head-servants, do sit every afternoon in the house.
"'Ordered that a committee of privileges be appointed, and it was appointed accordingly.
"'Complaint being made to the House that one Sir —— ——, Bart., a member of the House of Commons, had presumed to beat, kick, and cuff Mr Jeremy Strap, a member of this House, in manifest violation of the privileges of this House,
"'Ordered that the matter of the said complaint be referred to

DEVELOPMENTS IN JOURNALISM

the Committee of Privileges, and that they do immediately examine and report the same, with their Opinion thereupon, to the House.

"'The House being informed that Mrs Dripping from the Kitchen fire attended at the door, she was called in and presented to the House an estimate of the Charge of Victualling this House for half an hour. And then she withdrew.

"'And the said estimate being twice read,

"'Ordered that Mrs Dripping do immediately proceed to the victualling of this House, according to the said estimate.

"'The House being informed that Mrs Dripping from the Kitchen attended according to order,

"'Mrs Dripping was called in, and at the Bar presented to the House several dishes of pork-steaks, sausages, and black pudding, and then she withdrew.

"'Ordered that the said dishes be laid on the Table to be perused by the members of the House.

"'A motion being made, and the question being put, that much drink be now brought in,

"'It passed in the affirmative.

"'And much drink was brought in accordingly.

"'A petition was presented to this House and read, praying that a Bill be brought in for the more speedy and effectual payment of Mrs Dripping.

"Ordered that a Bill be brought in accordingly.

"'Mr John Brush from the Committee of Privileges reported the matter as it appeared to them, touching the complaint of Mr Jeremy Strap.

"'Resolved that Sir —— ——, by beating, kicking, and cuffing the said Mr Strap, is guilty of a notorious violation of the privileges of this House, and that Mr Strap in punishment of this matter, shall be at liberty to lay before this House, an exact and particular account of all the personal and family scandal relating to the said Sir —— ——, and also his table talk and familiar conversation, according to the constant usage of this House in such cases.

"'The House being informed that the House of Commons was just rising, Resolved *nem. con.* that this House do now adjourn.

"'And then the House adjourned till to-morrow afternoon at one of the clock.'"

The *Senator* ends with the thirty-second number. The essays throughout are of a mixed character. The author is preoccupied with *Caleb D'Anvers* and his *Craftsman*, but

THE EIGHTEENTH-CENTURY ESSAYISTS

gives also a fair number of papers in the manner of the *Spectator*.

The *Echo or Edinburgh Weekly Journal* (1729) was published in Edinburgh, as the sub-title indicates. It is not the least worthy of notice of the Edinburgh periodicals. The first number gives the aim of the paper: "No private character shall be personally wounded. We shall never meddle with the divine mysteries, or any controversies that may prove stumbling. Party jargon we have promised shall never be our theme." The paper falls into two sections, the one dealing with essays and answers to correspondents, like the earlier periodicals, the other giving home and foreign news. As well as *Mr Echo* (or Eccho, for the spelling varies in different issues) there is *Mrs Echo*, who is to have charge of her own department. "All ladies and gentlemen that deal in pieces of love, gallantry, criticism, humour, wit, and such-like subjects, are desired to make Mrs Eccho their correspondent." In addition to *Mr* and *Mrs Echo*, there is *Cousin Echo*, to whom letters are frequently sent. How near the essays adhere to the *Spectator* pattern will best be realised by naming a few of the more outstanding ones. The sixteenth number compares the world to a theatre; the twenty-first is on zeal; the forty-second on charity; the ninety-fourth on biography; and number one hundred and twenty-nine retails conversation at a friend's house. Events and happenings are recorded. The following is an instance: "A few days ago, a rogue went with a sham message to the Lady Clifton's in Great Marlborough Street, and while the servant went upstairs to his lady to deliver the message, the villain made off with all the servants' greatcoats and hats which hung in the passage." The paper continued to appear for several years up to the year 1734, and seems to have been deservedly popular. And the reason is not far to seek. Politics are excluded, and the majority of the papers continued the true aim and purpose of the essay periodical, and the reading public had not yet tired of them. The style, too, in many of the papers is admirably adapted to the theme discussed.

The *Echo* had been published in the capital of Scotland; the *Intelligencer* emanated from the capital of Ireland.

DEVELOPMENTS IN JOURNALISM

This periodical, by Dr Thomas Sheridan, was published in Dublin (1728). While Dublin never became the centre of such a brilliant literary coterie as distinguished Edinburgh in the eighteenth century, more than one of these essay periodicals were written and published in Ireland, and occasionally the contributors realised more than temporary fame. Swift, for example, contributed several papers to the periodical at present under review. Many of the features of the *Tatler* are reproduced in the *Intelligencer*—the usual characteristic dialogues and miscellaneous essays. The first number is credited to Swift, and there is nothing in the style to contradict such a belief. It is certainly written by one with a strong vein of sarcasm in his composition. The object and plan of the essay are given in this introductory number.

"There is a society lately established who, at great expense, have erected an officer of Intelligence, from which they are to receive weekly information of all important events and singularities, which this famous metropolis can furnish. Strict instructions are given to have the truest information. In order to which certain qualified persons are employed to attend upon duty in their several posts; some at the playhouse, others in Churches, some at balls, assemblies, coffee-houses, and meetings for Quadrille; some at the several courts of Justice, both spiritual and temporal; some at the College, some upon my Lord Mayor and Aldermen in their public affairs; lastly, some to converse with favourite chamber-maids, and to frequent those ale-houses and brandy-shops where the footmen of great families meet in a morning. Only the barracks and Parliament House are excepted, because we have yet found no *enfants perdus* bold enough to venture their persons at either. Out of these, and some other store-houses, we hope to gather materials enough to inform, or divert, or correct, or vex the town."

The third number, which is also attributed to Swift, is an interesting one, not so much for literary criticism as criticisms of morals. It deals with Gay's *Beggars' Opera*. Swift supports "this excellent moral performance of the celebrated Mr Gay" with much humour and sarcasm.

"I am assured," he writes, "that several worthy Clergymen in this city went privately to see the *Beggars' Opera* represented, and that the sneering coxcombs in the pit, amused themselves with making discoveries, and spreading the names of these gentlemen round the audience.

"I shall not pretend to vindicate a clergyman who would appear openly in his habit at a theatre, among such a vicious crew, as would probably stand around him, and at such lewd comedies and profane tragedies as are often represented. Besides I know very well that persons of their function are bound to avoid the appearance of evil, or of giving cause of offence. But when the Lords Chancellors, who are keepers of the King's conscience; when the judges of the land, whose title is Reverend; when ladies, who are bound by the rules of their sex to the strictest decency, appear in the theatre without censure, I cannot understand why a young clergyman who goes concealed out of curiosity to see an innocent and moral play should be so highly condemned; nor do I much approve the rigour of a great p....te who said, 'he hoped none of his clergy were there.' I am glad to hear there are no weightier objections against that Reverend body, planted in this city, and I wish there never may."

All the essays, however, are not conceived in the same spirit nor worked out with so masterly a literary touch, and the *Intelligencer* came to a close early in the year 1729. In the following year another periodical appeared which is interesting as showing the specialisation of interest which we have already mentioned. There was one main object in view in the publication of *Memoirs of the Society of Grub Street* (1730), and it was not a kindly one. The *Memoirs* were written to castigate all the minor and petty writers of the age. And such writers are numerous in any age. A number of the literary productions of Ralph Theobald (to be distinguished from Lewis Theobald whom we have had occasion already to mention) and others are reviewed and condemned. The *Memoirs* continued in life between two and three years. The first number introduces us to the *Society* which gives the periodical its name. *Giles Blunderbuss, Esq.*, corresponds to the *Mr Spectator* of Addison, and the society are determined to suppress all bad books. This would be a very commendable object indeed, but the impression is that impartiality in criticism is notable by its absence. While most of the sarcasm is justified, the aims and objects of true literary criticism are

DEVELOPMENTS IN JOURNALISM

not furthered in any way. Another periodical which was issued in the same year (1730) as the *Memoirs* is one which deserves only passing mention. The *Free Briton* is by Francis Walsingham of the Inner Temple. The *Free Briton* is a weekly paper. It appeared on Thursdays, and is very patriotic in tone, but the spirit of party politics is present. Political animus is displayed against the *Craftsman* of *Caleb D'Anvers* (Amherst). Amherst seems to have had the ill-fortune to raise against himself many enemies.

The *Free Briton*, obsessed as it is by politics, yields little purely literary material for our consideration.

A complete contrast to the *Craftsman* and the *Free Briton* is the *Comedian* (1732). The *Comedian* is one of those periodicals about which too much cannot be argued from its title. Its sub-title is a little unexpected, for the *Philosophical Enquirer* does not seem to be closely related to the *Comedian*. We do not usually associate fun and metaphysic. The periodical supplies much more serious reading than we would have expected. The *Comedian* was a monthly periodical commencing in April and continuing to the end of the year. The interval between each, as compared with the *Tatler* and the *Spectator*, is an unusually long one. The author explains the reason why. " An obligation to entertain the public, every week, with new compositions, is too great for the best genius to lay himself under, especially if such a writer has any other necessary avocation, as we may reasonably suppose most men have. When any single author imposes such a burden on himself, we should look for little more than a heap of crude sentiments inaccurately put together. So I shall take the space of one month betwixt the publication of every number of this work; a length of time sufficient for me to digest my thoughts into a proper order." " Agreeable to my subject, I shall look on the whole world as the scene of action in which a continual tragi-comedy is represented; and I shall exclude nothing therein, whether substantial or ideal, from being the subject of my pen." It is evident he is using the term the *Comedian* in the way Balzac was afterwards to apply it to his great series of novels *La Comédie Humaine*.

The first number contains a short essay on custom,

short remarks on philosophy, history, poetry, and oratory; and gives annals of the time. The papers are too sententious; while the " news " portion, though abundant, makes no literary appeal. The second issue, however, contains an essay in the form of a letter to Mr Pope, adversely criticising the latter's *Epistle* in verse to the Earl of Burlington. The opening sentences indicate the spirit of the criticism. " Friend Pope, thou hast discovered thyself to be as much like a poet in thy writing as in thy person thou art like an Adonis . . . I will give thee some admonitions concerning the use of certain English words which thou seemest to have forgot or never known." Pope's wrong use of the plurals of words, and misuse of others—in fact, his general lack of knowledge—are all detailed. While much of the criticism is of a verbal and somewhat crude character, the essay has a value in so far as it indicates a disposition (putting personalities out of account) to set aside the Popian standard of correctness. It may be taken as a foreshadowing of the end of the reign of neo-classicism. A set of papers in a serious vein is an inquiry into the immortality of the human soul. All the essays, however, are not purely literary; a number are of a political cast. The *Excise Bill* and the *Test Act* are discussed. But, taken as a whole, the *Comedian* is well above the average of these minor periodicals. The author, not too ambitious, has understood with something approaching accuracy the true nature of the periodical essay as it had been set forth by Steele and Addison at the very outset of its history.

The *Bee or Universal Weekly Pamphlet*, published in the following year (1733), arouses expectations from the name. But Goldsmith's *Bee*, though later in time, is vastly superior, both in matter and style. Yet this *Bee* has a catholic taste. The opening number informs us that there is to be something to suit every man's taste and principles. Begun in February, it was continued with success (though against opposition from Government) until the one hundred and eighteenth number. Afterwards the essays were gathered together into nine compact little volumes. The aim of the *Bee* is " to suck out the quintessence of every publick paper, rifling all its sweets, extracting its best parts, and rejecting the rest." Much the same plan had been adopted by the *London Magazine* the year before. Towards the close of the periodical Eustace Budgell acknowledges his identity as the prime mover in the undertaking. He adds that three have assisted him in the undertaking, but he is not at liberty to disclose their identity. Budgell sums up the *Bee* well. It is " an abridgment of everything material, and all the essays worth reading in the weekly papers; with some original compositions both in prose and verse." Budgell mentions that the number of papers and periodicals published is very great, and he hopes that this practice of his of selecting out the best things from them will tend to decrease the total number. Budgell had more than a little literary talent, and gives very interesting criticisms of some of the papers from which he takes extracts. Since contemporary opinion is always interesting and instructive, we may give a few of his criticisms. The *Craftsman*, by *D'Anvers*, he praises highly because of its outspokenness and the courage which it has shown through all political persecution. With reference to Fog's *Journal*, he says that the author has taken this assumed name in order to show that in defiance of authority he will continue the views of Nathaniel Mist, who has had to flee to France. The *Grub Street Journal* was designed, he tells us, for the amusement and diversion of the town. The *Universal Spectator* Budgell scathingly criticises. The title of *Spectator* is apt " to put people in mind of those pieces which were wrote (*sic*) some years since, and which are not very easily to be equalled; so that it is a sort of profaning the word *Spectator* to prefix it to anything mean or dull." It is not surprising to find that Budgell is jealous of the honour of the *Spectator*, since he is supposed to have written about thirty-seven of the papers himself. Similarly, the *London Tatler* does not equal those *Tatlers* formerly published by Sir Richard Steele. The *Auditor* is a new paper, and concerning it so far he has not much to say. The *Weekly Miscellany* is likewise a new paper, the author notifying that " after the example of Isaac Bickerstaff, Esq., and the *Spectator*, he shall think any pieces of inoffensive wit and humour perfectly consistent with his main design." This causes Budgell to break out in a reminiscent vein : " It is indeed hardly credible, how many authors have copied after those celebrated originals; the *Tatler*, *Spectator*, and *Guardian* have been translated into most European languages, and given birth to several papers in imitation of them in foreign countries. The French had for some time their *Babillard* or *Tatler* : the Dutch have at this day their *Spectator* : and the Germans had for some years together their *Guardian*. The majority of the many imitations of the *Spectator* in England have been extremely short-lived." He quotes with approbation Addison's own reference to his imitators, " that he looked upon the undertaking to write *Spectators* to be like the attempt of Penelope's lovers to shoot with the bow of Ulysses ; who soon found that nobody could shoot well with that bow but the hand which used to draw it." Finally, Budgell treats with a crushing sarcasm Read's *Weekly Journal*. Mr Read, he says, has apparently made a purchase of Mr Voltaire's *Life of the King of Sweden* and the *Sufferings of Mr Isaac Martin*, and retails these two books in portions to his customers every Saturday. " It is very possible that this procedure of Mr Read might give the first hint for printing *Rapin*, *Josephus*, *Sir Walter Raleigh*, Plutarch's *Lives*, and Bayle's *Dictionary* by piecemeal every week. We are informed that some religious persons have thoughts of printing the Bible after the same manner, and that the five first chapters of *Genesis* are ready for the press. The undertakers are in hopes that by this means many people who are frightened at the sight of a large volume, may be unwarily drawn in to read the Scriptures."

This is excellent. Budgell is writing with a sure hand. Something of the spirit of Addison seems to have passed into Budgell. The latter had been Addison's close friend. He went to Ireland with Addison as his clerk, and in his essays he closely imitated his master. An accumulation of troubles resulted in poor Budgell's suicide four years later. He left upon his desk the well-known words written upon a slip of paper :

> " What Cato did, and Addison approved,
> Cannot be wrong."

DEVELOPMENTS IN JOURNALISM

Thus even in his death Budgell revealed Addison's influence over him; though he mistook entirely Addison's teaching in the *Cato*.

Budgell carried out his project with consistency and zeal. Week by week the *Bee* contained articles from other periodicals, together with poetry and original essays. But in admitting lists of births, marriages, and deaths and general news he departed from the spirit and design of the *Spectator*, to which he more than once admiringly refers and to which he had himself contributed.

The *Weekly Amusement* (1734) admits even more of the miscellaneous element. The first number was published on 9th November 1734, and the design of the *Weekly Amusement* is stated to be " to instruct and entertain the world with what is serious, satirical, humorous and jocose." An interesting essay is given in the third number on song-writing, in which the author compares Sappho, Anacreon, and Horace with English poets. Passing to criticism of French poetry he says, "To do justice to the French, there is no living language that abounds so much in good songs." Waller and Donne and Cowley are criticised, and he quotes short songs and poems. It is not great criticism, but even the rudiments present of that system of comparative criticism, which has proved so powerful a literary engine in recent years, are worthy of note. A didactic or amusing story is included in each number, and there are papers on the fop, the precisian, and the beau. Some of the character sketches are really well executed. But overmuch space is devoted to home and foreign news to justify us in naming the *Weekly Amusement* a magazine of a purely literary nature.

A periodical of much more interest for us is *Commonsense* (1737), written by Chesterfield, Lyttelton, and Charles Molloy. Lord Chesterfield's is a noted name, and his work is always interesting. The first number was published on Saturday, 5th February 1737, and *Commonsense* continued to be issued weekly on the Saturday till 1739. The papers included have not all been separately allocated to the various contributors, but they are nearly all distinctly above the average. This periodical formed, no doubt, the literary training-ground for Lord Chesterfield's essay work, which shines so brilliantly, later on, in the *World*. In the first essay the writer (probably Molloy) discusses the other London magazines which may possibly interfere with *Commonsense* and humorously touches them off. Of the *London Journal* he says: "I was informed that paper of the same size and goodness, being to be had much cheaper unprinted and unstamped, and yet as useful to all intents and purposes, was now universally preferred. Fog's *Journal*, by a natural progression from Mist to Fog, is now condensed into a cloud, and only used by way of wet brown paper in cases of falls and contusions. The *Craftsman* was the only paper that gave me any concern, but I never observed *Mr D'Anvers* to be an enemy to *Commonsense*." A light and bright tone is at once struck—a style eminently suited for such essay work.

"The design of my paper is to take in all subjects whatsoever, and try them by the standard of common sense —*quicquid agunt homines* is my purpose." Thus he quotes the very motto used by Steele in the *Tatler*. The essays which follow are much above the average. Many of them are written in a clear and masterly fashion; often with a touch of satire; and there is ample lighter essay material mixed with the more serious discussions. Avarice, ambition, honour, and courtesy are dealt with; all the tricks and devices of fashion and dress are brought in; characters and sketches appear; and stories are frequently introduced. The names given to the characters suggest their nature. *Agrippina* has a sordid disposition, *Garulus* is talkative, and so on. These stories are usually didactic in aim. That of Lucinda (24th June 1738) is one of the best. A passage may be given from the issue for 11th February 1738. The subject is on "taste and eating": "Taste is now the fashionable word of the fashionable world, everything must be done with ' taste '—that is settled; but where, and what that taste is, is not quite so certain. They build houses in taste, which they cannot live in with conveniency. They suffer with impatience the music they pretend to hear with rapture, and they even eat nothing they like, for the sake of eating in ' taste.' The meal is now at once the most frivolous and most serious part of life—all useful or agreeable subjects of conversation are soon interrupted and overpowered by the ecstatic interjections of Excellent ! Exquisite ! Delicious ! Pray taste this, you never eat (*sic*) a better thing in your life. Is that good ? Is it tender ? Is it seasoned enough ? Would it not have been better so ? etc."—and these " Kitchen Critics " are keenly satirised. This is the kind of essay that is too seldom given, but is just right both in style and manner. It is light and amusing, and yet has an ulterior purpose in view which is made abundantly clear as the paper draws to a close. The essay is very probably the work of Chesterfield himself. It has the Chesterfield manner written all over it.

Commonsense proved so successful that it was re-issued in volume form. And we are not surprised at this success. As a periodical it comes close to the true ethos of its kind, and is a worthy forerunner of the better-known *World*, to which Chesterfield also contributed not a little of his finest wit and sarcasm.

Of the same year as *Commonsense* is the *Reveur* (1737), an Edinburgh periodical, which was published at Kincaid's shop opposite to the Parliament Cross. Issued weekly from November, it ended probably in May of the following year, since the British Museum has twenty-seven numbers, and no later copies can be traced. That the magazine was rather highly thought of is indicated by the following passage, from a writer in the *Scots Magazine* in the year 1787. He refers even the authors of the *Mirror* and the *Lounger* back to the *Reveur*, which " exhibits a favourable picture of Caledonian wit and humour, in which our brethren of the North have hitherto been supposed deficient." The first number of the *Reveur* makes most interesting reading. It opens with a reverie or allegorical vision in which Wisdom comes before the dreamer. He asks illumination from Her and She shows him the vast crowd of humanity passing by him in the eager pursuit of pleasure or of knowledge. Then " methought I saw a figure very like myself, with some half-sheets in his hand, which he was distributing to the passengers as they went along, to cheer and divert them. I was turning hastily to ask the meaning of this, but my cheek slipping from my hand, beat the spectacles off my nose; the heavenly vision disappeared, and I found myself in my old elbow-chair by the fireside, with my pen in my mouth, and the paper before me." Thus inspired he commences to write. The author is stated to have been Dr Robert Wallace, minister successively of New Greyfriars and the New North churches, Edinburgh. If not the sole, he was, at least, the principal contributor. The papers follow the *Spectator* pattern with some success. The eighth number is on vanity and avarice; the tenth on the vanity of riches; the eleventh on the true and the false lover. In the fourteenth number Wallace introduces something analogous to Steele's and Addison's *Club*. A number of characters are described. *Sir John Wischert* and his son, whom Wallace sets forth as examples to others; *Mr Jonathan Medley*, a bachelor of forty; *Mr Freeman*, a man of fortune; and, lastly, a clergyman. These Club members (if we may call them so) go walks through the town and have chats together in each other's houses. For example, at one of these meetings a sermon of the parson's (No. 27) is discussed.

It will be seen that the main features of the earlier periodicals are present. But the *Reveur* has a double interest, not only for itself, but as a forerunner in Edinburgh of the more famous *Mirror* and *Lounger* periodicals.

But the *Reveur* was not the only periodical being issued about this time in Edinburgh. Three others may be mentioned. The previous year (1736) had seen the publication of the *Conjurer*. We are not able to say much about the *Conjurer*, as time has dealt hardly with it, as it does with many conjurers, and only one number (No. 11), dated 16th January 1736, is now available for inspection. This issue is political in tone, being almost wholly taken up with a rather startling discussion with the Devil himself on the government and the constitution! The second periodical is both more ample and more interesting. It was issued two years later (1738) and is called *Letters of the Critical Club*. The *Letters* are the professed product of a Club of seven members. The first *Letter*, which is simply an essay of the *Spectator* pattern in all but name, gives a

DEVELOPMENTS IN JOURNALISM

description of this Club. The commencement is in verse form:

> " Now Muse, employ thy art, and tell
> The name of every beau and belle
> That met at Clara's house that day,
> And every character display."

And the aim of the Club is given: " We are friends to mankind, and love to encourage virtue and merit wherever it is found, by bestowing due encomiums upon it; and we take it upon us likewise to censure vice, but not in an ill-natured snarling way; for sometimes ridicule proves successful when other methods fail; it being most true, that some men will forbear being vicious for shame, when they cannot either be scared from vice or persuaded to lay it aside, by serious admonitions."

This was exactly Addison's method of attack, and a perfectly admirable one. The president of the Club is *Jack Plyant*; the others are *Will Portly, Dick Crotchet, Tom Meanwell*, the *Old Lady Courtly*, her daughter *Miss Jeanie*; and, lastly, the new member to whom the letter is addressed. These are only "ticket" names, and the characters have no real life. They are *nominum umbrae* but they show that the *Club* was still popular.

The second *Letter* contains reflections aroused by the coming in of the New Year 1738. This *Letter* is by *Will Portly*. The next is by *Dick Crotchet* on the subject of witches and enchantments; the next by *Jack Plyant* on disputes in general. A paper by *Ned Rhymer* renews the old contention between ancients and moderns: " Yet allowing the ancients the commendation due to them, as excellent copiers of nature; I think the moderns deserve a part of our applause, since they have been no less industrious, though perhaps not so successful, in promoting learning, and making several useful discoveries. Have we not had, of late, men of excellent parts, as might entitle them to almost an equal share of our esteem with the ancients? Among our poets, we may brag of Boileau, Molière, Tasso, Milton, Shakespeare, Pope, Addison, and Thomson." This is still at the low-water mark of criticism. Pope and Shakespeare are side by side, and Addison between

Pope and Thomson. But the *Letter* represents only once again the eighteenth century neo-classic views on correctness, as voiced by Boileau and by Pope. Letters on the theatre, on love, on wit, and on landskip (!) painting follow. There are thirty-six numbers in all, but the drawback of the elaborate Club idea is that it is never really developed. These *Letters* do not represent the manner and colour and dress which the actual characters would have had in real life. There is a uniformity about the essays which betrays the same hand, and the Club members remain lay figures; they never really live.

The third Edinburgh periodical of this period, the *Patriot* (1740), has still less interest from the literary point of view. It is, like the proverbial Irishman, always against the Government. One feature imitates the *Scots Magazine*, as the latter imitated the *London Magazine*, for the *Patriot* gives extracts from the *Craftsman* and *Commonsense*. But the periodical never had anything like the vogue in Edinburgh of the *Scots Magazine*.

The *Occasional Writer* (1738) maintains the form and method of the *Spectator*, though the subject-matter is largely political. It is dedicated to the citizens of London, and the author complains that other " occasional writers " had taken his title. Like the *Spectator*, he has been " a looker-on for some years past, at the great publi-political play-table," and observed the various moves which are adopted. His anger is aroused at much of what is going on, and in vigorous essays he reproves the rottenness of politics. He dropped in one day to a coffee-house, near the *Royal Exchange*, where the citizens were freely discussing their views, and he has dedicated his paper to them, because he wishes to give them good advice. The object is a laudable one, but the political prepossession is evident, and most of the papers have small intrinsic literary worth.

The *Citizen* of the following year is of somewhat the same type. It was published weekly on Fridays, commencing 9th February 1739. The author is " a plain citizen of London " and has joined himself with other merchants to meet occasionally and have converse together. They discuss their various businesses, and what they have learned as they have gone in and out amongst men. The political and commercial features become increasingly prominent in many of these periodicals. But they are to be combined " with such epistolary correspondence as treat of virtues and moral subjects, tending to improve the mind, and engage the passions on the side of justice, integrity, and humanity." It is from the habitual practice of these virtues the author holds that " we can only hope to support and preserve Society." But this latter promise of more varied essay subjects the author does not fulfil. The articles appearing each week are mainly political or trade articles. When they are of more general interest they are essays on Public Charity Schools, Hospitals and Infirmaries. But the sixteenth number, *Of the decay of the Drama*, is interesting. The author deplores the state into which the drama has fallen, extending his condemnation to poets and writers generally. The eighteenth, again, is of the *Spectator* pattern, being addressed to the ladies, warning them not to indulge in scandal. But the paper has a tendency more and more to become merely a trade journal, the commercial bias being increasingly evident.

In the same year appeared the *Universal Spy, or London Weekly Magazine*. The first number (Friday, 20th April 1739) has a verse motto that reads like an expansion of the *Tatler's* motto from Juvenal :

> " To show the various scenes of active life,
> The humours, follies, fashions, love and strife,
> That rule mankind, from youth to hoary age,
> And either sex in different whims engage,
> Is the great labour of our author's pen,
> And fill the treasures of our magazine."

The author writes under the pseudonym of *Timothy Truepenny, Gent.*, and the periodical is one of the earlier attempts to give a magazine of sorts. It must have been popular, for it had a fairly long run. Characters, stories, poetry, essays, foreign and domestic news are all given. The author apparently knows what will please his public. He gives an account of Dick Turpin, who had recently been executed at Tyburn, continued through several numbers, with ample detail. The story of a shipwreck is interesting. Another section of the magazine connects it with the earlier *Athenæum Oracle* : this is a section called the *Casuist*, " for receiving and resolving curious questions." The poetry which appears is of the stereotyped eighteenth-century pattern ; little songs and octosyllabic verses (addressed to the ladies), and didactic effusions on virtue and innocence and happiness. The *Universal Spy* is more a miscellaneous magazine than a periodical of the *Tatler* or *Spectator* type. There is, as time goes on, an increasing number of periodicals which diverge from the Queen Anne type. This was only natural as new ideas came into play and new needs demanded satisfaction.

The *Female Spectator* (1745) has an added interest from the fact that it was conducted by a woman. Eliza Haywood was not the first to write periodical essays. For example, mention has already been made of Mrs Manley. The *Female Spectator* is addressed " to Her Grace the Duchess of Leeds." The volume form in which the *Female Spectator* has survived to our day is divided into twenty-four issues. These came out separately at intervals during the years 1745 and 1746. The papers are largely made up of stories of a sentimental kind. Repeated warnings are given by the authoress to young people of her own sex to beware of the wiles of the male ! In her opening number Mrs Haywood refers to the periodical which had suggested the title of her own :

" It is very much by the choice we make of subjects for our entertainment that the refined taste distinguishes itself from the vulgar and more gross. Reading is universally allowed to be one of the most improving as well as agreeable amusements ; but then, to render it so, one should, among the numbers of books which are perpetually issuing from the Press, endeavour to single out such as promise to be most conducive to these ends. In order to be as little deceived as possible, I, for my own part, love to get as well acquainted as I can with an author, before I run the risk of losing my time in perusing his work. So I shall, *in imitation of my learned brother of ever-precious memory*, give some account of what I am."

She confesses she never was a beauty, and is now very far from being young ; " a confession," she adds, " which you will find few of my sex ready to make." But when she was in the hey-day of youth she had run through years of pleasure and frivolity, and is now left alone.

But she has associated with herself others who will assist her: *Mira*, a lady of family; a widow of quality; and a young lady, the daughter of a wealthy merchant. The *Club* is still the accredited machinery for such a periodical. Stories of *Tenderilla* and *Celinda* and *Fidelio* are varied by satires on Vauxhall, and by didactic papers; but the periodical lacks both lightness and variety, qualities essential for success in periodical essay work.

The *Female Spectator* does not deserve, from the literary point of view, the attention which it has actually received. It is the female authorship which has attracted notice to an otherwise undistinguished work, although other writers were associated with her in the composition of the paper.

The *Agreeable Companion, or A Universal Medley of Wit and Good-humour*, of the same year, is a collection of humorous essays, familiar dialogues, and a selection from humorous writers. It was published at intervals, and deserves but a passing notice. The *Penny Medley*, in the following year (1746), is a collection of stories and essays, and possesses little original material. For example, the first number gives Steele's famous tale of *Inkle and Yarico*; the story of the *Travels of a Shilling*; and the well-known incident of the *Ephesian Matron*. In later numbers extracts from Mandeville's *Travels* and pieces of history from various sources appear. The *Spectator* is often made use of in the same way. Miscellaneous paragraphs are usually added, but the vein of original composition is, in the case of this particular periodical, exhausted.

The *Parrot* (1746) was published weekly, and only nine numbers appeared. In the first an account is given of the birth of the *Parrot* in Java. It was carried thence to Batavia and passed into the possession of the governor of the island. The next to own the *Parrot* was a French lady living at Versailles. It then passed in succession into the possession of an Abbe, another lady, and a gentleman who was travelling in Germany. There is a piquancy and freshness about this account of the " bird's " history which makes it welcome and amusing. With such a wide and varied experience the *Parrot* is capable of giving information to every one. The accustomed feature of a letter to a friend in the country gives the tale of current events. The stories are of the typical " moral " kind and are marked by mawkish sentimentality. The title and the opening number lead us perhaps to expect too much of the *Parrot*. At any rate the author was not able to develop his idea in the way promised at the outset.

It is a welcome change to turn to the periodical essay work of one of the literary giants of the eighteenth century —and of all time. It is by his novels that Fielding is best known, but these only concern us indirectly. His essay work is greater in quantity than is commonly supposed, and he contributed to no fewer than four different periodicals—the *Champion*, the *True Patriot*, the *Jacobite's Journal*, and the *Covent Garden Journal*. Let us consider them in turn.

The *Champion* (1739) is the first of the four in point of time. It had been originated by James Ralph, and Fielding proved the " powerful auxiliary " to this later *Isaac Bickerstaff*. Fielding's work in the *Champion* has especial interest. It came before any of the great novels were written. *Joseph Andrews*, the first of them, did not appear till after the close of the *Champion*. The essay periodical had certainly done something to help the novel to success. Addison's work had been wholly in essay periodicals, but in a later period he might have been a novelist, as the *Sir Roger de Coverley* series of papers amply demonstrates. Fielding, on the other hand, while accomplishing good work in the essay periodical, gave his strength to the novel. The full title of this first periodical is the *Champion, giving a series of papers, humorous, moral, political, and critical*. There seems no doubt that many of the papers were written by Fielding himself, though there were other contributors, of whom James Ralph was naturally the chief. The first number is dated Thursday, 15th November 1739, and the *Champion* was issued thrice weekly. The essays fall into line with those of the *Tatler* and *Spectator*. The first number introduces the *eidolon*, Captain *Vinegar*, who presents himself: "I have now determined to lay aside the sword which, without vanity, I may boast to have used with some success, and take up the pen in its stead, with a design to do as much execution with the one, as I have already done with the other; or, in other words, to tickle now, as I before bruised men into good manners." He proceeds to give an account of his father, *Nehemiah Vinegar*, of his brother, his two sons, and his wife, and he states that they will look over the parts of the town which they frequent and send in the news they obtain. The *Lizard* family in the *Guardian* is at once recalled, and the close connection with the older periodicals made plain. Not only so, there are articles in almost direct imitation of the *beau's head* and the *coquette's heart* which Addison had done so inimitably before. The vices and follies of the time are considered with a light satiric touch, and a number of letters appear. Some papers call for special notice. In the issue for Saturday, 8th December 1739, *Captain Vinegar* describes his possession "of the club which Hercules rendered so famous, and with which he used to lay about him so heartily in defence of innocence and virtue, against the attacks of vice and oppression." A humorous history follows of the way the club has been effective at different periods in its strange, eventful history. In the issue dated Saturday, 22nd December, the author sets up a *Court of Justice* in the Addisonian manner. "Whatsoever is wicked, hateful, absurd, or ridiculous" is to be brought before the Court. The *vision* method is also continued. In the issue for 27th December, *Mr Nehemiah Vinegar* sends in an account of a dream he had had of his arrival at the gates of the *Palace of Wealth* and of what happened to him within the enchanted portals. Another notable paper is that dated 12th January 1740, where the underlying idea is that Jupiter and the other gods and goddesses come down again to earth.

The didactic papers are especially good. A paper on self-examination (2nd February 1740) and the conquest of one's self is admirably done. The "Eastern Tale," one of the most constantly recurring features in these later eighteenth-century periodicals, has freshness given to it likewise. That given under date 23rd February 1740 is

THE EIGHTEENTH-CENTURY ESSAYISTS

noteworthy. And there is an excellent and sensible *Apology for the Clergy* in the issue dated 19th April 1740. To give a fair idea of the nature of the *Champion* we transcribe a portion of the number dated 5th February 1740. It is an excellent example of the lighter essay of the periodical kind and deals with a familiar subject.

"I was waked this morning by a very great noise, which in my first confusion, I imagined to have been thunder; but, recollecting it was a season of the year when that rarely happens, I began to think that great guns were firing on some public solemnity, till at last I was very much surprised, and I believe the reader will be so too, to understand that this dreadful hurricane was nothing more than my wife Joan, who was laying about her with great vigour, and exercising her lungs on a maid-servant for the benefit of my family.

"This good woman is one of those notable housewives whom the careless part of the world distinguish by the name of a scold, this musical talent of hers, when we were first married, did not so well agree with me. I have often thought myself in the cave of Æolus, or perhaps wished myself there on account of this wind-music, but it is now become so habitual to me that I am little more alarmed at it than a garrison at the tatoo or reveille; indeed, I have, I thank God, for these thirty years last past seldom laid myself down, or rose up without it. All the capitulations I have made are that she would keep the garrison hours and not disturb my repose by such new performances. It hath been remarked by some naturalists that nature hath given all creatures some arms for their defence; some are armed with horns, some with tusks, some with claws, some with strength, others with swiftness, and the tongue may, I think, be properly said to be the arms which nature has bestowed on a woman.

"This weapon, however harmless it may appear, is generally found sufficient, as well for all offensive as defensive purposes. I think it is the wisest of men that says, 'Beware of an evil tongue.' A scold is very often dreaded by her whole neighbourhood, and I much question whether my wife's tongue be not as great a terror to all her acquaintance as my cudgel can be.

"My wife Joan tells me that on going into any family we may easily see by the regularity and order of affairs whether the mistress of the house be a scold or not, to which perhaps the old adage concerning the best mustard may allude.

"A very ingenious Clergyman of the Church of England hath

assured me that he found a very sensible alteration (for the better) in his parishioners upon the settlement of a very excellent scold among them. Whatever vice or enormity any in the Parish were guilty of, they were very sure of hearing it, as the proverb says, 'On both sides of their ears,' by this good woman, who, the Doctor very pleasantly assured me, did more towards the preservation of good manners by these daily lectures which she exhibited gratis in the streets than he could by all his sermons in the pulpit; (and) I do remember when I was a young fellow, to have heard a man excuse himself for retiring early from his debauched companions by saying, 'Gentlemen, you know I have a wife at home.'

"Notwithstanding what has been here said, it is very certain that this, as well as other customs, however good in itself, hath sometimes been used to evil purposes, and that a too sonorous tongue hath often made a pretty face a very disagreeable companion. On such occasions I have known several devices practised with good success, nor do I think I can sufficiently applaud the ingenuity of a certain Gentleman who used to accompany his wife's voice with a violin, thereby turning what another would have esteemed a harsh entertainment into a very agreeable concert."

The political element is apt to intrude overmuch—that feature which spoiled so many otherwise good periodicals. There is little work on literary criticism. Fielding's best contribution to that subject was shortly to appear. It is suggested in the complete title to his first novel, *The History of the Adventures of Joseph Andrews, and his Friend Mr Abraham Adams, written in imitation of the manner of Cervantes*. It is the last phrase which is significant of much. It was Fielding's work conceived and carried through in "the manner of Cervantes" that was to prove a powerful challenge to Popian correctness. The romantic atmosphere of *Don Quixote* carried over in this way to England helped that "renascence of wonder" which took place towards the close of the century. And many of the essays in the *Champion* give such a foretaste of Fielding's later style and manner of execution that we are justified in calling them his, and we link them on inevitably with the introductory chapters to each "book" of *Tom Jones*, where the author steps forward from behind the scenes and converses freely with the reader. It is not difficult to trace a relationship between the "asides" in *Tom Jones* to the essays of Fielding in the *Champion*.

Take, for example, Chapter I. of Book VII. of *Tom Jones*. The theme is a discussion of life as represented by the audience in a theatre who applaud or disapprove the various actions which are taking place upon the stage. The chapter (with the obvious exception of the references to the characters in the novel) might have been lifted bodily out of an issue of the *Champion*; or indeed, so far as treatment is concerned, out of the *Tatler* or *Spectator*. Even the casual reader who is not a pseudo-specialist in literature, trying to invent connections where none exist, is struck with the resemblance.

Fielding again exercised his talent for periodical essay work in the *True Patriot* (1745). This was a weekly paper, strongly *Whig* in politics, in professed opposition to the designs of the Pretender. It was the year of the '45 and feeling ran high. It is not always easy to decide which of the essays are from the pen of the novelist, but about ten (Nos. 1, 3, 4, 7, 9, 10, 11, 13, 23, 24) are probably his. The thirteenth number (Tuesday, 28th January 1746) is a typical number. It is by Fielding himself, and takes the form of a letter on a young *bowe* (*sic*) he met in the country. The essay, which is an indictment of the "notorious want of care in parents in the education of youth," is strongly didactic in tone. While one or two touches reveal the hand of the master, the essay as a whole is not so good as we might have expected from the writer of *Joseph Andrews*, *Jonathan Wild*, and a *Journey from this World to the Next*. It may have been that the essays of the *True Patriot* were more hurriedly written than the earlier *Champion* efforts, and Fielding for his opinions became known as the "pensioned scribbler." The same criticism holds for the *Jacobite's Journal* (1747). It was also political in tone, and is ostensibly produced by *John Trot-Plaid, Esq.*, in the usual manner of the periodical essay. At least two papers are by Fielding (Nos. 15 and 34). The former, dated 12th March 1748, though political in purpose, is excellently well done. It is a parody of Horace's *De Arte Poetica*. Fielding calls it *De Arte Jacobitica*, and sketches the weakness of the "other side" with a masterly style. Every word tells. But the *Covent Garden Journal* (1752), the last of the group we are considering, contains a larger amount of Fielding's work. He writes under the pseudonym of *Sir Alexander Drawcansir, Kt., Censor of Great Britain*. To the *Covent Garden Journal* Fielding contributed over two dozen essays, and some of them reveal him at his best. The third number (11th January 1752) deals with critics in a keenly sarcastic vein. The fourth is a humorous *glossary* of words. Here Fielding allows his wit free play: "*Author*: a laughing stock. It means likewise a poor fellow, and in general an object of contempt. *Modesty*: awkwardness, rusticity. *Promise*: nothing. *Sermon*: a sleeping time. *Sunday*: the best time for playing cards."

The eighth number glances at the importance of religion, and the tenth is on the scope of reading. The last-named subject, one would imagine, would have roused Fielding to something really fresh. But the perusal of it leaves one rather chill and disappointed. Not far from the commencement of the essay we are told that "the agreeable is to be blended with the useful." This was one of the stock phrases of the eighteenth-century criticism. Then the great triumvirate in satire—Lucian, Cervantes, and Swift—are mentioned, also Shakespeare and Molière as dramatists. Truth and decency (the oft-heard Horatian echo) are to be the end of writing. But these principles are not always observed, since Tom Brown and D'Urfey are read before Plutarch! Taste also is a quality which human nature is but slenderly gifted with, and, above all, "evil books corrupt at once both our manners and our taste." Perhaps Fielding had *Pamela* in view when he wrote these words. It was the publication of *Pamela* which had prompted Fielding to commence *Joseph Andrews*, disgusted as he was with the opportunist morality of Richardson's work. The thirty-third number (23rd April 1752) contains a notable description. A real love of Nature rather unusual for the time is displayed. The quiet of the country scene at the village inn is well contrasted with the swaggering and blustering and swearing of a young man from London, who is after-wards found serving in the metropolis in a linen-draper's shop. The reflections on this metamorphosis are strongly didactic in nature—there is "neither spirit nor good sense in oaths, nor any wit or humour in blasphemy." As far as these papers go, they are good, but the best examples of his essay powers in a modified form had been given several years before, in what we may name (borrowing the term from Southey's *Doctor*) the *interchapters* of *Tom Jones*. Coming fresh from the perusal of these, Fielding's periodical essays pale in comparison. These interchapters show Fielding at his best, and indicate that the novel was not yet entirely severed from the periodical. The bridge which bridged the gap between the *Sir Roger de Coverley* series and a novel like *Tom Jones* had not yet been destroyed.

Without doubt this transference of material to the novel seriously diminished the vitality of the essay periodical. The sketches of *Sir Roger*, of the *Tory Foxhunter*, of *Will Wimble*, and the rest, are worked up and reappear in the novels of Fielding. In plain language the *novel sucked the essay dry*, and the periodical essay, in its conservative *Spectator* pattern, in the end died of sheer inanition. The little tales and morals shrink into insignificance beside such full-blooded novels as *Joseph Andrews*, *Tom Jones*, and *Amelia*. It was not till the next century that the *magazine*, by breaking loose from the conservative pattern of the eighteenth-century periodical, and by including articles and stories of all descriptions, was able to compete with the novel which was running with it side by side. But as far as the period under consideration is concerned, the novel stole the best which Addison (who was a true novelist by nature) had been able to produce, and amplified and enlarged it till it grew and flourished into one of the mighty achievements of the eighteenth century. Hogarth's illustrations were another force competing with the periodical essay. In his great series of pictures Hogarth has given an imperishable series of *Essays on Canvas*—dealing with London and its life, and with the moral plainly open to view. He depicts a cock-fight in *Birdcage Walk*, and a dissection in the *Surgeon's Hall*; he takes us to reception-rooms in Arlington Street, and paints vivid and exact interiors of inns and taverns and bagnios. Using these scenes for background, he has delineated the types of the day, the beau, the rake, and the fine lady with her flounces and patches; but he has pictured them without any softening touches, exactly as they really were. Hogarth's striking series of paintings, *A Harlot's Progress* and *A Rake's Progress*, stand for many warning-papers by Steele. In point of fact, it has been stated that one of Steele's papers in the *Spectator* (No. 266) first suggested the former series to the great painter. The circulation of Hogarth prints acted for a time like a new *Tatler* or *Spectator,* and if not actually rivals, the pictures were a new source of attraction, and drew off attention from the printed page.

Literature of a wider sort was bound also to take a little from the essay periodical, for instance, William Law's *Serious Call to a Devout and Holy Life.* The various characters are portrayed there with a masterly touch of satire, with a characterisation of *La Bruyère* himself. They at once suggest Addison and Steele to us with their similar character drawing. *Flavia* and *Miranda, Mundanus* and *Fulvius,* could with very little alteration be reproduced in any of the essay periodicals. Consciously or unconsciously, the influence of the periodical essay made itself felt; but as other departments of literature or art assumed its features, its own vitality and freshness diminished.

CHAPTER V

JOHNSON'S PERIODICAL ESSAY WORK

DR SAMUEL JOHNSON has taken his place along with Swift and Fielding as one of the foremost literary figures of the period under review. To what extent this prominence is due to Boswell's *Life of Johnson* it does not rest with us to inquire, but about the middle of the century, before the commencement of the *Rambler*, Johnson was little known. His *Rambler* papers were really the first things to establish his reputation. The title which he chose for his periodical is an example of Johnson's downright way of setting about things. He accounts for it thus to his friend Reynolds, the great painter: "What must be done, sir, *will* be done. When I was to begin publishing that paper, I was at a loss how to name it. I sat down at night before my bedside, and resolved that I would not go to sleep till I had fixed its title. The *Rambler* seemed the best that occurred, and I took it." It was, all things considered, not the happiest title to have chosen. There is not that variety of contents present in the *Rambler* which we are led to expect from a title which the Italian translator named *Il Vagabondo*. Dr Johnson, great as are his merits, possessed a literary style which was scarcely fitted for unqualified success in the production of essays after the *Spectator* pattern. We have noted how the great success of the *Spectator* lay in its infinite variety; in the light and fanciful touches allowed in the writing; and, above all, in the humour and delicate irony with which the various foibles of society were hit off. Johnson has produced a long series of papers in the *Rambler*—over two hundred of them—and they form a splendid set of moral essays. But there is one drawback. Johnson's teaching was generally tinged with melancholy, his rather sad outlook on life being partly the result of physical defect and partly of temperament. Thus the *Rambler* essays do not give what had now come to be expected from the eighteenth-century essay periodical. They lack the light and easy touch of Addison. Lady Mary Wortley Montagu sarcastically suggested that the *Rambler* could not be held to follow the *Spectator* otherwise than as a pack-horse would follow a hunter. And Johnson himself came to recognise something of this truth. In his last number he writes: " As it has been my principal design to inculcate wisdom or piety, I have allotted few papers to the idle sports of imagination. Some, perhaps, may be found, of which the highest excellence is harmless merriment; but scarcely any man is so steadily serious as not to complain that the severity of dictatorial instruction has been too seldom relieved, and that he is driven by the sternness of the *Rambler's* philosophy to more cheerful and airy companions." The sheet itself was published at the price of twopence, twice weekly (every Tuesday and Saturday), from March 1750 until the same month two years later. Johnson received from the publisher, Payne, two guineas for each number, and with the exception of four, the *Rambler* papers were all his own composition. The sale of the *Rambler* was small compared to the thousands of the *Spectator*. Five hundred was about the normal issue, with the exception of Richardson's contribution (No. 97), which sold well. The author of *Pamela* and *Clarissa* was now famous, and this paper has, therefore, a more than passing interest. The subject which Richardson deals with is exactly the one which we might have expected from the author of *Pamela*—courtship. In that retrospective mood which sees the past in a halo of romance widely apart from the truth, he laments the degeneration of courtship in his own day.

"Oh, Mr Rambler! forgive the talkativeness of an old man! When I courted and married my Laetitia, then a blooming beauty, everything passed just so! But how is the case now? The ladies, maidens, wives, and widows, are engrossed by places of open resort, and general entertainment, which fill every quarter of the metropolis, and being constantly frequented, make home irksome. Breakfasting-places, dining-places; routs, drums, concerts, balls, plays, operas, masquerades for the evening, and even for all night; and, lately, publick sales of the goods of broken housekeepers, which the general dissoluteness of manners has contributed to make very frequent, come in as another seasonable relief to those modern time-killers. In the summer there are in every country-town assemblies: Tunbridge, Bath, Cheltenham, Scarborough! What expense of dress and equipage is required to qualify the frequenters for such emulous appearance?

" By the natural infection of example, the lowest people have places of sixpenny-resort, and gaming-tables for pence. Thus servants are now induced to fraud and dishonesty, to support extravagance, and supply their losses.

" As to the ladies who frequent those publick places, they are not ashamed to show their faces wherever men dare go, nor blush to try who shall stare most impudently, or who shall laugh loudest on the publick walks.

" The men who would make good husbands, if they visit those places, are frighted at wedlock, and resolve to live single, except they are bought at a very high price. They can be spectators of all that passes, and, if they please, more than spectators, at the expence of others. The companion of an evening, and the companion for life, require very different qualifications."

Richardson in this passage is still consistent to his earlier principles as developed in his first book.

Johnson's style has been much discussed and much criticised. That he could write in a simple manner cannot be denied. He is at his best in this direct style in the *Lives of the Poets*. A perfect example is the *Life of Savage*. But in the *Rambler* the heavier and more Latinised style of Johnson is predominant. This is obvious from the outset. In the first number, for example, he commences by stating the difficulty of settling the form of address to his readers: " Judgment was wearied with the perplexity of being forced upon choice when there was no motive to preference, and it was found convenient that some method of introduction should be established, which, if it wanted the allurement of novelty, might enjoy the security of prescription." This is the second sentence in the opening paper. It is typical of thousands. There had been nothing quite like it before, but it is a style which comes rather strangely from one who counselled others to give their days and nights to the study of Addison. Because there can be no doubt Johnson's heavily Latinised style was not the best suited for periodical essay work. Macaulay goes so far as to say: "As soon as he took his pen into his hand to write for the public, his style became systematically vicious. All his books are written in a learned language, in a language which nobody hears from his mother or his nurse, in a language in which nobody ever quarrels, or drives bargains, or makes love, in a language which nobody ever thinks. When he wrote for publication, he did his sentences out of English into Johnsonese. Like those unfortunate Chiefs of the Middle Ages who were suffocated by their own chain-mail and cloth of gold, his maxims perish under that load of works which was designed for their defence and their ornament." This is clever, but not nicely balanced criticism. Johnson in the best examples of his style shows beautifully balanced phrases and well-judged antithesis, and his work is enriched by a certain dignity and weight which make his sentences, when read aloud, have a peculiarly impressive effect. His work is well worthy the close attention of the striver after a good style. Johnson carefully revised the essays before their publication in volume form, and the general thoroughness of his work, "in the making," is seen by comparing specimens of first drafts, kept by Boswell and others, with the finished production. A large number of minute verbal alterations were made. In these earlier dark days, of which Johnson would never speak, he had almost certainly contributed to one or other of the periodicals and magazines which we have mentioned in the previous chapters, and though this periodical essay work was never disinterred and is now impossible to trace, that early training all told on the general cumulative effect of the *Rambler* essays.

It is not difficult to classify the main features of the *Rambler*. The majority of the papers deal with moral reflections on life, the fleeting nature of happiness, the regulation of the thoughts, the proper means of repressing overmuch sorrow, and the necessity of attending to the duties of common life. Johnson's *Visions* and *Allegories* are specially well done, though they cannot be called a new feature in periodical literature, since Addison, as in most things, had led the way here; but the *Voyage of Life* (No. 102) and *An Allegorical History of Rest and Labour* (No. 33) are peculiarly Johnson's own. The following extract from the former of these two papers gives a fair idea of the style and manner of execution of these *Rambler* essays :—

"'Life,' says Seneca, 'is a voyage, in the progress of which we are perpetually changing our scenes; we first leave childhood behind us, then youth, then the years of ripened manhood, then the better and more pleasing part of old age.' The perusal of this passage having incited in me a train of reflections on the state of man, the incessant fluctuation of his wishes, the gradual change of his disposition to all external objects, and the thoughtlessness with which he floats along the stream of time, I sunk into a slumber amidst my meditations; and, on a sudden, found my ears filled with the tumult of labour, the shouts of alacrity, the shrieks of alarm, the whistle of winds, and the dash of waters.

"My astonishment for a time repressed my curiosity; but soon recovering myself so far as to inquire whither we were going, and what was the cause of such clamour and confusion, I was told that they were launching out into the ocean of life, that we had already passed the streights of infancy, in which multitudes had perished, some by the weakness and fragility of their vessels, and more by the folly, perverseness, or negligence of those who undertook to steer them; and that we were now on the main sea, abandoned to the winds and billows, without any other means of security than the care of the pilot, whom it was always in our power to choose among great numbers that offered their direction and assistance.

"I then looked round with anxious eagerness; and first turning my eyes behind me, saw a stream flowing through flowery islands, which every one that sailed along seemed to behold with pleasure; but no sooner touched than the current, which, though not noisy or turbulent, was yet irresistible, bore him away. Beyond these islands all was darkness, nor could any of the passengers describe the shore at which he first embarked.

"Before me, and on each side, was an expanse of waters violently agitated, and covered with so thick a mist, that the most perspicacious eye could see but a little way. It appeared to be full of rocks and whirlpools, for many sunk unexpectedly while they were courting the gale with full sails, and insulting those whom they had left behind. So numerous, indeed, were the dangers, and so thick the darkness, that no caution could confer security. Yet there were many, who, by false intelligence, betrayed their followers into whirlpools, or by violence pushed those whom they found in their way against the rocks.

"The current was invariable and insurmountable; but though it was impossible to sail against it, or to return to the place that was once passed, yet it was not so violent as to allow no opportunities for dexterity or courage, since, though none could retreat back from danger, yet they might often avoid it by oblique direction.

"It was, however, not very common to steer with much care or prudence; for by some universal infatuation, every man appeared to think himself safe, though he saw his consorts every moment sinking round him; and no sooner had the waves closed over them, than their fate and misconduct were forgotten; the voyage was pursued with the same jocund confidence; every man congratulated himself upon the soundness of his vessel, and believed himself able to stem the whirlpool in which his friend was swallowed, or glide over the rocks on which he was dashed: nor was it often observed that the sight of a wreck made any man change his course: if he turned aside for a moment, he soon forgot the rudder, and left himself again to the disposal of chance.

"This negligence did not proceed from indifference or from weariness of their present condition; for not one of those who thus rushed upon destruction, failed, when he was sinking, to call loudly upon his associates for that help which could not now be given to him; and many spent their last moments in cautioning others against the folly by which they were intercepted in the midst of their course. Their benevolence was sometimes praised, but their admonitions were unregarded.

"The vessels in which we had embarked being confessedly unequal to the turbulence of the stream of life, were visibly impaired in the course of the voyage; so that every passenger was certain, that how long soever he might, by favourable accidents, or by incessant vigilance, be preserved, he must sink at last.

"This necessity of perishing might have been expected to sadden the gay, and intimidate the daring, at least to keep the melancholy and timorous in perpetual torments, and hinder them from any enjoyment of the varieties and gratifications which nature offered them as the solace of their labours; yet in effect none seemed less to expect destruction than those to whom it was most dreadful; they all had the art of concealing their danger from themselves; and those who knew their inability to bear the sight of the terrors that embarrassed their way, took care never to look forward, but found some amusement for the present moment, and generally entertained themselves by playing with HOPE, who was the constant associate of the voyage of life."

Dr Johnson often turns to the trials and difficulties which beset the lot of literary men and how their hopes are liable to disappointment, as, for example, in the second number. He discusses the difference between an author's writings and his conversation (No. 14), and the dangers and misery of literary eminence (No. 16), while he warns students that the study of life is not to be neglected for the sake of books (No. 180). His critical papers are specially worthy of note. Dr Johnson in the *History of Criticism* must rank along with Ben Jonson, Dryden, and Pope as representing distinct and important epochs in the seventeenth and eighteenth centuries. He possessed a thoroughly critical mind; he was well and widely read; his faults are due rather to his period, and to certain prepossessions influenced perhaps a little by his physical defects—his defective eyesight and lack of " ear." In No. 2 of the *Rambler* he points out to the literary aspirant the various forces of idle and envious critics all tending to depress and hurry his work out of sight. He laments the degradation of criticism (No. 3), and continues in the same vein (No. 22) under the guise of an *Allegory on Wit and Learning*, and (No. 93) on the responsibilities of the critic. But he soon leaves these generalities and comes to that actual examination of literature, wherein the critic inevitably reveals his true quality *qua* critic. His criticisms on Milton are interesting, from this " time " point of view. No. 86 discusses Milton's heroic verse. Here Johnson practically assumes that *the* medium of poetry must be the regular end-stopped decasyllabic couplet—with the iamb as base, and practically no mixed measure allowed except to avoid monotony. Hence it comes about that he censures lines from *Paradise Lost* which we now consider triumphs of prosodical effect. Especially unfortunate does the censure of the trochee inserted in Cowley's line seem to us now:

" And the soft wings of peace *cover* him round."

JOHNSON'S PERIODICAL ESSAYS

Following out the same principles in No. 88, he discusses Milton's licence of elision, and he declares Milton " has left our harsh cadences yet harsher " ! and in No. 90, since he is convinced of the need for a regular cæsura, he objects to the varied pauses of Milton, apparently not understanding the great achievement which the latter has accomplished in this constant varying of the pause and in the construction of his verse paragraph. " To imitate the fictions and sentiments of Spenser can incur no reproach, for allegory is perhaps one of the most pleasing vehicles of instruction. But I am very far from extending the same respect to his diction in his stanza." His style was in his own time allowed to be vicious, so darkened with old words and peculiarities of phrase, and so remote from common use that Johnson boldly pronounced him *to have written no language.* "His stanza is at once difficult and unpleasing: tiresome to the ear by its uniformity, and to the attention by its length. It was at first formed in imitation of the Italian poets, without due regard to the germs of our language." There is scarcely a phrase in this passage which at the present time we would subscribe to. But it would be unfair to say that here we have the true critical stature of Johnson. Elsewhere in his papers there are not only good critical *dicta*, but statements which show that he was in nowise hide-bound to any scheme of neo-classicism, but rises above his time to the eternal principles upon which criticism rests. Take, for example, No. 156, where he attacks any servile following of the three unities in drama, culminating in the last paragraph where he boldly asserts : " It ought to be the first endeavour of a writer to distinguish nature from custom ; or that which is established because it is right from that which is right only because it is established ; that he may neither violate essential principles by a desire for novelty, nor debar himself from the attainment of beauties within his view, by a needless fear of breaking rules which no literary dictator had authority to enact." In such a passage as this, Dr Johnson far outstrips in critical value the papers of Addison. In the *Milton* papers Addison simply attempted a justification of the poet by quoting passages which had a certain similarity to those of Virgil; and in the *Pleasures of the Imagination* series Addison defines Imagination in a manner which precludes its application to poetry or indeed to literature at all. But in these *Rambler* papers we have not only direct applications of the critical tenets of the time to literary texts; but incidentally great critical flashes of insight which are worthy of the best of the Romantic critics of the following century.

The number of Johnson's papers which are concerned with the fair sex would not have been sufficient to have called down the ire of Swift, if he had been alive. Johnson's women characters are ticketed with rather formidable Latin names, and have not the lightness and vivacity of Steele's delineations of womankind. There is more than a little truth in what Garrick said on this very point that his women characters "were all Johnsons in petticoats"; and the paper (No. 39) headed *The Unhappiness of Women whether single or married*, while truly Johnsonian, is scarcely calculated to give satisfaction to his female readers! But when he leaves these more general exhortations and comes to the direct description of some one he has in his mind to satirise, his touch comes out more clearly. Take, for example, No. 200, *Asper's Complaint of the Insolence of Prospero*, where Johnson bitterly comments on the changed attitude of his old friend Garrick to him, when the wheel of fortune had turned in the actor's favour. During *Asper's* visit to *Prospero's* house he is subjected to a series of "insults"—the cloth covering the carpet is turned up at the corner to show the brightness, colour, and richness of the pattern; and "pride not being easily glutted with persecution" he is given only second-rate tea, and asked to admire the beautiful Dresden china, but told to set them down "for they who were accustomed only to common dishes, seldom handled china with much care." "You will, I hope," adds Johnson, in the character of *Asper*, "commend my philosophy when I tell you that I did not dash his baubles to the ground." This paper is equal to the best of the *Tatler* and *Spectator* papers for briskness and humour. Other attempts at humorous or semi-humorous treatment are No. 12, giving an amusing account of a servant-girl's troubles whilst endeavouring to get a situation in London; and No. 161, giving an account of the successive occupants of a garret (a tailor, a young lady of doubtful reputation, an apparently respectable man who turns out to be a coiner, an author, and two sisters). A clever paper describes a young trader's attempts at politeness (No. 116), and an account of a Club of Antiquaries (No. 177) is good. Thus the strictly moral and didactic contributions are relieved on not a few occasions by papers of a lighter nature. In one sense the *Rambler* may be said to supplement the *Tatler* and *Spectator*, and the three taken together make a notable contribution to the literature of the periodical essay in the eighteenth century. The charge against the *Rambler* that it attains neither the kaleidoscopic variety nor the bright treatment of the earlier periodicals has, however, truth on its side. On the other hand, we can well understand that Johnson looked back upon his work with pride and satisfaction; the essays form a notable bundle of moral and didactic reading. They carry home their lessons with an impressive force scarcely to be surpassed in any work of a similar kind.

To complete our estimate of Dr Johnson's essay periodical work, it will be convenient to consider the *Idler* along with his earlier work. Six years after the conclusion of the *Rambler* there began to appear the *Universal Chronicle, or Weekly Gazette*, published by Newbery every Saturday, and in this newspaper appeared a series of papers called *Idlers*. These were the mainstay of the venture; at any rate, the paper having run for two years, stopped soon after Johnson ceased sending in his weekly essays. This method of contribution had been in operation earlier, as in the case of Mist's *Weekly Journal*. Exception has again been taken to the rather misleading name given to his work, though the papers are much shorter and certainly a little lighter in tone and more varied in character than the *Rambler* essays. The *eidolon* in the *Rambler* had been the merest *nominis umbra*. Here also the *Idler's* character is of the very vaguest description. The *Idler* is not wholly the composition of Dr Johnson. In addition to one or two papers which are anonymous, there are three by Thomas

THE EIGHTEENTH-CENTURY ESSAYISTS

Warton. One of this last group, the *Journal of a Senior Fellow* (No. 33), is a delightful ironic description of the Epicurean life of a college don. It is no doubt reminiscent of the *diaries* in the *Spectator*, but there are original touches which redeem it from the charge of plagiarism, and the style is right—light, easy, and humorous. Take the following passage :—

"*Monday*, 11 *a.m.*—Went down into my cellar. *Mem.*—My *Mountain* will be fit to drink in a month's time. *N.B.*—To remove the five-year-old port into the new bin on the left hand.

"1 *p.m.*—Dined alone in my room on a soal (*sic*). *N.B.*—The shrimp-sauce not so good, as Mr H. of Peterhouse and I used to eat in London last winter at the *Mitre* in Fleet Street. Sat down to a pint of Madeira. Mr H. surprised me over it. We finished two bottles of port together, and were very cheerful. *Mem.*—To dine with Mr H. at Peterhouse next Monday. One of the dishes a leg of pork and peas, at my desire."

There is a series of three papers by Sir Joshua Reynolds on *False Criticism on Painting* (No. 76), on *The Grand Style of Painting* (No. 79), and on *The True Idea of Beauty* (No. 82). In these Reynolds discusses in an interesting way the rule *imitate nature* in painting, and pleads for more than mere accuracy and realistic detail. The highest art is not that a "cat or fiddle is painted so finely that it looks as if you could take it up." What he pleads for is the sublime style of Michael Angelo, whom he calls the *Homer of Painting*. This series of papers in an essay periodical was really something new—a widening of subjects suitable for discussion in such essays. When an authority like Reynolds deigned to give short and interesting papers on the subject of which he was master, there was an increased importance and position implied for the essay periodical.

Johnson in the *Idler* has given little sketches of a great many characters; *Treacle, Drugget, Whirler, Betty Broom, Mrs Savecharge, Dick Shifter*, and *Miss Heartless*. Each of these sketches hits off some fault or defect of character, and some are decidedly amusing. *Molly Quick*'s complaint of her mistress (No. 46) is excellent. She will never give her a direct order, but works by innuendoes and opposites till the poor girl is simply distracted : " When she would have something put in its place, *she bids me lay it on the floor.* If she would have me snuff the candles, she asks *whether I think her eyes are like a cat's* ? If she thinks her chocolate delayed, she talks of the *benefits of abstinence.* If any needle-work is forgotten, she supposes *that I have heard of the lady who died by pricking her finger.*"

Moral and didactic papers are naturally frequent. The titles, *Self-Denial Necessary* (No. 52), *Expectations of Pleasure Frustrated* (No. 58), *What have ye done ?* (No. 88), and *Physical Evil Moral Good* (No. 89), are not belied by their contents; they give a recasting of all Dr Johnson's wisdom and wide outlook on life.

Literary criticism is not so prominent as in the *Rambler,* but Johnson's two papers on *Minim the Critic* (Nos. 60 and 61) are quite comparable to Addison's *Tatler* papers on *Ned Softly,* though not perhaps in so deliciously humorous a vein. Many of the hits made against the readily equipped and instantaneously trained critic and his rules, seem to expose the weaknesses of some of Johnson's own critical positions. The remarks on the Academy of Criticism, and those regarding rhyme and sense sacrificed to sound, and " how the best thoughts are mangled by the necessity of confining or extending them to the dimensions of a couplet," are particularly apposite. The following passage will serve to illustrate the tone of the two papers :—

"Dick Minim, after the common course of puerile studies, in which he was no great proficient, was put an apprentice to a brewer, with whom he had lived two years, when his uncle died in the city, and left him a large fortune in the stocks. Dick had for six months before used the company of the lower players, of whom he had learned to scorn a trade, and, being now at liberty to follow his genius, he resolved to be a man of wit and humour. That he might be properly initiated in his new character, he frequented the coffee-houses near the theatres, where he listened very diligently, day after day, to those who talked of language and sentiments, and unities and catastrophes, till by slow degrees he began to think that he understood something of the stage, and hoped in time to talk himself.

"But he did not trust so much to natural sagacity as wholly

to neglect the help of books. When the theatres were shut, he retired to Richmond with a few select writers, whose opinions he impressed on his memory by unwearied diligence ; and, when he returned with other wits to the town, was able to tell, in very proper phrases, that the chief business of art is to follow nature ; that a perfect writer is not to be expected, because genius decays as judgment increases ; that the great art is the art of blotting ; and that, according to the rule of Horace, every piece should be kept nine years.

" Of the great authors he now began to display the characters, laying down as an universal position, that all had beauties and defects. His opinion was, that Shakespeare, committing himself wholly to the impulse of nature, wanted that correctness which learning would have given him ; and that Johnson, trusting to learning, did not sufficiently cast his eye on nature.

" He blamed the stanza of Spenser, and could not bear the hexameters of Sidney. Denham and Waller he held the first reformers of English numbers ; and thought that if Waller could have obtained the strength of Denham, or Denham the sweetness of Waller, there had been nothing wanting to complete a poet."

The growth of the *Eastern Tale* and of the *Allegory* is quite a remarkable feature in these eighteenth-century periodicals. Frequent in the *Spectator* of Addison and Steele, they reappeared in the *Rambler*, and in the *Idler* Johnson has continued the practice. A typical tale is No. 99, entitled *Ortogrul of Basra*.

" As Ortogrul of Basra was one day wandering along the streets of Bagdad, musing on the varieties of merchandise, which the shops offered to his view, and observing the different occupations which busied the multitudes on every side, he was awakened from the tranquillity of meditation by a crowd that obstructed his passage. He raised his eyes, and saw the Chief Vizier, who, having returned from the divan, was entering his palace. Ortogrul mingled with the attendants, and being supposed to have some petition for the vizier, was permitted to enter. He surveyed the spaciousness of the apartments, admired the walls hung with golden tapestry, and the floors covered with silken carpets, and despised the simple neatness of his own little habitation.

" Surely, said he to himself, this palace is the seat of happiness, where pleasure succeeds to pleasure, and discontent and sorrow can have no admission. Whatever Nature has provided for the delight of sense, is here spread forth to be enjoyed. What can mortals hope or imagine, which the master of this palace has not obtained ? The dishes of Luxury cover his table, the voice of Harmony lulls him in his bowers ; he breathes the fragrance of the groves of Java, and sleeps upon the down of the cygnets of Ganges. He speaks, and his mandate is obeyed ; he wishes, and his wish is gratified ; all whom he sees obey him, and all whom he hears flatter him. How different, Ortogrul, is thy condition, who art doomed to the perpetual torments of unsatisfied desire, and who has no amusement in thy power that can withhold thee from thy own reflections ! They tell thee that thou art wise ; but what does wisdom avail with poverty ? None will flatter the poor, and the wise have very little power of flattering themselves. That man is surely the most wretched of the sons of wretchedness, who lives with his own faults and follies always before him, who has none to reconcile him to himself by praise and veneration. I have long sought content, and have not found it ; I will from this moment endeavour to be rich.

" Full of his new resolution, he shuts himself in his chamber for six months, to deliberate how he should grow rich ; he sometimes proposed to offer himself as a counsellor to one of the kings of India, and sometimes resolved to dig for diamonds in the mines of Golconda. One day, after some hours passed in violent fluctuation of opinion, sleep insensibly seized him in his chair ; he dreamed that he was ranging a desert country in search of some one that might teach him to grow rich ; and as he stood on the top of a hill shaded with cypress, in doubt whither to direct his steps, his father appeared on a sudden standing before him. ' Ortogrul,' said the old man, ' I know thy perplexity ; listen to thy father ; turn thine eye on the opposite mountain.' Ortogrul looked, and saw a torrent tumbling down the rocks, roaring with the noise of thunder, and scattering its foam on the impending woods. ' Now,' said his father, ' behold the valley that lies between the hills.' Ortogrul looked, and espied a little well, out of which issued a small rivulet. ' Tell me now,' said his father, ' dost thou wish for sudden affluence, that may pour upon thee like the mountain torrent, or for a slow and gradual increase, resembling the rill gliding from the well ? ' ' Let me be quickly rich,' said Ortogrul ; ' let the golden stream be quick and violent.' ' Look round thee,' said his father, ' once again.' Ortogrul looked, and perceived the channel of the torrent dry and dusty ; but following the rivulet from the well, he traced it to a wide lake, which the supply, slow and constant, kept always full. He waked, and determined to grow rich by silent profit and persevering industry.

THE EIGHTEENTH-CENTURY ESSAYISTS

" Having sold his patrimony, he engaged in merchandise, and in twenty years purchased lands, on which he raised a house, equal in sumptuousness to that of the vizier, to which he invited all the ministers of pleasure, expecting to enjoy all the felicity which he had imagined riches able to afford. Leisure soon made him weary of himself, and he longed to be persuaded that he was great and happy. He was courteous and liberal; he gave all that approached him hopes of pleasing him, and all who should please him hopes of being rewarded. Every art of praise was tried, and every source of adulatory fiction was exhausted. Ortogrul heard his flatterers without delight, because he found himself unable to believe them. His own heart told him its frailties, his own understanding reproached him with his faults. ' How long,' said he, with a deep sigh, ' have I been labouring in vain to amass wealth which at last is useless. Let no man hereafter wish to be rich, who is already too wise to be flattered.' "

Papers of this nature suggest reflections upon what we may term the gradual orientalisation of the eighteenth century. Walpole writes his *Chinese Letter*, Goldsmith composes his *Citizen of the World* papers, Dr Johnson writes his *Rasselas* as well as these tales in the *Rambler* and *Idler*, and the *Arabian Nights Entertainments* themselves were first translated by Gulland into French between 1704 and 1707. Later in the century (1786) we recall the curious history of Beckford, the author of *Vathek*, with its gorgeous scenes and closing with the gloomy impressiveness of the *Hall of Eblis*. It is doubtful whether this " orientalising " tendency was a healthy one. Beckford himself was more or less insane, and the robust Fielding would never have gone to the East for his " local colour." But this " Eastern " mode of expression obtained a firm hold upon the literary practice of the time. In Germany a collection of Eastern Tales was made by Goethe himself, and the far inferior but highly imaginative Hoffman (who is ably dealt with by Sir Walter Scott in one of his essays) was under the same influence. In the nineteenth century we can mention only two examples. Fitzgerald gave us his excellent translation (and more than translation) of *Omar Khayyam*, and the earlier tendency reappeared in George Meredith in his curious batch of tales *The Shaving of Shagpat*. In the eighteenth century itself this orientalisation was only one of the ways along which the reaction that was gradually growing in strength against neo-classicism revealed itself.

The *Idler* is about half the size of the *Rambler*. Though lighter in bulk, it had the advantage at times in its shorter papers and lighter tone. There is very little actual repetition in the second periodical even when somewhat similar subjects are discussed. Taken together the *Rambler* and *Idler* are a notable production in the sphere of the essay periodical.

A comparison inevitably suggests itself at this point between the two literary giants, Johnson and Addison. Addison is the *Horace* of the period, while Johnson is rather the *Juvenal*. Addison has the Horatian sense of fun, and is lighter and more playful in tone, even in his ironic touches, while Johnson excels in a heavier satire, almost saturnine in tone; he is (externally at least) more of the bear, and Addison more of the gentleman. But another, and more important point is that Addison keeps more " outside of himself," so to speak, and looks on the world with the keen searching eye of the novelist himself—for Addison had the true disposition of a Fielding or a Scott. But Johnson does not manage to do this; he is more personal; he cannot get away from himself, and *Dr Johnson* is ever in his thoughts. He is not so successful in his essay productions in that he lacks this almost necessary quality of detachment. But both did great work in their kind, and deserve to be ranked as the princes of their age.

CHAPTER VI

THE *ADVENTURER, WORLD, CONNOISSEUR,* AND OTHERS

We are naturally loth to leave the company of Dr Johnson, so well-beloved a figure, but several lesser lights, interesting in their own way, must now engage our attention.

Some years before the advent of the *Idler*, and just after the conclusion of the *Rambler*, the *Adventurer* was issued under the supervision of Dr Hawkesworth. It had been plainly evident that the scheme of the *Rambler* was too monotonous and heavy to succeed with a public nourished on *Tatler* and *Spectator* traditions, and Johnson himself gave assistance in the drawing-up of the various departments of this new venture. In a letter to Dr Joseph Warton, brother of the Warton we have mentioned, he puts the scheme very well. " We have considered that the paper should consist of pieces of imagination, pictures of life, and disquisitions of literature, . . . and the latter province of criticism and literature they are very desirous to assign to the commentator on Virgil." With the assistance of Warton, Johnson himself, and Bathhurst, Hawkesworth produced a paper which aimed at giving more variety than had been the case with the *Rambler* and the *Idler*. Hawkesworth's career presents some points of interest. The story of it makes a curious narrative. He was commissioned by the Admiralty to draw up a connected account, in literary form, of the discoveries then recently made by Captain Cook and others in the South Seas. Hawkesworth received for this work the enormous sum of £6000 (worth considerably more than twice that amount to-day), but he was greatly chagrined by the action of enemies who issued plates illustrating certain practices and customs of the natives, which he had described in his book. It is said that the charge, one practically of immorality, so affected him as to shorten his life.

Of the *Adventurer*, Hawkesworth wrote no less than half the number of papers, which totalled one hundred and forty in all. In the first number, Hawkesworth introduces his *Adventurer*. A rather clever rigmarole on Courage contrasts his situation as an author with the Knight Errant of old. He is setting out to do battle, " for he knows he has not far to go before he will meet some fortress which has been raised by sophistry for the asylum of error, some enchanter who lies in wait to ensnare innocence, or some dragon breathing out his poison in defence of infidelity; he has also the power of enchantment which he will exercise in his turn; he will sometimes crowd the scene with ideal beings; sometimes recall the past, and sometimes anticipate the future." This recalls the aim of Addison himself in the *Spectator*. It is more varied than that proposed by Johnson in the *Rambler*, and Hawkesworth promises, in addition, stories and imaginative pieces of work. The *Adventurer*, as a personage, remains at the vanishing point. His character is not developed; he is not made use of as *Isaac Bickerstaff* or *Nestor Ironside* had been in the earlier periodicals. But this was really no drawback, a greater literary freedom was thereby given.

The bulk of the papers being by Hawkesworth, we consider his work first. It has often been said that his style is a close imitation of Johnson's, and strong traces of resemblance in weight and balance of sentence, especially in the didactic papers, may be noted. When we consider his friendship with the great man, and the direct influence Johnson seems to have exercised in the preparation and execution of the *Adventurer*, we need not be surprised that Hawkesworth's enthusiastic appreciation of Dr Johnson carried him, consciously or unconsciously, to imitate his method and style. But Boswell's remarks on this point in his *Life of Johnson* are unjust. There is more than a little originality in Hawkesworth's work. For example, the majority of the imaginative pieces were by Hawkesworth himself, most of the stories being allegorical, and setting forth, with appropriate apparatus, the various virtues and vices. And he excels in his Eastern Tales and domestic narratives. He tells the story of *Melissa*, who, after various trials, marries happily; the story of *Opsinous*, and the story of *Flavilla*, while Agamus's account of his daughter is a really powerful, if gloomy, setting of a rather unpleasant theme. Mrs Chapone's contribution, called the *History of Fidelia*, follows the same lines. All these are directly didactic in their purpose.

Of the Eastern Tales, *Amurath* is one of the best and runs through three numbers, and the *History of Nouraddin and Amana* is well done. A number of allegorical tales founded on religion and the virtues are also cast in Eastern form. Typical examples of these are the *Story of Yamodin and Tambra* and *Almarine and Shelimala*. Although they develop features of their own, most of these tales can be traced to their ancestry in the *Spectator*. The tales and allegories of Addison, who excelled in this class of work, are their source and fount. It may just be that the prevalence of these tales in the *Adventurer* was due to the fact that Hawkesworth's wife kept a boarding-school for girls, and that he provided these tales for the guidance and instruction of the pupils.

The subjects of some of his papers recall Dr Johnson's *Rambler*. For example, *The Distresses of an Author invited to read his Play* (No. 52) makes amusing reading, but invites comparison with Johnson's paper on *The Scholar's Complaint of his own Bashfulness* in the *Rambler* (No. 157).

This paper of Hawkesworth's is an unexcelled example of the style of much of this class of work. The poet enters the room where he is to read his play with " an enormous queue of brown paper, which some mischievous brat had, with a crooked pin, hung between the two locks of his major periwig." His appearance of course creates merriment, but his troubles have only just begun, for he describes his bow to the lady of the house thus : " At the same time bowing with the most profound reverence, unhappily I overturned a screen, which, in its fall, threw down the breakfast-table, broke all the china, and crippled the lap-dog. In the midst of this ruin I stood torpid in silence and amazement, stunned with the shrieks of the ladies and the yelling of the dog, and the clattering of the china, and while I considered myself as the author of such complicated mischief, I believe I felt as keen anguish as he, who, with a halter about his neck, looks up, while the other end of it is fastening to the gibbet." While reading, the poet is ruthlessly interrupted. He is holding the audience with pathetic voice as he approaches the climax of distress in his play when one of the company suddenly remembering something, " which, if he did not communicate, he might forget, desired me to stop half a moment ; and then turning to his companion, ' Jack,' says he, ' there was sold in Smithfield, no longer ago than last Saturday, the largest ox that ever I beheld in my life.' The ridicule of this malicious apostrophe was so striking, that pity and decorum gave way, and my patroness herself burst into laughter." His manuscript is then torn from his hand by a young buck, who mimics his reading to the amusement of the company, and finally the poor author takes his leave in the extreme of distress and perplexity.

Bathurst is the reputed humorist of the *Adventurer*. Some of his papers are very good, in particular the fifth, which gives a new version of the application of the theory of the transmigration of souls. He relates the adventures of an eldest son who becomes in succession a mongrel puppy, a bullfinch, a cockchafer, and an earthworm. The plan of a new memorandum book for the use of ladies (No. 23) is fresh, and a similar scheme for a paper called the *Beaumonde* is both witty and satirical.

His *Adventures of a Halfpenny*, while it inevitably suggests comparison with the earlier *Adventures of a Shilling*, is good and is a typical example of Bathurst's work.

" I was led to the consideration of this subject by some halfpence I had just received in change : among which one in particular attracted my regard, that seemed once to have borne the profile of King William, now scarcely visible, as it was very much battered, and besides other marks of ill-usage had a hole through the middle. As it happened to be the evening of a day of some fatigue, my reflections did not much interrupt my propensity to sleep, and I insensibly fell into a kind of half-slumber ; when to imagination the halfpenny which then laid before me upon the table, erected itself upon its rim, and from the royal lips stamped on its surface articulately uttered the following narration :—

"'Sir! I shall not pretend to conceal from you the illegitimacy of my birth, or the baseness of my extraction; and though I seem to bear the venerable marks of old age, I received my being at Birmingham not six months ago. From thence I was transported, with many of my brethren of different dates, characters, and configurations, to a Jew-pedlar in Dukes Place, who paid for us in specie scarce a fifth part of our nominal and extrinsic value. We were soon after separately disposed of, at a more moderate profit, to coffee-houses, chop-houses, chandler shops, and gin-shops.

"'I had not been long in the world, before an ingenious transmuter of metals laid violent hands on me; and observing my thin shape and flat surface, by the help of a little quicksilver exalted me into a shilling. Use, however, soon degraded me again to my native low station; and I unfortunately fell into the possession of an urchin just breeched, who received me as a Christmas-box of his god-mother.

"'A love of money is ridiculously instilled into children so early, that before they can possibly comprehend the use of it, they consider it as of great value: I lost, therefore, the very essence of my being, in the custody of this hopeful discipline of avarice and folly; and was kept only to be looked at and admired; but a bigger boy after a while snatched me from him, and released me from my confinement.

"'I now underwent various hardships among his play-fellows, and was kicked about, hustled, tossed up, and chucked into holes; which very much battered and impaired me; but I suffered most by the pegging of tops, the marks of which I have bourne about me to this day. I was in this state the unwitting cause of rapacity, strife, envy, rancour, malice, and revenge, among the little apes of mankind; and became the object and the nurse of those passions which disgrace human nature, while I appeared only to engage children in innocent pastimes. At length, I was dismissed from their service, by a throw with a barrow-woman for an orange.

"'From her, it is natural to conclude, I posted to the gin-shop; where, indeed, it is probable I should have immediately gone, if her husband, a foot-soldier, had not wrestled me from her, at the expense of a bloody-nose, black-eye, scratched face, and torn regimentals. By him I was carried to the Mall in St James's Park; where—I am ashamed to tell how I parted from him—let it suffice that I was soon after safely deposited in a night-cellar.

"'From hence I got into the coat-pocket of a Blood, and remained there with several of my brethren for some days unnoticed.

THE ADVENTURER AND OTHER PERIODICALS

But one evening, as he was reeling home from the tavern, he jerked a whole handful of us through a sash-window into the dining-room of a tradesman, who he remembered had been so unmannerly to him the day before, as to desire payment of his bill. We reposed in soft ease on a fine Turkey carpet till the next morning, when the maid swept us up; and some of us were allotted to purchase tea, some to buy snuff, and I myself was immediately trucked away at the door for the *Sweetheart's Delight*.

"'It is not my design to enumerate every little accident that has befallen me, or to dwell upon trivial and indifferent circumstances, as is the practice of those important egoists, who write narratives, memoirs, and travels. As useless to the community as my single self may appear to be, I have been the instrument of much good and evil in the intercourse of mankind: I have contributed no small sum to the revenues of the crown, by my share in each newspaper; and in the consumption of tobacco, spirituous liquors, and other taxable commodities. If I have encouraged debauchery, or supported extravagance, I have also rewarded the labours of industry, and relieved the necessities of indigence. The poor acknowledge me as their constant friend; and the rich, though they affect to slight me, and treat me with contempt, are often reduced by their follies to distresses which it is ever in my power to relieve.'"

Bathhurst has caught the right spirit in which to write such a paper. His style is clear, simple, and straightforward, and it was largely the occurrence of such papers that enhanced the popularity which the *Adventurer* deservedly attained.

Johnson, in addition to his assistance at the outset, wrote a good deal for the *Adventurer*. The story of Misargyrus (Nos. 34 and 41) is in his best didactic vein: the concerns and miseries of literary men are again touched upon (Nos. 85, 95); his essay on *Sleep* is good; and the eighty-fourth number is worthy of note because it shows Johnson in a lighter mood. It is well worth reading. It is the old *Tatler* or *Spectator* idea of going to town in a stage-coach. This allows an account of the adventures on the way. Johnson introduces fresh touches. He described very well the "standoffishness" of the company inside the coach, and how, on their arrival at the inn, they simulate a greatness which by no means belongs to them. If Dr Johnson had written more of this style of work for the *Rambler* he would have had greater success with it and gone further to supply that variety and humour which the periodical essay requires.

The *Adventurer* has quite a number of general papers which refuse exact classification. Take, for example, the *Various Transmigrations of a Flea* (No. 5) and a *Visit to Bedlam with Dean Swift* (No. 109) by Warton, and the *Adventures of a Louse* (No. 121), which proves to be a rather melancholy story, told by Hawkesworth himself; *A Description of Characters at Bath* (No. 129), by Warton, is both fresh and smart. In this paper various types of men are satirised under the suggestive ticket-names of *Inertio, Crito, Dr Pamper, Spumosius, Mr Gull*, and *Captain Gairish*.

The criticism of literature is not forgotten. The critical papers which Dr Johnson wished Warton to write did actually appear. These papers are important because they supply clear premonitions of the coming revolt against Popian correctness and the neo-classic *régime* generally. In the *Adventurer* he gives a most interesting set of papers, though he often speaks with uncertain and hesitating voice. Towards the close of the undertaking Warton tells us (No. 139) that these essays were introduced to correct taste. Philosophy had come out of closets and libraries to dwell in Clubs and at tea-tables as Addison wished, but had degenerated into what was little less than common prattle. The pendulum had swung to the other side. Warton endeavours to bring criticism back to its true level.

It is a little disappointing to see him open his series of papers with *A Parallel between Ancient and Modern Learning* (No. 49). The reference is still to the long and dreary war in which Swift helped his patron, Sir Wm. Temple, many years before, by writing his *Battle of the Books*. Warton's paper is one of the last guns to fire over the almost deserted battlefield. In it Warton criticises adversely French critics, though he makes an exception of Fenelon and one or two others. His estimate of Montaigne is obviously coloured by " moral " consideration when he says : " But these blemishes of Montaigne are trifling and unimportant compared with his vanity, his indecency, and scepticism. That man must totally have suppressed the natural love of honest reputation which is so powerfully felt by the truly wise and good, who can calmly sit down to give a catalogue of his private vices, and publish his most secret infirmities, with the pretence of exhibiting a faithful picture of himself, and of exactly portraying the minutest features of his mind." A later paper (No. 51) makes mention of Longinus, who is in some respects one of the most significant figures in the whole history of criticism. In his treatise *On the Sublime* Longinus refers to the Old Testament phrase, " Let there be light," and Warton expands this reference of Longinus into a fresh and enlarged criticism of Holy Scripture cast into the literary form of a supposed " find." The title of the essay explains the device: *Translation of a Manuscript of Longinus lately discovered containing a Comparison of Celebrated Passages in Pagan and Jewish Writers.* Warton makes a sound statement when he asserts that many passages of Scripture have equal (if not greater) merit compared with outstanding passages in Greek dramatists. Erasmus, as Warton indicates at the forefront of his paper, had also explained the literary pre-eminence of the Bible. Longinus is supposed to write to his friend *Terentianius* in the following strain : " You may remember that in my treatise *On the Sublime*, I quoted a striking example of it from Moses the Jewish lawgiver, ' Let there be light, and there was light ! ' I have since met with a large volume translated into Greek by the order of Ptolemy, containing all the religious opinions, the civil laws and customs of that singular and unaccountable people, and, to confess the truth, I am greatly astonished at the incomparable elevation of its style, and the supreme grandeur of its images, many of which excel the utmost efforts of the most exalted genius of Greece." The literary device exemplified in Warton's paper has been repeated by later writers, but at the time the method was fresh and original. A third essay of Warton (No. 63) contains reference to Pope, and reveals a disposition no longer to accept either Pope's poetical position or his retailed theories unquestioningly. Both here and elsewhere Warton is outspoken on the subject. Three later numbers (Nos. 75, 80, 83) are devoted to a discussion of the *Odyssey*. Warton recommends it especially for school use. Milton is dealt with (No. 101) somewhat after the same manner as in the essays of Dr Johnson, passages being quoted; while Shakespeare comes under review in some five papers. *The Tempest* and *Lear* are discussed largely in the form of " re-telling " the story with illustrative passages, but with no great critical result. With the one hundred and fourteenth number, dated 9th March 1754, the *Adventurer* came to a close. Sufficient has been said to indicate that it includes within its pages a greater variety of subject-matter than Johnson was able to give to a composition wholly his own. Hawkesworth and Johnson had in a measure " run " the *Adventurer* together, and the combination had proved singularly successful, and the happy choice of coadjutors in Warton and Bathhurst had done something to add to this success. An honest attempt had been made to reproduce the best features of the Queen Anne periodicals without a slavish imitation of them; and although the *Adventurer* is little known to-day, Hawkesworth was animated by principles which are as sound now as when they were written. " As I was upon these principles to write for the young and the gay; for those who are entering the path of life, I knew that it would be necessary to amuse the imagination while I was approaching the heart; and that I could not hope to fix the attention, but by employing the passions. I have, therefore, sometimes led them into the regions of fancy, and sometimes held up before them the mirror of life; I have concatenated events, rather than deduced consequences by logical reasoning; and have exhibited scenes of prosperity and distress as more forcibly persuasive than the rhetoric of declamation. Time, which is impatient to date my last paper, will shortly moulder the hand that is now writing it in the dust, and still the breast that now throbs at the reflection: but let not this be read as something that relates only to another; for a few years only can divide the eye that is now reading from the hand that has written. This awful truth, however obvious, and however reiterated, is yet frequently forgotten: for surely, if we did not lose our remembrance, or at least our sensibility, that view would always predominate in our lives, which alone can afford us comfort when we die."

THE ADVENTURER AND OTHER PERIODICALS

Warton's criticism marks one of the many stages in eighteenth-century criticism of Shakespeare. Warton's is a transition stage, the final one is exemplified in Coleridge.

The next periodical which falls to be considered, the *World*, carries our history a step further, and gives a new turn to the essay periodical. The *World* possesses quite a style of its own, and includes several fresh features. The title seems to suggest its more varied character. The *World* was begun before the *Adventurer* ceased to be issued, the first number appearing at the opening of the year 1753. After a long run of over 200 numbers it came to an end on almost the last day of the year 1756.

The design, as stated in the first number, is " to ridicule with novelty and good humour, the fashions, foibles, vices, and absurdities of that part of the human species which calls itself the *World* and to trace it through all its business, pleasures, and amusements." These words serve to recall the aim of Addison in the *Spectator*. The grave tone of the *Rambler*, of the *Adventurer* even, is obviously being reacted against; and the introduction of a new set of contributors, men of fashion and social position, is a notable feature. This first number indicates the tone of the periodical as a whole; it is bright and amusing, with many sly asides aimed at the readers themselves, the discussions of religion and politics, the question of mottoes in Latin and Greek, and the wits who will exercise their ingenuity over the title. These last the author himself forestalls : "*Advertisement to the Wits.*—Whereas it is expected that the title of this paper will occasion certain quips, cranks, and conceits at the *Bedford* and other coffee-houses in this town: this is therefore to give notice, that the words, *this is a sad world, a vain world, a dull world, a wretched world, a trifling world, an ignorant world, a damned world:* or that *I hate the world, am weary of the world, sick of the world*, or phrases to the same effect, applied to this paper, shall be voted, by all that hear them, to be without wit, humour, or pleasantry, and be treated accordingly."

No critical papers appear in the *World*, unless Dodsley's essay on criticism (No. 32) be considered an exception. In that paper criticism is called a disease, and Dodsley says:

THE EIGHTEENTH-CENTURY ESSAYISTS

"It is not more true that every man is born in sin than that he is born in criticism." Few essays can be called wholly serious, and irony is the usual weapon employed, vices being turned into ridicule under the rather dangerous guise of defence or apology—for sometimes the irony was misread or misunderstood. The paper was eagerly read, exercised considerable influence at the time, and remains easily the best example of the *lighter* eighteenth-century periodical. The *World* was projected by Edward Moore, who shows real editorial capacity. He did not write all the papers, as Johnson did in his *Rambler*: he did not even compose the majority, only sixty-one out of two hundred and nine; but he managed to call to his aid a new set of writers, men of high rank in life, the Earl of Chesterfield, the Earl of Bath, the Earl of Cork, Horace Walpole, Soame Jenyns, and Owen Cambridge. This was a new departure, for before this date the men who contributed regularly to the essay periodical were members of the middle class. Even Addison and Steele were not received in the highest society, and it will be remembered how Addison was sneered at by Pope and others for his marriage, late in life, with his pupil's exalted mother. Thus the paper was drawn into a position of prominence in upper circles which previous similar productions had not enjoyed. Its popularity no doubt aided the favourable reaction which was taking place in regard to the social position of authors. Previously authors and the literary profession had not ranked very high. Even as late as the period of Southey himself we find complaints of the small remuneration given to writers. Moore still continues the *eidolon* of which *Isaac Bickerstaff* forms the prototype. This is *Adam Fitzadam*, whose name is chosen, no doubt, as a play on the title of the *World*—Adam being the *World's* progenitor. But the character is not developed, and he is the merest *nominis umbra* and does not occupy a prominent position. His presence seems more a carrying on of a long-honoured tradition than anything else. Moore received three guineas for each paper from Dodsley the publisher. With Lord Lyttelton's aid and patronage he obtained the aid of those writers we have mentioned and others. The majority of them would not accept any cash payment, so the money fell to Moore. The *World* appeared once a week.

In his judgment of contemporary literature, Horace Walpole (perhaps because he was himself a contributor) ranks the *World* as written by " our first writers." This phrase provoked Macaulay, who, in his essay on Walpole's *Letters to Sir Horace Mann*, takes the occasion to say: " Our first writers, it seems, were Lord Chesterfield, Lord Bath, Mr W. Whithed, Sir Charles Williams, Mr Soame Jenyns, Mr Cambridge, Mr Coventry. Of these seven personages, Whithed was the lowest in station, but was the most accomplished tuft-hunter of his time. Coventry was of a noble family. The other five had among them two seats in the House of Lords, two seats in the House of Commons, three seats in the Privy Council, a baronetcy, a blue riband, a red riband, about a hundred thousand pounds a year, and *not ten pages that are worth reading*. The writings of Whithed, Cambridge, Coventry, and Lord Bath are forgotten. Soame Jenyns is remembered chiefly by Johnson's review of the foolish essay on the *Origin of Evil*. Lord Chesterfield stands much lower in the estimation of posterity than he would have done if his letters had never been published. The lampoons of Sir Charles Williams are now read only by the curious, and though not without occasional flashes of wit, have always seemed to us, we must own, very poor performances." Such a statement is lacking in true historical perspective. It is not a just summing up of the value of the *World* as an essay periodical.

Moore contributed papers dealing with many varied subjects. They range from whist, pantomimes, the marriage question, and punning, to the uses of learning. They are all tinged with a light satire and are usually most successful. One example of his style will suffice. The subject is Sunday Observance (No. 21). " I can just remember that before Christianity was entirely reasoned out of these kingdoms, it was a mighty custom for young folks to go to church on that day; and indeed I should have thought there was no manner of harm in it, if it had not been plainly proved, as well by people of fashion as others, that going to church was the most tiresome thing in the world; and that consequently it was notoriously perverting a day set apart solely for rest. . . . I am for the strict observance of all institutions; and as we have happily got rid of the religious prejudices of our forefathers, and know but one way of keeping Sunday as it ought to be kept—the lying in bed all that day; and that permission be given to those who cannot sleep in their beds to go to church and sleep there." Moore can also write pleasing tales in an easy and unaffected style. A little picture of "back to the land," producing domestic happiness, is given in the sixteenth number, while the ludicrous experiences of a "Simple-Simon" clergyman (Nos. 31, 186) are told in happy style; Moore's ironic method of presentation is prominent in *A Tale of Scandal* (No. 139) and the story of *A Perfidious Lover* (No. 145). The last paper supplies a melancholy coincidence. In the paper Moore tells how *Fitzadam*, in turning aside to gaze at his lady friend *Mrs Cooper*, ran his horse against a post, and got himself so severely injured that death ultimately ensued. Whilst a collection of the *World* essays was being made in volume form, Moore died, in the act of revising *the same paper* for the press.

The contributions which Chesterfield made to the *World* naturally raise expectations. If anyone knew the *World*, surely it was the polite and diplomatic Chesterfield. He had contributed to earlier periodicals, as we have had occasion to mention, but it was just a chance that his first paper to the *World* was accepted at all. He had sent it in anonymously, and Moore was passing it over altogether, but Lyttelton recognised the handwriting and informed Moore of the identity of the anonymous contributor. This was the first of twenty-three papers which were received from him. Chesterfield excels in a certain delicate ironical method of attack and in his description of Society and its manners and morals, of which he was so acute a critic and judge. The letters which he sent to his son, Philip Dormer Stanhope (however little the latter may have profited by the good advice tendered), are but another evidence of the father's consummate knowledge of men and affairs. Chesterfield's first contribution (No. 18) describes a gentleman's tour to Paris with his family. He cautions men not to carry their wives and children with them when going abroad, and illustrates his warning by an amusing series of anecdotes. He satirises (No. 29) the practice of sending young men abroad to finish their education (a criticism of his own method with his son), while *Ironical Recommendation of the Present Times* (No. 49) is in his best vein. A single sentence is sufficient to show the subtle irony of Chesterfield's style. In *Different Opinions of this Paper* (No. 111) his opening sentence is : " It is very well known that religion and politics are perfectly understood by everybody, as they require neither study nor experience." Chesterfield's essays must be read carefully. The irony is so finely pitched that it may be misunderstood. He is at his best when he defines the *gentleman* :

" A GENTLEMAN, which is now the genteel synonymous term for a MAN OF HONOUR, must, like his Gothic ancestors, be ready for and rather desirous of a single combat. And if by a proper degree of wrong-headedness he provokes it, he is only so much the more jealous of his HONOUR, and more of a GENTLEMAN.

"He may lie with impunity, if he is neither detected nor accused of it; for it is not the lie he tells, but the lie he is told of, that dishonours him. In that case he demonstrates his veracity by his sword, or his pistol, and either kills or is killed with the greatest HONOUR.

" He may abuse and starve his own wife, daughters, or sisters, and he may seduce those of other men, particularly his friends, with inviolate HONOUR, because, as Sir John Brute very justly observes, he wears a sword.

" By the laws of HONOUR he is not obliged to pay his servants or his tradesmen ; for, as they are a pack of scoundrels, they cannot without insolence demand their due of a gentleman ; but he must punctually pay his gaming-debts to the sharpers who have cheated him ; for those debts are really debts of HONOUR.

"He lies under one disagreeable restraint ; for he must not cheat at play, unless in a horse-match ; but then he may with great HONOUR defraud in an office, or betray a trust.

"A Gentleman, is every man, who with a tolerable suit of cloaths, a sword by his side, and watch and snuff-box in his pockets, asserts himself to be a gentleman, swears with energy that he will be treated as such, and that he will cut the throat of any man who presumes to say the contrary."

The subjects Chesterfield discusses are Duelling, Clubs,

Gambling, Civility, and Good Breeding. Two outstanding papers are those (Nos. 100, 101) in which Chesterfield recommends Johnson's *Dictionary*, which was then being published. They are couched in terms of high praise, as the following passage shows :—

"I heard the other day with great pleasure from my worthy friend, Mr Dodsley, that Mr Johnson's *English Dictionary*, with a grammar and history of our language prefixed, will be published this winter in two large volumes in folio. . . . Many people have imagined that so extensive a work would have been best performed by a number of persons who should have taken their several departments, of examining, sifting, winnowing (I borrow this image from the Italian *Crusca*), purifying, and finally fixing, our language, by incorporating their respective funds into one joint stock. But whether this opinion be true or false, I think the public in general, and the republic of letters in particular, greatly obliged to Mr Johnson for having undertaken and executed so great and desirable a work. Perfection is not to be expected from any man; but if we are to judge by the various works of Mr Johnson already published, we have good reason to believe that he will bring this as near to perfection as any one man could do. I, therefore, recommend the previous perusal of it to all those who intend to buy the dictionary, and who, I suppose, are all those who can afford it."

This is high praise indeed, but it is seen in another light when we read the letter of reply which it called forth from Johnson, in which he recalls the treatment he received in the waiting-room of his lordship, half a score of years before. He repudiates Chesterfield's long-delayed offer of patronage in memorable words :—

"Is not a patron, my Lord, one who looks with unconcern on a man struggling for life in the water, and when he has reached ground, encumbers him with help ? The notice which you have been pleased to take of my labours had it been early, had been kind; but it has been delayed till I am indifferent, and cannot enjoy it; till I am solitary, and cannot impart it; till I am known, and do not want it. I hope it is no very cynical asperity not to confess obligations where no benefit has been received, or to be unwilling that the public should consider me as owing to a patron which Providence has enabled me to do for myself."

After the letter was received, no more papers recommending Johnson's *Dictionary* appeared in the *World*.

THE ADVENTURER AND OTHER PERIODICALS

Owen Cambridge contributed almost as many papers to the *World* as Chesterfield, and added a humorous element to the periodical. His two papers on *Hearers* (Nos. 54, 56) are witty; and the essays on *Books and Novels* (No. 170) and *Ambition for Trifles* (No. 72) are both very good. Articles on subjects so varied as gardening and turtle feasts help to give variety to the paper. Horace Walpole, dilettante and cultivator of belles-lettres and landscape gardener of Strawberry Hill, wrote several of the *World* essays. He sent in nine papers to Moore, but does not always exhibit great delicacy of taste; two at least of his papers (Nos. 28 and 160) are scarcely free from the censure which Robert Louis Stevenson applied in our own day, when he said that the " racy sermon against lust " was a feature of the age. His *Recommendation of Theodore, King of Corsica, to the Liberality of the Public* (No. 8) is interesting from the historical standpoint, and also his essay on the *Change of Style* (No. 10), in which he discusses the reformation of the calendar. He humorously calls upon all " to unite their endeavours with mine in decrying and exploding a reformation, which only tends to discountenance good old practices and venerable superstitions." The fourteenth number, also by Walpole, *On the Composition of Letters*, is interesting, since the author is one of our most voluminous (and withal charming) letter-writers. He declares that men are usually deficient in the art of letter-writing, while, on the other hand, " it is the Fair part of the creation which excels in that province." He illustrates this by example from *Eloisa*, Madame de Sevigné, an Italian *Lucretia Gonzago*, and also quotes specimens of absurd letter-writing. The last-mentioned essay of Walpole leads us to discuss how far letter-writing acted, if not actually as a rival, to the essay periodical, at least almost as an extension of it. The eighteenth century was an age of letter-writers and of letter-writing, and if we look into Walpole's voluminous correspondence we will find that many of the letters are of the *Spectator* pattern, and with a little adjustment could be made to stand in any of the periodicals. Byron, Scott, Sydney Smith, and Thackeray all join in singing the praises of Walpole's letters as witty but valuable pictures of the times. There is no doubt Walpole wrote them with an eye to future publication; there are distinct references in his letters to this effect; and even at the time they were handed about. These letters give us the scandal of the town, the annals of a quiet neighbourhood, literary criticism, political intelligence, and social gossip—all the features of the essay periodical. Indeed, we could construct " headings " out of the subject-matter of the letters similar to those prefixed to the essays of the *World* or *Connoisseur*. Here is such a précis of one of Walpole's letters to the Earl of Hertford :—*Periwigmakers in Distress—Headgear of the Ladies—Opening of Almack's—The Printer of the " North Briton " in the Pillory*—and so on. Walpole affects to despise literature, yet he discusses in his letters Richardson's *Pamela*, Gray's new poems, his own *Castle of Otranto*, and Voltaire's *Criticism of Shakespeare*, and Bishop Percy's *Old Ballads*. And earlier in the century Pope had made use of elaborate devices, not always very creditable, to get his letters published. But more important still were the interesting and amusing letters of Lady Mary Wortley Montagu, which were published as early as 1763. These must have had a great influence, giving as they do such bright pictures of foreign travel. And Chesterfield's letters to his son were published (rather to the annoyance of the Earl's family) about the same time. Their popularity was so great that five editions were sold within twelve months.

All these and other similar examples had their effect in diverting at least the upper classes from contributing to these essay periodicals. Their letters are really little essays; but the difference lies in this—while the essayists (like Addison in the *Spectator*) took the public immediately into their confidence, other letter-writers wrote rather with a view to their work being read by posterity than by the present generation. Their letters were only read in the first instance by their friends.

An interesting number in the *World* supplies a new subject and new treatment. It is the seventeenth, entitled *An Account of the Races and Manners of Newmarket*. The Earl of Bath, the author, not only gives a brilliant and " on the spot " description of the whole scene, but extends his remarks to the breeding of horses. Soame Jenyns supplied five papers, all good. Soame Jenyns has been hardly treated by critics. Dr Johnson passed a rather severe criticism upon him, and Lamb, in one of his essays, includes his work among his "books which are not books." Soame Jenyns' *Origin of Evil* and *Evidences of the Christian Religion* were well known in his own day, and one of his *World* papers deals with the transmigration of souls. This last-named subject, which had been treated before by the periodical essayists, was usually a matter for fun and ridicule, but in this case Jenyns seems to have believed the doctrine, for he treats it seriously. Other contributors, Coventry (who also wrote a novel), Parratt, Williams, Loveybond, Marriott, Herring, and Dalrymple are not individually of great importance, but they each gave one or two papers to the *World*, and added in this way to its variety. Taken as a whole, the *World* is one of the most readable of the eighteenth-century periodicals. Its lightness and crispness and wealth of ironical suggestion are features all its own. The *World* marks a distinct advance towards our modern magazines, and the rank of its main contributors, their style and treatment, all unite to give the *World* a unique place in this progression of periodical literature.

There had been great and renewed interest and activity in this special department of literature since Johnson's *Rambler* was published. The *Connoisseur*, a periodical similar to the *World*, ran contemporaneously with it. It was undertaken by two young men, Colman and Thornton, who worked together in a manner which reminds us of Erckmann and Chatrian in France at a later date. They seem to have composed even single papers together, and it is difficult to distinguish the work of each. Their position was clearly indicated in the closing number: "We have not only joined in the work taken together, but almost every single paper is the joint product of both; and as we have laboured equally in erecting the fabric, we cannot pretend that any one particular part is the sole workmanship of either." The first number appeared in January 1754. The *Connoisseur* continued to be published weekly, on Thursday, till September 1756, when the 140th number was reached. The full title is the *Connoisseur, by Mr Town, Critic and Censor General*. In the same issue there also appears a *Mr Village*, "who will try to do for the country" what *Mr Town* has to do for the city. But these "characters" in no way interfere with the freedom of the authors in composition. In point of fact, it is not until the last number that any description is given of *Mr Town*, and then it is a most amusing composite one. "Mr Town is a fair, black, middle-sized, very short man. He is about thirty years of age, and not more than four and twenty. He is a student of the law, and a bachelor of physic. He was bred at the University of Oxford; where, having taken no less than three degrees, he looks down on many learned professors as his inferiors." The great majority of the papers are by the two friends, and considering their comparative youth and inexperience, the variety of their papers is surprisingly good. Few serious papers appear; the majority deal with the chat of the town, and the various clubs and taverns. One or two tales appear: a satirical hit at the *white man* being related in the Hottentot story of *Touassouw and Knonmquaihe* (No. 21), while in No. 26, on *The Amusements of Sunday*, there is an echo of Swift's essay on *The Abolishing of Christianity in England*, since Christianity is apparently out of place in an age of frivolity and infidelity.

An extract or two from this paper will give an idea of the style of the *Connoisseur* paper. The heading, along with a quotation from Horace is:

> "Of all the days are in the week,
>   I dearly love but one day;
> And that's the day that comes between
>   A Saturday and Monday."

The essay opens by satirising the practice of thousands who leave the town to spend the day in the country, to swallow beer at country inns, observing, with Tom Brown, "that the Sabbath is a very fine institution, since the very breaking of it is the support of half the villages about our metropolis." A humorous extract is then given from the diary of one of these noble city gentlemen, and the paper proceeds:

THE ADVENTURER AND OTHER PERIODICALS

"Going to Church may, indeed, be reckoned among our Sunday amusements, as it is made a mere matter of diversion among many well-meaning people, who are induced to appear in a place of worship from the same motives that they frequent other public places. To some it answers all the purposes of a rout or assembly, and from their bows, nods, courtesies, and loud conversation, one might conclude that they imagined themselves in a drawing-room. To others it affords the cheap opportunity of showing their taste for dress. Not a few, I believe, are drawn together in our cathedrals and larger churches by the influence of the music rather than the prayers; and are kept awake by a jig from the organ-loft, though they are lulled to sleep by the harangue from the pulpit. A well-disposed Christian will go a mile from his own house to the Temple Church, not because a Sherlock is to preach, but to hear a solo from Stanley.

"But though going to church may be deemed a kind of amusement, yet upon modern principles it appears such a very odd one, that I am at a loss to account for the reasons which induced our ancestors to give into that method of passing their Sunday. At least it is so wholly incompatible with the polite system of life, that a person of fashion (as affairs are now managed) finds it absolutely impossible to comply with this practice. Then again, the service always begins at such unfashionable hours, that in the morning a man must huddle on his clothes, like a boy to run to school, and in an afternoon must inevitably go without his dinner. In order to remove all these objections, and that some ritual may be established in this kingdom, agreeable to our inclinations, and consistent with our practice, the following scheme has been lately sent me, in order to submit it to the serious consideration of the public.

"Imprimis, It is humbly proposed, that Christianity be entirely abolished by Act of Parliament, and that no other religion be imposed on us in its stead; but as the age grows daily more and more enlightened, we may at last be quite delivered from the influence of superstition and bigotry.

"Secondly, That in order to prevent our ever relapsing into pious errors, and that the common people may not lose their holiday, every Sunday be set apart to commemorate our victory over all religion; that the churches be turned into free-thinking meeting-houses, and discourses read in them to confute the doctrine of a future state, the immortality of the soul, and other absurd notions, which some people now regard as objects of belief.

"Thirdly, That a ritual be compiled exactly opposite to our present liturgy; and that, instead of reading portions of Scripture, the first and second lessons shall consist of a section of the Posthumous Works of Lord Bolingbroke, or a few pages from the writings of Spinoza, Chubb, Maundeville, Hobbes, Collins, Tindal, etc., from which writers the preachers shall also take their text.

"Fourthly, That the usual feasts and fasts, viz. Christmas Day, Easter Sunday, Trinity Sunday, etc., be still preserved; but that on those days discourses be delivered suitable to the occasion, containing a refutation of the Nativity, the Resurrection, the Trinity, etc.

"Fifthly, That instead of the vile melody of a clerk bawling out two staves of Sternhold and Hopkins, or a cathedral choir singing anthems from the psalter, some of the most fashionable cantatas, opera airs, songs, or catches, be performed by the best voices for the entertainment of the company.

"Lastly, That the whole service be conducted with such taste and elegance, as may render these free-thinking meeting-houses as agreeable as the theatres; and that they may be even more judiciously calculated for the propagation of atheism and infidelity than the Robin Hood Society, or the Oratory in Clare Market."

This extract is sufficient to indicate that Colman and Thornton had caught up the manner and style of the earlier periodicals. The same satiric note appears, the same aim to reform by ridiculing the vices and foibles of Society. A familiar feature of the earlier periodicals also reappears in the ninety-fifth number, *The Bride-Cake—a Vision*. It is a satire on the inequality of the couples hastening forward to matrimony. *The Temple of Usury* (No. 117) is a humorous account of the humble pawnshop " to strip the citizens of their most valuable effects, and for a small reward to deposit them as offerings." Literary criticism scarcely appears. The nearest approach to it is when satiric references are made (No. 27) to the prevailing habit of using hard words, and an eloquent appeal is made for simplicity in the written and spoken word; the eighteenth-century taste for Shakespeare is illustrated (No. 16) when the original ballad from which Shakespeare was supposed to have borrowed part of the plot of the *Merchant of Venice* is given; and in the forty-second number the *Study of the English Language* is recommended.

But Colman and Thornton were not the only contributors to the *Connoisseur*. The Earl of Cork (who wrote for the *World*) did good work here also, and several papers sent in by the poet Cowper are of special interest. They mark the early stage of Cowper's career, before the later period when his brain was clouded by the effects of religious melancholia, and his literary productions practically ceased. His first contribution (No. 111), *A Letter, containing the Character of the delicate Billy Suckling*, is aimed against those *molly-coddles* who never leave their mother's apron-strings. His second essay (No. 119), on *Keeping a Secret*, inveighs against tale-telling. " The first lesson our little masters and misses are taught, is to become blabs and tell-tales; they are bribed to divulge the petty intrigues of the family below stairs to papa and mamma in the parlour, and a doll or a hobby-horse is generally the encouragement of a propensity which could scarcely be atoned for by a whipping," and closes with the good if rather obvious advice, " That no man may betray the counsel of his friend, let every man keep his own." But his *Letter from Mr Village* (No. 134) is undoubtedly the best of the group. It gives *An Account of the present state of the Country Churches, their Clergy, and their Congregations*, and is a well-written account of the state of church services at the period. A portion of this paper will serve at once as a picture of the period and an illustration of Cowper's style.

" It is a difficult matter to decide, which is looked upon as the greatest man in a country church, the parson or his clerk. The latter is most certainly held in higher veneration, where the former happens to be only a poor curate, who rides post every Sabbath from village to village, and mounts and dismounts at the church door. The clerk's office is not only to tag the prayers with an amen, or usher in the sermon with a stave; but he is also the universal father to give away the brides, and the standing god-father to all the newborn bantlings. But in many places there is a still greater man belonging to the church, than either the parson or the clerk himself. The person I mean is the 'Squire, who, like the king, may be styled head of the church in his own parish. If the benefice be in his own gift, the vicar is his creature, and of consequence entirely at his devotion; or, if the care of the church be left to a curate, the Sunday fees of roast beef and plum pudding, and a liberty to shoot in the manor, will bring him as much under the 'Squire's command as his dogs and horses. For this reason the bell is often kept tolling, and the people waiting in the churchyard, an hour longer than the usual time; nor must the service begin till the 'Squire has strutted up the aisle, and seated himself in the great pew in the chancel. The length of the sermon is also measured by the will of the 'Squire, as formerly by the hour-glass; and I know one parish, where the preacher has always the complaisance to conclude his discourse, however abruptly, the minute that the 'Squire gives the signal, by rising up after his nap.

"In a village church, the 'Squire's lady or the vicar's wife are perhaps the only females that are stared at for their finery; but in the larger cities and towns, where the newest fashions are brought down weekly by the stage-coach or waggon, all the wives and daughters of the most topping tradesmen vie with each other every Sunday in the elegance of their apparel. I could even trace the gradations of their dress, according to the opulence, the extent, and the distance of the place from London. I was at church in a populous city in the North, where the mace-bearer cleared the way for Mrs Mayoress, who came sidling after him in an enormous fan-hoop, of a pattern which had never been seen before in those parts. At another church, in a corporation town, I saw several Negligees, with fur-belowed aprons, which had long disputed the prize of superiority; but these were most woefully eclipsed by a burgess's daughter, just come from London, who appeared in a Trolloppee or Slammerkin, with treble ruffles to the cuffs, pinked and gymped, and the sides of the petticoat drawn up in festoons. In some lesser borough towns, the contest, I found, lay between three or four black and green bibs and aprons; at one a grocer's wife attracted our eyes, by a new-fashioned cap, called a Joan; and at another they were wholly taken up by a mercer's daughter, in a Nun's Hood.

"I need not say anything of the behaviour of the congregations in these more polite places of religious resort; as the same genteel ceremonies are practised there, as at the most fashionable churches in town. The ladies immediately on their entrance, breathe a pious ejaculation through their fan-sticks, and the beaux very gravely address themselves to the haberdashers' bills, glewed upon the linings of their hats. This pious duty is no sooner performed, than the exercise of bowing and curtsying succeeds: the locking and unlocking of the pews drowns the reader's voice at the beginning of the service; and the rustling of silks, added to the whispering and tittering of so much good company, renders him totally unintelligible to the very end of it."

His last paper (No. 138) is on the well-worn theme of *Conversation*, in which the *Smirkers and Smilers*, the *Wits*

THE ADVENTURER AND OTHER PERIODICALS

and the Whistlers, the *Tatlers and the Swearers*, are keenly satirised. The *Tatlers*, for example, are those whose pliable pipes are admirably adapted to " the soft parts of conversation," and sweetly " prattling out of fashion," make very pretty music from a beautiful face and a female tongue; but from a rough manly voice and coarse features, mere nonsense is as harsh and dissonant as a jig from a hurdy-gurdy. The *Swearers* I have spoken of in a former paper; but the *Half-Swearers* who split, and mince, and fritter their oaths into gad's bud, ad's fish, and demme; the *Gothic Humbuggers*, and those who " nick-name God's creatures," and call a man a cabbage, a crab, a queer cub, an odd fish, and an unaccountable muskin, should never come into company without an interpreter. But I will not tire my reader's patience by pointing out all the pests of conversation; nor dwell particularly on the *Sensibles*, who pronounce dogmatically on the most trivial points, and speak in sentences; the *Wonderers*, who are always wondering what o'clock it is, or wondering whether it will rain or no, or wondering when the moon changes; the *Phraseologists*, who explain a thing by all that, or enter into particulars with this and that and t'other; and lastly, the *Silent Men*, who seem afraid of opening their mouths, lest they should catch cold, and literally observe the precept of the Gospel by letting their conversation be only yea, yea; and nay, nay." This group of periodical essays by Cowper is admirably done, and interesting when we consider the small bulk we possess of Cowper's early work. His later prose work as exemplified in his letters (amplifying as they do the very smallest details) makes some of the pleasantest reading of its kind in English literature, and this quality is seen even here.

As a whole the *Connoisseur* falls below the level of the *World*. Both periodicals show a gradual dropping off in a section which had been a prominent feature in the *Tatler* and *Spectator*, namely, that class of paper which was really a light sermon; Addison's *Saturday* papers had been written in a simple religious vein and had been very effective. The tendency now was (in entire opposition to the *Rambler*) to drop papers of that nature entirely and write directly for amusement by describing new fashions and occupations without attempting any moral reflections. And in this way one of the prominent features of the magazines of the succeeding century was adumbrated.

In addition to these larger and more important essay periodicals,—the *Rambler*, the *Idler*, the *Adventurer*, *World*, and *Connoisseur*,—a large number of periodicals of less note were published about the middle of the century. It may have been that the example of Johnson stimulated some; others obviously went back to the earlier models, the *Tatler* and *Spectator*, and imitated them; while a minority were able to introduce features which were new and fresh. We shall occupy the remainder of the chapter with a review of a number of these little-known essay periodicals.

First of all comes the *Student* (1750), issued monthly at Oxford. The *Student* contains speeches, letters, essays, and poetry, and tends to become more general in nature than is usual with the essay periodical, and forecasts the development of the modern magazine. The first number was issued on 31st January 1750, and it was not regular in its publication, and only eighteen numbers were published. The *Student* in point of time preceded the *Rambler* by about two months, and when the latter appeared the *Student* was loud in its praises: " A work that exceeds anything of the kind ever published in this kingdom, some of the *Spectator's* excepted—if indeed they may be excepted —everything is easy and natural, yet everything is masterly and strong." It is indeed some merit in mediocrity to perceive the quality of the work of a master, but this is the most striking feature of the *Student*. Otherwise it savours overmuch of a compilation, and when even speeches are given it departs from the limits which had become by this time generally recognised for the essay periodical.

The *Inspector* appeared in the following year. The author was the rather notorious Sir John Hill, a man whose history exhibits ups and downs which are stranger than fiction. These papers are examples of the " insert " method, being first published in the *London Daily Advertiser*. They appeared regularly every morning for two years. Such a record displays the unwearied activity and industry of

THE ADVENTURER AND OTHER PERIODICALS

Hill at this time. The subjects covered in these papers are very varied, and Hill indulged in scandal and satire to such an extent that it is recorded that he once received corporal punishment in Ranelagh Gardens because of the offensive nature of one of his papers. But the *Inspector* essays are not all by any means in this libellous vein. Hill was a natural historian of some merit, and his best papers relate to insects, fish, and fossils; his work as *Inspector* was thus a varied one, relating not only to mankind, but also to the animal world.

Another periodical worthy of mention was *Gray's Inn Journal* (No. 1, 21st October 1752), issued weekly for two years down to 12th October 1754. Each number contained an essay in the *Spectator* pattern, and a division headed *True Intelligence*. The latter department gave scope for ironical and humorous strictures on human life. The paper was written by Arthur Murphy, who wrote plays and practised (after some difficulty owing to his previous connection with the stage) as a Barrister. The "character" assumed by Murphy is Charles Ranger, Esq., who introduces himself as the Member of a Club of Originals. But little use is made of this *Club*. His papers are varied in character, and the subjects dealt with include *Beauty, Routs, Coquettes, Style, Lying, Criticism, Poetry, and Painting, Love, Duelling* —in fact, most of the subjects of the periodical essayists of those days. Here is the account given of *Charles Ranger, Esq.* (No. 10): " I have, perhaps, as many whims in my turn of mind, as any man whatever, and they adhere to me so tenaciously, that I cannot disengage myself from them. Notwithstanding all the pains I have been at, I cannot induce myself to carry a supernumerary ace in my pocket to a brag-table; I could never contract an intimacy in a gentleman's family in order to debauch his daughter, or carry on a design upon his wife; I had rather lose my joke at any time, than my friend; and I am so awkward that I cannot attempt to bilk a box-keeper. Add to this, I am far from being a Freethinker, notwithstanding the very great reputation to be acquired by it. I am sensible that these are unaccountable oddities, and it does not escape me, that in so enlightened and accomplished an age as this, they must set a man in a very disadvantageous light; but the truth of it is, they have taken such root in my mind, that I am apprehensive I shall never be able to attain that elegance of life and taste which is remarkable in some of my neighbours." This is the true spirit of Addison *redivivus*, and the style is good—simple, with a strong flavour of sarcasm intermingled. Drake, commenting on this journal, says: " In humour, invention, and variety, the *Gray's Inn Journal* is often superior to the contemporary papers of Hill and Fielding; but the early numbers are too much occupied by a useless contest with the authors of the *Inspector*. The periodical circulation of this Journal was not inconsiderable, and in 1752 it was republished in two volumes dedicated to the Hon. Robert Nugent." Drake's comment is just. *Gray's Inn Journal* is superior to many of the others, both in style and execution, and indicates that the legal training of its author was no bar but an assistance to the success of the periodical.

A somewhat similar essay periodical production was the *Scourge, by Oxymel Busby, Esq.* It is a single sheet, and each issue contains generally but a single essay. The *Scourge* was published three times a week, the first number appearing on Tuesday, 28th November 1752. The initial essay possesses the traditional features: " Custom hath established as a Law, that the first papers of every periodic kind should be appropriated to the acquainting the public of the person, circumstances, and capacity of its writers, the plan on which he proceeds, and what they may expect from him. In compliance, therefore, with that law, I shall confine this paper to myself and family, and proceed without any further preamble." With these opening words the author proceeds to say that he is descended from *Dr Busby* who " scourged " learning and morals into many of the most firm pillars of Church and State; and he likewise will not scruple to apply the lash when necessity seems to require it. His Christian name *Oxymel* (Greek for a mixture of sour and sweet) indicates his double character. He gives his aim practically in the same words as Addison and Steele, and in his detailed method of working out his plan, he closely follows the older scheme. The second

THE ADVENTURER AND OTHER PERIODICALS

number of the *Scourge* discusses marriage, and the remarks are illustrated by a suitable story of *Rivelia*, the daughter of a wealthy merchant. The third number deals with religion, the fourth is a lighter paper on hats; then follows a succession of essays covering the familiar subjects of the Queen Anne periodicals: epitaphs, the theatre, a chat in a coffee-house, character sketches, and a dream of Father Christmas. It will be instructive to give a typical *moral* paper (No. 22) of this periodical, because it represents, about the middle of the eighteenth century, the kind of essay which was considered " right " so far as ethics were concerned:

"As I shall hereafter have frequent occasion to mention my mother and wife, to avoid confusion of *Mrs Busby, Senior,* and *Mrs Busby, Junior,* I shall from henceforth name the former Stella and the latter Maria.

"The other morning, myself and Maria with our son and daughter had just placed ourselves at the tea-table, when Stella came in. 'Children,' said she, 'I am come to breakfast and chat with you.' She had scarce seated herself when, seeing Maria's work lying in the window, without further ceremony she turned to her. 'Bless me,' she said, 'how pretty the network looks. It is very tedious to do, is it not. When will you have finished it?' 'Oh, madam,' returned Maria, 'it will not be so long in hand as you imagine. My daughter Kitty helps me, when at home from school. Every day lessens the remainder, as we every day do something towards it. I have learned that the most arduous works are to be accomplished by time and application.' 'Nay, child,' answered Stella, 'think not I discommend a work, because it is long—no—in my days the length of the work was in some degree a measure of its excellence. I sat three years towards finishing a bed, and was engaged two more in a settee and six chair bottoms all in tent stitch. You don't practice tent stitch now, I fancy 'tis all out—well, everything has its fashion. I remember so many things that were quite the mode in my girlish days, which are so now, and have been in and out twice or thrice. But, my dear,' continued she, 'I must approve your taking your daughter in for a work-mate, she will by that means not be displeased at the task, but be proud you permit her to join with you. She should never be idle.' 'Indeed, madam,' replied the little Harriet, 'I hate idleness, and have ever since I worked my sampler, for I got by heart such pretty verses I worked there, that they have quite

THE EIGHTEENTH-CENTURY ESSAYISTS

kept me from it, and will do so I'm sure so long as I think of them. If Papa pleases, I'll tell you what they were.'

"'Oh! my little dear,' replied Stella, 'I don't doubt but your Papa will be glad to hear any witness of your memory, I mean of what is good, so you need not fear his consent.' 'I don't know that,' said Harriet, 'for indeed, to tell you the truth, I have told them so often, I begin to think Papa will grow tired of them—and last night he bade me hold my tongue.'

"'Wonderful,' replied Stella, stifling a laugh, 'that Papa could bid you hold your tongue—but I suppose you were talking either what you should not, or when you should not.'

"'I must own,' said Harriet, 'Papa was writing, and indeed Mama told me I must never say anything to anybody, be it ever so pretty, unless I was asked, and then to do it directly without twice asking; and now, ma'am, to let Mama see I haven't forgot what she said, if you will but bid me once, upon my word you shan't twice.'

"As soon as Stella could recover her countenance, she said, 'Well, Harri, what were these very pretty verses.'

"Harriet, rising and making an obeisance to all present, repeated as follows :—

"'How doth the little busy bee
  Improve each shining hour?
And gather honey all the day
  From every opening flower?

How skilfully she builds her cell!
  How neat she spreads the wax,
And labours hard to store it well
  With the sweet food she makes.

In works of labour, or of skill,
  I would be busy too,
For Satan finds some mischief still
  For idle hands to do.

In books, or work, or healthful play,
  Let my first years be past,
That I may give for every day
  Some good account at last.

May love through all my actions run,
  And all my words be mild;
Live like the blessed Virgin's Son,
  That sweet and lovely child.'

When she had done, Stella kissed her, thanked her, and said she

THE ADVENTURER AND OTHER PERIODICALS

must have a copy. 'Yes,' Maria answered, 'Harriet shall tell them to her brother, and he shall write them out, that both may have equal share of your commendations.'

"When breakfast was over, we insensibly fell into discourse upon the subject of Harriet's sampler. 'I can never enough approve,' said my dear Maria, ' the prudence in making such things the subject of work, or writing, for learners. When we take pains to form every composing letter, it imprints strongly on our mind the purport and meaning of the words, and children of any capacity will always form some conclusion from whatever words they copy. Idleness of all other inlets to vice is the greatest, and as the verses justly observe:

> "' Satan finds some mischief still,
> For idle hands to do. . . .'"

The *Scourge* had a fairly long life—as length of life is measured in these minor periodicals. Over eighty essays in all were issued, and among them are quite a number containing excellent material.

The *New Universal Magazine,* started two years later and continued for five years, is of a more general nature. The initial clause does not err on the side of modesty: "The whole is intended to restore the declining state of magazines by a constant supply of true knowledge and real pleasure." Only a section of each issue is relevant to our purpose. The style of the magazine will be best understood by the consideration of one of the numbers, that for August 1754. There is a short essay on happiness, of which the opening sentence will suffice to indicate its nature: "Though happiness is the end which all mankind seek after, how few are there who take the right path to obtain it!" It is the stock essay of the period. The second essay gives " the character of a true hero "; the third, remarks on marriage; the fourth, the taking of oaths; and parliamentary proceedings and songs conclude the number.

Occasionally we get articles not only in exact imitation of *Spectator* essays, but even the essay taken bodily out of the *Spectator* without any acknowledgment! For example, in the issue for December 1754, an essay headed " *Modern Anatomy — the beau's head and the coquette's heart dissected,*" is nothing more nor less than one of Addison's better-known papers, almost word for word! It is, however, its own best defendant. For it is quite an oasis in the desert. How refreshing it is for the reader to come upon it, brimful as it is of fine irony and delicate wit, in the midst of so much that is barren and mediocre!

The *Monitor* again, of the following year 1755, by Richard Beckford, is an example of the political periodical. Beckford says: "My intention is to commend good men and good measures, and to censure bad ones, without respect of persons, to awaken the spirit of liberty and loyalty, for which the British nation was anciently so distinguished." No less than one hundred and four numbers of the *Monitor* appeared, and many of the essays contained in them are vigorous and trenchant, so far as style is concerned, but the political preoccupation is obvious, and their appeal is an extra literary one.

In the *Old Maid*, of the same year, we have a paper which returns more closely to the *Tatler* and *Spectator* kind. It was written by a lady, Frances Brooke, under the pseudonym of *Mary Singleton, Spinster* (No. 1, Saturday, 15th November 1755). It compares favourably with Eliza Haywood's *Female Spectator* of ten years before. In her opening remarks the authoress says: "Amidst the glut of essay papers, it may seem an odd attempt in a woman, to think of adding to the number; but as most of them, like summer insects, just make their appearance, and are gone, I see no reason why I may not buzz amongst them a little; though it is possible I may join the short-lived generation, and this day month be as much forgot as if I never existed. Be that as it may, in defiance of all criticism, I will write." In this number, *Mary Singleton* gives an account of herself. She confesses she has turned fifty, is a hopeless "old maid," but relates how she, in her youth, had an engagement which had been ruthlessly broken off by her suitor; so she had remained single. In the second essay she gives an account of her niece *Julia*, whom she had brought up and educated practically as her own child.

It is interesting to read the remarks of Frances Brooke on contemporary periodicals. A paper in the *Connoisseur* on *Old Maids* had offended her. She says: "As I take in no

THE ADVENTURER AND OTHER PERIODICALS

essay paper but the *World*, I should have remained ignorant of this very dull and scurrilous abuse, which is contained in an obscure paper called the *Connoisseur*." In the third number " the present lack of genius in the country" is lamented on. The seventh number discusses marriage, relative to the approaching nuptials of her niece Julia. The succeeding number contains an article on Virgil's poetry, based on remarks made by Dr Johnson in his *Rambler*, but contains little fresh in the way of literary criticism. Further on (No. 12) there is an interesting eulogy of one of Beaumont and Fletcher's songs (" Hence all ye vain delights ") :

"The images," she remarks, " are heightened with all the beauty of colouring and ornament of the most exquisite poetry; and the versification, allowing for the distance of time, surprisingly smooth and harmonious, even to modern ears, though accustomed to the studied correctness of these latter days." She compares passages from Milton's *Il Penseroso* with the song. The remarks on the versification are characteristic of the eighteenth-century views on correctness, but give a hint of a longing for better things. The eighteenth number contains a criticism of *King Lear*. That literary taste is not wanting is shown in the following criticism: " It has always been a great astonishment to me, that both the theatres have given Tate's wretched alteration of *King Lear* the preference to Shakespeare's excellent original." The *Old Maid* adheres to the *Spectator* design, and is much above the average minor periodical.

The *Critical Review, or Annals of Literature*, which commenced to appear in the following year (1756) and of which there were seventy volumes in all, is interesting mainly on account of two circumstances. In the first place, Tobias Smollett was the originator of it, and in the second place the criticisms and reviews given are interesting as forecasting, to some extent, the *Edinburgh Review* (1802) itself. Take an example of the criticism offered. In the number dated March 1756 occurs a criticism of the *Winter's Tale* of Shakespeare, with alterations by Charles Marsh. " The practice of altering Shakespeare is like that of mending an old Roman causeway by the hands of a modern paviour; though far less excusable, because not undertaken for use

THE EIGHTEENTH-CENTURY ESSAYISTS

and convenience." Some of these criticisms form quite a long essay of four or five pages; and it is not difficult to see a germ in them of the modern nineteenth-century *Reviews*.

The *Test* (1756) is a paper of a different character. In the first number (it appeared weekly) the author says he is not stirred by " a momentary itch of scribbling," but writes upon " the true principles of Whiggism as they were felt by Mr Steele, Mr Addison, and the noble band of patriots in Queen Anne's reign." This surely is a misrepresentation, and emphasises only one small feature of Addison's and Steele's work. The essays are almost all political. The third on *Liberty* promises better, but degenerates into a discussion of the precarious state of politics at the time; and of the tarnished glory of the British flag. There are no essays of a general social or domestic value, and the interest of the paper is extra-literary. The *Prater* also appeared in the same year (1756), and is a brightly written periodical. *Nicholas Babble, Esq.*, is the " Editor." Thirty-five numbers of the *Prater* appeared, and there is a pleasing variety in subject and a great deal of humour. The motto given in the first number is:

> " Let them censure, what care I,
> The herd of critics I defy " (Prior),

and *Mr Babble* gives the usual account of himself. " I am an oldish man," he writes, " sixty odd; but have all my senses perfect and enjoy a large share of health. I was always of an inquisitive, communicative disposition, and have been so long celebrated by my club companions for my facetiousness, that I begin to think myself qualified to ' prate ' to a larger circle." In the course of years he has gathered together a huge volume of observations not much smaller than a volume of Johnson's *Dictionary*, and from this he will give selections. This periodical is a welcome relief from the heavier " moral " essays which form the principal bulk of the eighteenth-century type of essay. A monthly publication of the same year, 1756, is called the *Universal Visiter* (sic) and possesses a miscellaneous character. But essays are included along with other matter which make up quite a respectable monthly magazine. One of the

THE ADVENTURER AND OTHER PERIODICALS

undertakers of this miscellany was Christopher Smart, and other writers were David Garrick and Dr Percy. Dr Johnson sometimes assisted his friend Christopher Smart by sending him in essays. Boswell refers to this fact in the *Life*. He quotes Johnson as saying: " I wrote for some months in the *Universal Visitor* for poor Smart while he was mad, not then knowing the terms on which he was engaged to write, and thinking I was doing him good. I hoped his wits would soon return to him. Mine returned to me, and I wrote in the *Universal Visitor* no longer."

The *Centinel* of the following year (1757) comes nearer the *Tatler* and *Spectator* pattern. The *Centinel* was a weekly paper, and commenced early in the year (No. 1, Thursday, 6th January). The copy examined by the present writer had this note, dated 1780, written in faded ink by a former owner, Mr J. Reed: " A hundred and forty numbers in all were published. This paper was commenced soon after the *World* was discontinued. The author was Dr Thomas Franklin. Mr Steevens tells me he wrote some numbers, particularly Nos. 5, 12, and 18."

In the first number Dr Franklin discusses his position as a *centinel*. " He proposes to watch the progress of the human mind; to keep the passions within the bounds of temperance to prevent their intoxication or irregularity; and should his authority prove ineffective, he at least will give timely warning at the approach of vice, folly, and impertinence."

This seems to indicate the strong influence the issue of Dr Johnson's *Rambler* was having on the minds of his brother essayists, for this is simply a repetition of the moral purpose set forth in the *Rambler*.

The second number of the *Centinel* gives a letter from a disappointed lover, and the *Centinel* improves the occasion with an appropriate fable from La Motte. The third paper indicates another source of influence. Franklin quotes from his *brother-centinel Mr Fitzadam*, and he says that everyone is trying to find out who he is. The fourth paper gives a vision in the Addisonian style—the eternal contest between the forces of *Truth* and *Falsehood*; the fifth (with the motto, " Confiteor, si quid prodest delicta fateri ") tells the melancholy story of a young man who was forced by an ambitious parent to give up the hand of the woman he loved for place and position; the sixth satirises, as Chesterfield did in the *World*, the practice of sending young men abroad, especially when accompanied (as in the case of *Clodio* here) by an ignorant and vicious tutor; the tenth has similar reflections on female education; while the eleventh resembles one of Addison's papers in the *Guardian* on naked bosoms, for a new craze, gauze handkerchiefs, an artifice "very easily seen through and detected," is satirised. The next number treats of the stock subject, marriage.

But the thirteenth number is rather novel. It is a letter from *Captain Sentry*, nephew to *Sir Roger de Coverley*, who writes that he is now in possession of Coverley Hall. The *Centinel* answers this letter with some reminiscences (No. 15). Another letter (No. 26) continues the correspondence from *Captain Sentry's son*, in which he traces out the further history of the widow and of *Will Wimble*. The propriety of taking up characters which Addison and Steele had created may well be questioned. The attempt is not altogether a success, and scarcely deserves to be, though the same device has been employed later. For example, after *Pickwick Papers* had been published some one had the audacity to write *Pickwick Abroad*. An illustration of the attempt, however, may be given from the fifteenth number, as it will also serve as an example of the style of the *Centinel* essays. It will be seen that an endeavour is being made to carry on the Addisonian tradition.

" Having received two ingenious letters from my cousin Sentry of Coverley Hall in Worcestershire, now at Bath, with which I entertained my readers the last fortnight, I flatter myself they will not be displeased if I lay before them this week my answer to my worthy kinsman, which they shall have verbatim, without addition or mutilation, as follows :—

" ' To Roger Coverley Sentry
    at Bath in Somersetshire.
                " ' LONDON, *April 9th*, 1757.

" ' GOOD SIR,—I hope the important concern I have upon my hands will sufficiently apologise for my not answering your first obliging and entertaining letter, before I received the second favour;

but as you already seem sufficiently apprised that the welfare of these great Kingdoms, which depends so much upon my vigilance, is not to be neglected for mere matters of ceremony, my excuse, I dare say, is already pleaded in your breast before I have committed it to paper. After returning you the sincerest and warmest thanks for the assistance you have already afforded, and the flattering promises you have given of still continuing so valuable a friendship and correspondence, I must congratulate myself, my family, and my country (for I have a lively sense of your abilities), that my very good friends, Sir Roger de Coverley and Captain Sentry, have left all their amiable qualities, as well as their fortunes, to me who will make so proper a use of both in the service of his country.

"'It is now, cousin, I very well remember it, thirty-two years ago last Candlemas, since I was at Coverley Hall; you was then a little round jolly boy, which shape I find you still retain, just put into breeches. Ah! could your worthy father have lived to have seen this day;—but he is gone after his worthy friend the Spectator, who, I have often heard my cousin Bridget say, was your Godfather; and she used to attribute the roundness of your face when a child, to the accidental circumstance of that sponsor's putting his remarkable short countenance over the font at the ceremony of the christening; which, poor man, I find he survived only six weeks. If there is really any power (as your maiden aunt always believed there was) of a godfather's conveying a mental similitude, as well as a corporeal one, to the favoured infant, by looking down upon the holy water, I and the world shall still have further obligations to my deceased friend of transmitting his *lucubrating* spirit one generation lower to chastise the vicious, to laugh the giddy out of their follies, and forward and establish the good in their pursuit of happiness through the paths of virtue. I am afraid I shall become ridiculous to the spirit of infidelity that reigns at present in the world, by confessing that I begin to have some faith in this affair myself; nay, since I have begun to own the forwardness of my belief, I will farther fairly acknowledge that more than once I have imagined there was a secret virtue even in the Spectator's reading-glass, which your father, of ever respected memory, gave me, and in the tobacco box and silver-tipped stopper of his venerable predecessor Isaac Bickerstaff, Esq., which latter was sent me as a present, when I first entered into my office as Centinel-general, from the public-spirited executors of that greatly revered antiquarian Thomas Hearne of Oxford. I have particularly observed that every paper I have written, when I used those inestimable moveables, breathes a superior spirit to the rest.

THE EIGHTEENTH-CENTURY ESSAYISTS

"'These low-minded people, who are contented with nothing but what is accounted for by reason, may turn such thoughts into derision; but let me tell the scoffers, there is more in these things than is *dreamt of in their philosophy*, as Hamlet says.

"'The assistance you have already afforded, has not only laid an obligation upon me, but has, I find, given great pleasure to the generality of your readers, many of whom, dissipated as the times are, have a very respectful remembrance of the good old Worcestershire baronet, your great-uncle; nay, some of them had a personal acquaintance both with him and my ever honoured friend your father Captain Sentry. But as infidelity is a principal characteristic of the present age, there are numbers in this metropolis, and, I make no doubt, many even where you now are, who make a doubt whether there ever were such people; and still further, if my information be true, several gentlemen, who have been from the beginning of the season at Bath, have wrote word to their inquiring correspondents in London, that there neither is now, nor has been any such person as Mr Sentry there this year, and the whole of the two letters so subscribed is a gross imposition both upon me and the public. What will this world come to? In a day or two more I suppose the nonentity even of my person will be maintained and some sagacious coffee-house orator will confidently advance and perhaps be believed, for we have those who have faith for the grossest absurdities, that the very existence of the Centinel-general of Great Britain is purely imaginary; but I give my country this fair warning, that if this heretical sect gains ground, I will desert my important post for ever, and leave them to the care of these envious malignants! which if I do, the world may cry out with the fact.

"'. . . Quis custodiat ipsos, custodes. . . .'"

One of the features of the *Centinel* is its strong didactic infusion, suggesting the influence of the *Rambler*; individual papers are well and carefully written. One of the characteristics which strikes one most forcibly in reading these minor periodicals is the extraordinary ingenuity shown in inventing new names for them. For example, in the same year as the *Centinel*, the quaintly named *Crab-tree* was published. The first number appeared on Tuesday, 26th April 1757, price twopence. The motto is a courageous one: "Omnia, te adversum, spectantia nulla, retrorsum." The author elaborates two islands—*Brit-land*, so-called from its brightness, and *Anger-land*, which takes its name undoubtedly from

THE ADVENTURER AND OTHER PERIODICALS

the passionate temper of its inhabitants. They are beautiful islands, " situate in one of the largest fresh-water lakes of North America." This is a novel beginning. And in several numbers the author supplies details concerning their inhabitants, their manners and customs. The inevitable conclusion is that he is keeping closely in view Swift's *Gulliver's Travels*. But stripped of this attractive allegory, the papers resolve themselves into pieces of political satire. *Farmer Crabtree*, the *eidolon*, airs his views on coinage, the state of the market, and the general condition of the country and government. There is little that is purely literary, but the paper is preferable to those papers which are purely and nakedly political and do not even employ the literary device of allegory.

An additional paper of the same year is one of an entirely different stamp. The *Monitor, or Green-room laid open*, was published at intervals at the price of threepence, and the subject-matter is purely theatrical. The author wishes to stir up the people to " save the situation " in the theatrical world. *Covent Garden* has become obnoxious, and he fears the same for the *Haymarket* theatre. " There certainly is not a department of public truth," he says, " much more consequential or more necessary to be appropriated with such a choice than the playhouses, where genius, wit, humour, virtue, and satire ought to be displayed in live portraits, to form the improvement of mankind both in sentiment and behaviour." A stirring indictment of the degenerate state of the stage is given. Addison had more than once touched on the stage ; Steele had made it more or less his principal purpose in the *Theatre*, for Steele was himself a successful writer of plays ; but the *Monitor* is probably the first paper written for purely theatrical ends.

During the period under consideration in this chapter, Edinburgh was not behindhand in literary production. It is not generally known that the famous *Edinburgh Review*, which started practically with the nineteenth century, had a predecessor nearly fifty years before that date. Yet so it was. The *Edinburgh Review* appeared in the year 1755, and though only two numbers, published at an interval of six months, saw the light, it forms a noteworthy issue. The design of the work was " to lay before the public from time to time a view of the progressive state of learning in this country. The great number of performances of this nature sufficiently proves that they have been found useful." The contributors to it formed a rather brilliant group: Wedderburn, afterwards Lord Chancellor of England, was at the head of it, and with him were associated Adam Smith, Robertson the historian, and Dr Blair. The articles are largely reviews of books. These reviews are usually long and discursive, and undoubtedly forecast the manner of the famous nineteenth-century magazine. For example, there is an interesting review of Dr Johnson's *Dictionary*. It is thought that the reason why so brilliant a beginning had so soon an ending was that discussion was entered upon of the most delicate subject of all—religion. Some Secession publications were handled severely in the review by an Edinburgh minister, Dr John Jardine, and great indignation was aroused, and Wedderburn was forced to withdraw his review.

Two years later came from the same place a magazine of a more general kind. This was the *Edinburgh Magazine*, which ran with great success between the years 1757 and 1762. The editor, Walter Ruddiman, jun., writes: " To gratify that appetite for novelty which is natural to the human mind, by an agreeable variety, has been our constant aim." The opening essay is in the form of a letter of advice to the publishers, and discusses the subjects that may be profitably dealt with in a magazine of this kind. " Of these the most universal and most important is religion "; then come politics, commercial interests, and monthly occurrences, and " the works of imagination and fancy whether poetry or prose. A spirited tale, or elegant poem, will sometimes employ a vacant hour, even of the most severe recluse. Instruction and entertainment being your aim, good manners and religion will disappoint the rake and libertine of what would suit their taste." Memoirs, pages from history, and extracts from London journals and magazines are also given, together with a record of affairs both at home and abroad. The *Spectator* type of essay is still there, but the

THE ADVENTURER AND OTHER PERIODICALS

periodical widens out into the general magazine, and is vastly different from the simple sheet of the Queen Anne essayists. Another type of magazine was the chronicle of the times and record of history and literature. Take one example; the *Annual Register*, which has continued to this day, and occupies seventy volumes in the British Museum Library, was begun in the year 1758. It contributes an account of the best books published during each year, and summarises a history of current events. The literary development of the magazine, with its greater bulk and more varied contents, was to constitute the greatest rival of the essay periodical. At this stage of its history the magazine may be dull, lack originality and crispness, but by the opening of the nineteenth century its growth and vitality were assured.

CHAPTER VII

THE PERIODICAL ESSAY WORK OF GOLDSMITH

OLIVER GOLDSMITH, whose periodical essay work falls next to be discussed, is one of the best known and most beloved figures in literature. But we need only refer to the details of his life to deduce one fact. In his travels over Europe, and during his stay in London, Goldsmith gathered together material taken direct from life. His keen observation and gift of humour combined with his native genius to produce just the right style for periodical essay-writing. There had been nothing quite like it since Addison. He possessed the faculty, which Fielding had in still larger degree, of giving to his characters those touches of humanity which cause them to stand out living from the pages. At a time when *sensibilité* was being overdone, Goldsmith revealed a command of true pathos which ranks him very high; but the essence of his charm lies in a most elusive quality, a *je ne sais quoi* which defies exact definition and is peculiarly his own.

Goldsmith, in the same year (1759) in which he published his *Inquiry into the Present State of Polite Learning in Europe*, commenced and completed a short series of miscellaneous essays for a periodical called the *Bee*. The *Bee* had been started by the bookseller Wilkie as a periodical of essays, dramatic criticisms, and work of a similar nature. It was a weekly paper, and was published on Saturdays at 3d. a number. The *Bee* had only a short existence (from 3rd October to 24th November), but was succeeded by others like the *Busybody*, to which Goldsmith also contributed. The contents of the *Bee* are very various. Goldsmith indulges in a number of stories, original or twice-told: *The Story of Alcander and Septimius*, translated

THE PERIODICAL ESSAYS OF GOLDSMITH

from a Byzantine historian, and the famous *History of Hypatia*, which recalls Kingsley's novel of a later date. He writes on the theatre, and on dress, on justice and generosity, the same subjects in fact as had been dealt with often before, but in an admirable style relieved by many touches of humour. For example, the third number is a paper on *The Use of Language*, and its style may be appreciated from the following extract :—

"The principal use of language, it is usually said, is to express our wants, so as to receive a speedy redress. Such an account may satisfy grammarians well enough, but men who know the world maintain very contrary maxims; they hold, and I think with some show of reason, that he who best knows how to conceal his necessity and desires is the most likely person to find redress, and that the true use of speech is not so much to express our wants, as to conceal them."

The fourth number includes a very fine *City Night Piece* in which Goldsmith describes a walk through the town at dead of night.

"The clock has just struck two, the expiring taper rises and sinks in the socket, the watchman forgets the hour in slumber, the laborious and the happy are at rest, and nothing wakes but meditation, guilt, revelry, and despair. The drunkard once more fills the destroying bowl, the robber walks his midnight round, and the suicide lifts his guilty arm against his own sacred person."

Goldsmith has also, in these papers, *A Reverie on Literary Fame*, in a style which he developed later; and in his remarks on *Education* (No. 6) he speaks of schoolmasters as "a people whom, without flattery, I may in other respects term the wisest and greatest upon earth! . . . and I will be bold enough to say, that schoolmasters in a state are more necessary than clergymen, as children stand in more need of instruction than their parents." A paper on literary history, entitled *An Account of the Augustan Age in England*, touches upon a whole host of names from L'Estrange and Dryden to Addison and Steele. These essays of Goldsmith's in the *Bee* are a real success: he has understood the true *ethos* of the periodical essay, and has produced papers short, light, witty, and yet informative, including a wide variety of subject-matter.

It was the publication of these and other contributions to the *Busybody*, the *Lady's Magazine*, and the *Critical Review* which attracted the publisher Newbery to his work, and it was for Newbery's paper, the *Public Ledger*, that Goldsmith, commencing on 24th January 1760, contributed the famous series of *Chinese Letters*, afterwards collected and published under the general title of the *Citizen of the World*. The idea of supposing a Chinaman to record his various observations of London was not new; Tom Brown had employed the same idea, only under the guise of an Indian; and in France Montesquieu had published, forty years before, his *Lettres Persanes*; Addison had used the method in the *Spectator*; and, nearer Goldsmith's own time, Horace Walpole three years before had published a letter from *Xo Ho*, a Chinese philosopher at London, to his friend *Lien Chi* at Peking.

These considerations, however, do not detract from the positive merit of Goldsmith's work. He wrote no fewer than a hundred and twenty-three of these letters, and they are all readable, though some are slight in construction, giving the impression that Goldsmith had on more than one occasion nearly written himself out. These marks of haste in construction and style were no doubt difficult to avoid, when the essays had to be in for a certain day. Goldsmith was, unlike Addison, very unmethodical in his literary work. A few of the more interesting of these Chinese letters deserve special notice. A satire on newspapers (Letter V.) supplies information like the following: "Edinburgh—we are positive when we say 'that Saunders M'Gregor, who was lately executed for horse-stealing,' is not a Scotsman, but born at Carrickfergus." Letter XII. supplies a direct reminiscence of Addison's *Spectator* articles on his visit to Westminster Abbey; Letter XXI. gives an interesting account of the theatre and the arrangements in force at that time. In Letter XXXI. Goldsmith returns to a favourite *Spectator* form in an allegory on *Virtue and Vice*, while Letter LI. is an exceedingly amusing paper and strikes a new note. It tells of a visit to a publisher, and a discussion regarding the books that sell best includes humorously sarcastic reference to eccentric styles as, for example, that of Sterne's. The publisher shows the visitor a book, "Here it is; dip into it where you will, it will be found replete with true modern humour. Strokes, sir; it is filled with strokes of wit and satire in every line." "Do you call these dashes with the pen strokes," replied I, "for I must confess I can see no other." "And pray, sir," returned he, "what do you call them? Do you see anything good now-a-days, that is not filled with strokes— and dashes? Sir, a well-placed dash makes half the wit of our writers of modern humour."

Three papers further on *Beau Tibbs* is introduced. The description of this immortal character is unique, and *Beau Tibbs*, along with the *Man in Black* (who is not quite so successfully sketched), are the two best known characters in the set of papers. The Chinaman is walking with his friend in one of the public walks when the latter seizes him and endeavours by fast walking to evade an undesirable acquaintance, but in vain. *Beau Tibbs* comes up: "His hat was punched up with peculiar smartness; his looks were pale, thin, and sharp; round his neck he wore a broad, black riband, and in his bosom a buckle studded with glass; his coat was trimmed with tarnished twist; he wore by his side a sword with a black hilt; and his stockings of silk, though newly washed, were grown yellow by long service."

Letter LXXI. is one of the most successful of the papers of this set—*Mr* and *Mrs Tibbs*, the *Man in Black*, a pawnbroker's widow with whom the latter is in love, and *Lien Chi Altangi* himself, go to Vauxhall, and the misadventures there are inimitably described.

"The people of London are as fond of walking as our friends at Pekin of riding; one of the principal entertainments of the citizens here in summer is to repair about nightfall to a garden not far from town, where they walk about, show their best clothes and best faces, and listen to a concert provided for the occasion.

"I accepted an invitation a few evenings ago from my old friend, the Man in Black, to be one of a party that was to sup there; and at the appointed hour waited upon him at his lodgings. There I found the company assembled, and expecting my arrival. Our party consisted of my friend, in superlative finery, his stockings rolled, a black velvet waistcoat, which was formerly new, and a gray wig combed down in imitation of hair; a pawnbroker's widow, of whom, by the by, my friend was a professed admirer, dressed out in green damask, with three gold rings on every finger; Mr Tibbs, the second-rate beau I have formerly described; together with his lady, in flimsy silk, dirty gauze instead of linen, and an hat as big as an umbrella.

"Our first difficulty was in settling how we should set out. Mrs Tibbs had a natural aversion to the water, and the widow, being a little in flesh, as warmly protested against walking; a coach was therefore agreed upon; which being too small to carry five, Mr Tibbs consented to sit in his wife's lap.

"In this manner, therefore, we set forward, being entertained by the way with the bodings of Mr Tibbs, who assured us he did not expect to see a single creature for the evening above the degree of a cheesemonger; that this was the last night of the gardens, and that consequently we should be pestered with the nobility and gentry from Thames Street and Crooked Lane; with several other prophetic ejaculations, probably inspired by the uneasiness of his situation.

"The illuminations began before we arrived, and I must confess, that upon entering the gardens I found every sense overpaid with more than expected pleasure: the lights everywhere glimmering through the scarcely moving trees—the full-bodied concert bursting on the stillness of the night—the natural concert of the birds, in the more retired part of the grove, vying with that which was formed by art—the company gaily dressed, looking satisfaction—and the tables spread with various delicacies—all conspired to fill my imagination with the visionary happiness of the Arabian lawgiver, and lifted me into an ecstasy of admiration. 'Head of Confucius,' cried I to my friend, 'this is fine! this unites rural beauty with courtly magnificence! If we except the virgins of immortality, that hang on every tree, and may be plucked at every desire, I do not see how this falls short of Mahomet's Paradise!'—'As for virgins,' cries my friend, 'it is true they are a fruit that do not much abound in our gardens here; but if ladies, as plenty as apples in autumn, and as complying as any Houri of them all, can content you, I fancy we have no need to go to heaven for Paradise.'

"I was going to second his remarks, when we were called to a consultation by Mr Tibbs and the rest of the company, to know in what manner we were to lay out the evening to the greatest advantage. Mrs Tibbs was keeping the genteel walk of the garden, where, she observed, there was always the very best company; the widow, on the contrary, who came but once a season, was for securing a good standing-place to see the waterworks, which she assured us would begin in less than an hour at farthest; a dispute therefore began, and as it was managed between two of very opposite characters, it threatened to grow more bitter at every reply. Mrs Tibbs wondered how people could pretend to know the polite world, who had received all their rudiments of breeding behind a counter: to which the other replied, that though some people sat behind counters, yet they could sit at the head of their own tables too, and carve three good dishes of hot meat whenever they thought proper; which was more than some people could say for themselves, that hardly knew a rabbit and onions from a green goose and gooseberries.

"It is hard to say where this might have ended, had not the husband, who probably knew the impetuosity of his wife's disposition, proposed to end the dispute by adjourning to a box, and try if there was anything to be had for supper that was supportable. To this we all consented; but here a new distress arose: Mr and Mrs Tibbs would sit in none but a genteel box—a box where they might see and be seen—one, as they expressed it, in the very focus of public view; but such a box was not easy to be obtained, for though we were perfectly convinced of our own gentility, and the gentility of our appearance, yet we found it a difficult matter to persuade the keepers of the boxes to be of our opinion; they chose to reserve genteel boxes for what they judged more genteel company.

"At last, however, we were fixed, though somewhat obscurely, and supplied with the usual entertainment of the place. The widow found the supper excellent, but Mrs Tibbs thought everything detestable. 'Come, come, my dear,' cries the husband, by way of consolation, 'to be sure we can't find such dressing here as we have at Lord Crump's or Lady Crimp's; but, for Vauxhall dressing, it is pretty good; it is not their victuals, indeed, I find fault with, but their wine; their wine,' cried he, drinking off a glass, 'indeed, is most abominable.'

"By this last contradiction the widow was fairly conquered in point of politeness. She perceived now that she had no pretension in the world to taste; her very senses were vulgar, since she had praised detestable custard, and smacked at wretched wine; she was therefore content to yield the victory, and for the rest of the night to listen and improve. It is true, she would now and then forget herself, and confess she was pleased; but they soon brought her back again to miserable refinement. She once praised the painting of the box in which we were sitting, but was soon convinced that such paltry pieces ought rather to excite horror than satisfaction ; she ventured again to commend one of the singers, but Mrs Tibbs soon let her know, in the style of a connoisseur, that the singer in question had neither ear, voice, nor judgment.

"Mr Tibbs, now willing to prove that his wife's pretensions to music were just, entreated her to favour the company with a song ; but to this she gave a positive denial—' for you know very well, my dear,' says she, ' that I am not in voice to-day, and when one's voice is not equal to one's judgment, what signifies singing ? Besides, as there is no accompaniment, it would be but spoiling music.' All these excuses, however, were overruled by the rest of the company, who, though one would think they already had music enough, joined in the entreaty. But particularly the widow, now willing to convince the company of her breeding, pressed so warmly, that she seemed determined to take no refusal. At last, then, the lady complied, and after humming for some minutes, began with such a voice, and such affectation, as, I could perceive, gave but little satisfaction to any except her husband. He sat with rapture in his eye, and beat time with his hand on the table.

"You must observe, my friend, that it is the custom of this country, when a lady or gentleman happens to sing, for the company to sit as mute and motionless as statues. Every feature, every limb, must seem to correspond in fixed attention ; and while the song continues, they are to remain in a state of universal petrifaction. In this mortifying situation we had continued for some time, listening to the song, and looking with tranquillity, when the master of the box came to inform us that the waterworks were going to begin. At this information I could instantly perceive the widow bounce from her seat ; but correcting herself, she sat down again, repressed by motives of good breeding. Mrs Tibbs, who had seen the waterworks an hundred times, resolving not to be interrupted, continued her song without any share of mercy, nor had the smallest pity on our impatience. The widow's face, I own, gave me high entertainment ; in it I could plainly read the struggle she felt between good breeding and curiosity ; she talked of the waterworks the whole evening before, and seemed to have come merely in order to see them ; but then she could not bounce out in the very middle of a song, for that would be forfeiting all pretensions to high life, or high-lived company, ever after. Mrs Tibbs, therefore, kept on singing, and we continued to listen till at last, when the song was just concluded, the waiter came to inform us that the waterworks were over.

THE PERIODICAL ESSAYS OF GOLDSMITH

"'The waterworks over!' cried the widow; 'the waterworks over already! that's impossible! they can't be over so soon!' 'It is not my business,' replied the fellow, 'to contradict your ladyship; I'll run again and see.' He went, and soon returned with a confirmation of the dismal tidings. No ceremony could now bind my friend's disappointed mistress. She testified her displeasure in the openest manner; in short, she now began to find fault in turn, and at last insisted upon going home, just at the time that Mr and Mrs Tibbs assured the company that the polite hours were going to begin, and that the ladies would instantaneously be entertained with the horns.—Adieu."

It is interesting to note that Letter CXVII. is practically a repetition of the *City Night Piece*, which appeared in the *Bee* some time before; perhaps Goldsmith was pressed for time, or wished to give the paper a wider circulation. Taken as a whole, the *Citizen of the World* papers make up a unique series of essays, and they have taken their place as a classic in our literature.

But these papers do not exhaust Goldsmith's contribution to periodical literature. For years before he had been contributing articles to various papers, endeavouring in this way to eke out a miserable existence. It is not possible to identify all these essays simply by internal evidence. Johnson's position is very similar. But in 1765 Goldsmith gathered together the best of them with unerring taste and published them in a volume. In the *Preface* Goldsmith complains that they had been frequently reprinted without due acknowledgment, and it is to vindicate his own claims that he now gathers them together. "Yet after all, I cannot be angry with any who have taken it into their heads to think that whatever I write is worth reprinting, particularly when I consider how great a majority will think it scarcely worth reading. *Trifling* and *superficial* are terms of reproach that are easily objected, and that carry an air of penetration in the observer. These faults have been objected to the following essays; and it must be owned, in some measure, that the charge is true. However, I could have made them more metaphysical had I thought fit; but I would ask whether in a short essay it is not necessary to be superficial? Before we have prepared to enter into the depths of a subject in the usual forms, we have got to the bottom of one scanty page, and thus lose the honours of a victory by too tedious a preparation for the combat." Goldsmith was perfectly justified in this defence of the slight nature of the essay, and these words show he realised aright its true nature and purpose as a literary kind.

Smollett, in particular, had been attracted by his work, as well as Newbery, and it was to the former's paper, the *British Magazine*, that he contributed perhaps his best known essay, the famous *Reverie at the Boar's Head Tavern in Eastcheap*, which has been enjoyed by all lovers of literature since. The fullness of the description at the Inn is notable in an age before Balzac or Dickens, though Smollett had shown this faculty of amplifying detail more than once. The *Reverie* describes how the author falls asleep in his chair; and the ghost of Mrs Quickly appears, and Mrs Quickly gives a history of the varied fortunes of the *Tavern*. Everything combines to make it a delightful essay, easy, fanciful, and humorous to a degree, as the following extract serves to show:—

"The improvements we make in mental acquirements only render us each day more sensible of the defects of our constitution: with this in view, therefore, let us often recur to the amusements of youth, endeavour to forget age and wisdom, and, as far as innocence goes, be as much a boy as the best of them.

"Let idle declaimers mourn over the degeneracy of the age; but in my opinion every age is the same. This I am sure of, that man in every season is a poor fretful being, with no other means to escape the calamities of the times but by endeavouring to forget them; for if he attempts to resist he is certainly undone. If I feel poverty and pain, I am not so hardy as to quarrel with the executioner, even while under correction; I find myself no way disposed to make fine speeches while I am making wry faces. In a word, let me drink when the fit is on, to make me insensible; and drink when it is over, for joy that I feel pain no longer.

"The character of old Falstaff, even with all his faults, gives me more consolation than the most studied efforts of wisdom: I here behold an agreeable old fellow forgetting age, and showing me the way to be young at sixty-five. Sure I am well able to be as merry, though not so comical, as he. Is it not in my power to have, though not so much wit, at least as much vivacity? Age, care, wisdom, reflection, begone—I give you to the winds! Let's have t'other bottle: here's to the memory of Shakespeare, Falstaff, and all the merry men of Eastcheap!

"Such were the reflections that naturally arose while I sat at the Boar's-Head Tavern, still kept at Eastcheap. Here, by a pleasant fire, in the very room where old Sir John Falstaff cracked his jokes, in the very chair which was sometimes honoured by Prince Henry, and sometimes polluted by his immoral merry companions, I sat and ruminated on the follies of youth; wished to be young again, but was resolved to make the best of life while it lasted; and now and then compared past and present times together. I considered myself as the only living representative of the old knight, and transported my imagination back to the times when the Prince and he gave life to the revel, and made even debauchery not disgusting. The room also conspired to throw my reflections back into antiquity: the oak floor, the Gothic windows, and the ponderous chimney-piece, had long withstood the tooth of time; the watchman had gone twelve; my companions had all stolen off; and none now remained with me but the landlord. From him I could have wished to know the history of a tavern that had such a long succession of customers; I could not help thinking that an account of this kind would be a pleasing contrast of the manners of different ages; but my landlord could give me no information. He continued to doze and sot, and tell a tedious story, as most other landlords usually do, and though he said nothing, yet was never silent; one good joke followed another good joke; and the best joke of all was generally begun towards the end of a bottle. I found at last, however, his wine and his conversation operate by degrees: he insensibly began to alter his appearance; his cravat seemed quilled into a ruff, and his breeches swelled out into a fardingale. I now fancied him changing sexes; and as my eyes began to close in slumber, I imagined my fat landlord actually converted into as fat a landlady. However, sleep made but few changes in my situation; the tavern, the apartment, and the table, continued as before: nothing suffered mutation but my host, who was fairly altered into a gentle-woman, whom I knew to be Dame Quickly, mistress of this tavern in the days of Sir John; and the liquor we were drinking seemed converted into sack and sugar.

"'My dear Mrs Quickly,' cried I (for I knew her perfectly well at first sight), 'I am heartily glad to see you. How have you left Falstaff, Pistol, and the rest of our friends, below stairs? Brave and hearty, I hope?' 'In good sooth,' replied she, 'he did deserve to live for ever; but he maketh foul work on't where he hath flitted.

Queen Proserpine and he have quarrelled for his attempting a rape upon her divinity; and were it not that she still had bowels of compassion, it more than seems probable he might have been now sprawling in Tartarus.'

"I now found that spirits still preserve the frailties of the flesh; and that, according to the laws of criticism and dreaming, ghosts have been known to be guilty of even more than platonic affection; wherefore, as I found her too much moved on such a topic to proceed, I was resolved to change the subject, and desiring she would pledge me in a bumper, observed with a sigh, that our sack was nothing now to what it was in former days. 'Ah, Mrs Quickly, those were merry times when you drew sack for Prince Henry; men were twice as strong, and twice as wise, and much braver, and ten thousand times more charitable, than now. Those were the times! The battle of Agincourt was a victory indeed! Ever since that we have only been degenerating; and I have lived to see the day when drinking is no longer fashionable, when men wear clean shirts, and women show their necks and arms. All are degenerated, Mrs Quickly; and we shall probably, in another century, be frittered away into beaux or monkeys. Had you been on earth to see what I have seen, it would congeal all the blood in your body—your soul, I mean. Why, our very nobility now have the intolerable arrogance, in spite of what is every day remonstrated from the press—our very nobility, I say, have the assurance to frequent assemblies, and presume to be as merry as the vulgar. See, my very friends have scarcely manhood enough to sit to it till eleven; and I only am left to make a night on't. Prithee, do me the favour to console me a little for their absence by the story of your own adventures, or the history of the tavern where we are now sitting; I fancy the narrative may have something singular.'"

But the other essays are also good. One gives a description of various clubs, the *Humdrum Club*, the *Muzzy Club*, the *Harmonical Society*, and a club of *Fashion*. The story-with-a-moral is exemplified in *Ascm, an Eastern Tale*. Other noteworthy papers are the *Adventures of a Strolling Player; Rules to be observed at a Russian Assembly*; and *A Biographical Memoir*, supposed to be written by an "Ordinary" of Newgate, which humorously describes three methods of running into debt. A set of essays on the cultivation of *Taste*, the *Origin of Poetry*, on *Metaphor*, on *Hyperbole*, and on *Versification*, can scarcely be ranked very high. The discussion on taste had been a favourite, if elusive, subject with the eighteenth-century essayists, and Goldsmith scarcely forwards the matter very much. One or two references are made to prosody (for example, a not very happy one to Milton's blank verse), but there are no critical *loci*, such as occur in Shenstone's *Essays*, and in the " fragments " of criticism left by Gray. Goldsmith's life and temperament debarred him from becoming a literary critic. His *metier* was not that of a critic.

There is one problem associated with the life of Goldsmith which is always discussed by every critic on the work of Goldsmith, and that is the discrepancy between the fine literary quality of his written work and the alleged fatuity of his conversation. Everyone is familiar with the saying that Goldsmith " wrote like an angel and talked like poor Poll." He seems to have been made fun of in the society of that period. Boswell in his *Life of Johnson* preserves a number of anecdotes and incidents where *Goldy*, as he was familiarly called, is ridiculed. And Boswell is not the only writer to minimise Goldsmith's merit as a talker. Rogers the poet recalls the judgment of one who knew Goldsmith well : " Sir, he was a fool. The right word never came to him. If you gave him back a bad shilling, he'd say, ' Why, it is as good a shilling as ever was *born* ! ' You know he ought to have said *coined*. *Coined*, sir, never entered his head. He was a fool, sir." And others have given similar testimony. The true explanation of the apparent paradox lies in this : that Goldsmith was, like Dickens, a man of great heart and tender sensibility, and that he was misunderstood by the society of that time, which was artificial and intellectual, but which could not understand the true delicacy and sensitiveness of Goldsmith. Thus the latter was like a fish out of water in that coffee-house society, and blunders were inevitable. A significant passage occurs in his edition of his *Citizen of the World* papers which clearly defines his position. " I might have taken my station in the world, either as a poet or a philosopher, and made one in those little societies where men club to raise each other's reputation. But at present I belong to no particular class. I resemble one of these animals that has been forced from its forest to gratify human curiosity. My earliest wish was to escape unheeded through life; but I have been set up for halfpence, to fret and scamper at the end of my chain. Though none are injured by my rage, I am naturally too savage to court any friends by fawning, too obstinate to be taught new tricks, and too unprovident to mind what may happen. I am appeased though not contented, too indolent for intrigue and too timid to push for favours, I am—but what signifies, what am I ?" He has summed up his own life, and if he blundered in the society where he was ridiculed, it was a society which was not worthy of him. But with regard to the quality of his essay periodical work, there can be no cavil nor question—Goldsmith must take a foremost position in the history of the periodical essay in the eighteenth century. There can be no doubt that he had acquired the right touch for this kind of essay-writing. Godwin, in his essay on *Intellectual Abortion* in his *Thoughts on Man*, says: " Goldsmith's prose flows with such ease, copiousness, and grace that it resembles the Song of the Sirens." This is too enthusiastic an appreciation for sober criticism; but the phrase, *resembles the Song of the Sirens*, fixes for us in some measure that quality of Goldsmith's prose too elusive to characterise, which makes us say that he accomplished almost all that could be desired by way of successful essay-writing.

In connection with Goldsmith's periodical work, we made mention of the *Busybody* (1759). Only twelve numbers were published. The first number refers to the large family of busybodies in the world, and gives a satiric account of the particular branch to which the author belongs. Being laid up with a broken leg, the author has had the plan of this paper suggested to him as an occupation for his enforced leisure. The second number gives some stories of traders he has known, and their characteristics. The third gives a vigorously written account of some " choice spirits " and the club to which they belong. For example, the second rule of the Club is, " That no member get drunk before nine of the clock, upon pain of forfeiting threepence, to be spent by the company in tobacco." The fifth number publishes *The Logicians Refuted*, a poem by Dean Swift, which the *Busybody* says has never before been

THE PERIODICAL ESSAYS OF GOLDSMITH

printed, and which he received from a nobleman. Two issues (Nos. 11 and 12) also relate some rather doubtful anecdotes on the slovenly dress and figure of Swift, in relation to *singular men, odd men, and hippish men,* whom he is satirising. But the majority of the papers have a political bias, and thus the literary interest of the *Busybody* diminishes.

The *Court Magazine* of two years later, issued monthly, contains a rather miscellaneous selection of material. Sentimental love stories of the usual type appear, and an interesting essay dealing with the most remarkable periods of English literature, in which the writer touches upon the Chaucerian period, Elizabethan literature, Restoration drama, and the novelists. As seems almost inevitable with contemporary writers of any period in English literature, the author of this article takes a pessimistic view of " the present state of letters." In each issue there is also given an essay under the heading of *The Green-Room,* and plays are discussed.

The *Court Magazine* resembles more closely the newer magazine kind becoming very popular than the simpler essay periodical.

But in the following year there was issued a paper of more interest. This was the *Auditor* (1762). The first essay is both fresh and interesting : " It has ever been my opinion that the writers of periodical papers have, for the most part, begun at the wrong end. They conceived it expedient, it seems, to introduce themselves to their readers, by formally acquainting them with the various circumstances of their birth and education, the singularities of their tempers, the proportion of their features, and the texture of their skins." He satirically suggests the appointment of a master of ceremonies who would perform the introduction, " This, Ladies and Gentlemen, is *Mr Spectator,* a person of a round visage, great erudition, and profound taciturnity ! "

He holds that Addison's opening description of the *Spectator* (which he quotes) is wrong, and that it should have been delayed ; for " curiosity is seldom awakened about any adventurer till he has given some proof of his abilities." In due time, if the public see fit, the author will publish an essay on his life and genius; meanwhile the title of a humble *Auditor* is sufficient. He wishes to tell the world what, as an auditor, he hears. But this is simply *mutatis mutandis* the *Spectator* in the guise of an *Auditor*. The second paper is a satirical sketch on the favourites of the fickle crowd. The next two or three papers are political; but the eighth offers some variation. It is what the author terms " a sleeping reverie, where the imagination takes the hint from reason, and echoes back to her all her most sober reflections in a sportive and whimsical manner." He adapts part of Swift's *Gulliver's Travels* and supposes himself at Brobdingnag, where he discusses English politics.

The author of the *Auditor* is evidently striving to write a clear Addisonian style, and his satiric touch is often quite effective. For example, in the twelfth number he gives a political dictionary for the year 1762, and his definitions are often amusing: for example, " *The People of England*: Not the mass of the people, and their representatives in Parliament, as has been vainly imagined. By this phrase is meant the grand pensioners, Lord Gawkee, Alderman Sugarcane, Colonel Squinturn, an illiterate bookseller, a city attorney, a drunken parson, and a broken poet."

In the fourteenth number the present state of literature is discussed, and the lament is made that writers who do not know how to hold a pen rush into print. In the first number the *Auditor* had said that his topics would range from the spirit of Faction to the spirit of Cock-Lane, but he forgets this promise, for he soon limits himself to politics, and the literary value of the periodical becomes very small.

The *Schemer*, again, was originally published in the *London Chronicle* at various intervals covering a period of more than two years, and was reprinted in 1763 in volume form. The " Editor " is *Helter van Scelter*. The object of the *Schemer* is " to ridicule the glaring follies of mankind, in the various departments of Literature, Philosophy, and Politics. The author is particularly severe upon the political essayists. Advertisements, various " characters," and the female sex all fall to be discussed, and the *Schemer* is simply one other weak imitation of the Queen Anne essay periodical.

THE PERIODICAL ESSAYS OF GOLDSMITH

A paper of a more general type was the *Weekly Amusement* (1763), which continued for a year. It is partly a set of original papers, partly a collection from different sources. It will be sufficient to indicate its nature to say that the first number alone includes subjects ranging from rules and reflections for the conduct of life to directions for curing rank grass in meadows. The second issue has an interesting *vision* on the gymnosophists of India. Stories and essays from the *Plain Dealer*, the *North Briton*, and the *Monitor* are also included. This method of "extracts" seemed to be getting more popular, and one or two features of the modern magazine are already observable. For example, there is an account (rather exaggerated and unreal) of strange animals to be seen in Brazil, and crude illustrations are given, and the departure from the essay periodical kind is increasingly evident.

The paper was reissued in 1766 and 1767 in a modified form. It is smaller; the extracted portions are fewer; and there is always a story told in each number. In this form the magazine maintained a steady popularity for over a hundred numbers.

A paper closer to the essay periodical pattern, about the same time, was the *Plain Dealer*. We have already noticed an earlier magazine of the same name. The first number, like Steele's *Tatler*, was given away *gratis*. The paper came out weekly on Saturdays, beginning on 14th May 1763. In the first number the author, like the *Auditor*, makes a slight deviation from the traditional opening. "It has been customary," he says, "for the writers of periodical papers to begin their work with some account of themselves, but however general the practice, I cannot prevail on myself to comply with it." His aim is to defend the liberty of the people, and in the second number urges the maxim " that the first subject in this kingdom, equally with the lowest, is amenable to justice." The third number is a little pessimistic: "I have not philosophy enough to laugh at the follies, or to weep over the vices of the world: I am a *Plain Dealer*: they tempt me to be a misanthrope." The opening of this magazine is promising, but it does not proceed on purely literary lines. Discussions of the social and political conditions of the people are indulged in, and the paper tends to develop a strong political bias, and diverges from the true aim of the essay periodical.

But the *Spendthrift* (1766) returns to the *Spectator* type. In the collection of *Spendthrifts* given in the British Museum Library, the former owner of them, Mr Isaac Reed, has the following note written at the top of the first number: "Most of these papers are supposed to have been written by Lord Holland. Mr Nichols, who printed them, informs me that the copy always came from that nobleman's house." Mr Reed also gives, pasted on the cover, two letters from Dr Hawkesworth (of *Adventurer* fame) to Mr Dodsley, Bookseller, Pall Mall, London. They seem to indicate that he also contributed once or twice to the *Spendthrift*. Here is the first of these two letters.

"SIR,—I send you a paper upon a popular subject, *Taste*. Pray let me know, by a line, what your authors say to it. I beg that, if it is printed at all, it may be printed without any alteration. I shall send all my papers under this express condition. The sequel you shall have by next post. Mark all my papers at the bottom with an ' X.'—I am, S^r. Y^r. Obed. Humble Servt.,

(Sgd.) JNO. HAWKESWORTH.

"BROMLEY, 10*th May* 1766."

The *Spendthrift* is, in form, almost an exact imitation of the *Tatler* or *Spectator*. In the first number the *Spendthrift* introduces himself as being in a state of destitution, and the idea of a periodical paper struck him as a hopeful way in which to repair his broken fortunes. He finds that the present age is dull, and he longs for the days of Charles II., and thinks that there are "two wants at the present time, namely, tolerable productions for the stage, and weekly papers *not* political." This introduction seems to promise well. He is evidently going to exclude politics, and he prefers trifling to serious subjects. Nor do the papers disappoint this hope, as the variety of the first half-dozen or so will indicate. The second number is on *self-love*; the third has the motto, "each pleasure has its price," and is an excellent paper with a sound moral; the fourth deals with the marriage state: the fifth on *looking out of the window*, recalls the later essay by Leigh Hunt with the like title; the next number considers life from a more serious point of view; while numbers seven and ten tell a rather melancholy story in the form of letters.

Hawkesworth's articles (Nos. 8 and 13) on taste are rather disappointing. He commences by stating, truly enough, "I know of no topic that has more frequently employed the writers of essays than *taste*, nor any that has given them more trouble to less purpose," but he proves himself unable to avoid the dangers into which the earlier writers had fallen. His discussion of the idea of beauty does not carry us very far, and when in the second paper he continues his subject as far as it relates to *painting*, he shows himself still hidebound by the Popian "correctness," for he criticises Hogarth severely for placing on canvas such *disagreeable* subjects. It was one of the maxims of the eighteenth century, that only certain subjects should be dealt with by the artist. It will more correctly represent this paper to give the fourteenth number as a specimen extract. It is the *Diary of a Macaroni*. This was not an entirely new theme. Earlier periodicals had dealt with the diary of a citizen, the diary of a lady of fashion, and the diary of a fellow of a college. But the essay deserves credit for its style and its freshness of treatment.

"Though these papers are chiefly calculated to expose the vices and follies of the age, I hope my readers will allow me to digress a moment from the original intention of them, in order to pay that tribute of praise which real merit has a right to claim, and express my most profound admiration for the characters of these fashionable Gentlemen, who are so considerable an ornament to the Beau Monde, and are commonly distinguished by the title of macaronies. I must confess myself remiss in not having already taken notice of so respectable a body, and having foolishly mis-spent my time to a subject of so much greater importance.

"Though the polite world are sufficiently acquainted with the lives and manners of this extraordinary race of men, there are many parts of this Metropolis in which (I flatter myself) these papers are read, where, though their fame may have extended, the particulars of their characters are wholly unknown; for the information, therefore, of the inhabitants of such places I think it necessary to give some account of them, which I shall do in as few words as possible.

"A macaroni is a gentleman who, having finished his travels, on his return to England, devotes his life partly to the attendance of the ladies, partly to drinking, but chiefly to the gaming-table, and in general to every fashionable debauchery. In Italy he has contracted every kind of vice; in France he has picked up all sorts of folly and foppery; and in England he is habituated to a life of indolence and activity. His principles are debauched; his constitution is ruined, and his fortune often spent before he is five and twenty. With this he is a perfect connoisseur in painting, music, and all the polite arts; and well versed in a kind of superficial common-place conversation, with which he never fails to entertain the fair sex.

"Amiable and accomplished as this character may appear, it has not been able to escape the censure of the malicious. Such is the envy which the world bears to superior excellence. Of the spotless innocence of their lives I am, indeed, a proper judge, from a Journal of one of these gentlemen which by accident fell into my hands, and which, though it can afford no great amusement to my readers, I shall present them with, as it may serve to prove what I have now advanced, and show how they (as the poet expresses it)

"'Pass away
In gentle inactivity the day.'

"'THE MACARONI'S JOURNAL

"'*Monday morn, 8 o'clock.*—Returned from Almack's. Lost all my money. Woke at two with a damned headache. Rode into Hyde Park to cure it. Came home something better, but monstrously tired with my ride. Obliged to dine at home to nurse myself for the evening. Went to Ranelagh in my new French frock.

"'*Tuesday.*—Woke at twelve, pretty well. Walked out till two. Came home to cut my hair. Turned off my perruquier for not using perfumed powder. Not a creature at the Opera. Set up at Almack's. Lost a little.

"'*Wednesday.*—Got up at three. Like my new perruquier. Was dressed *a la Grecque*. Caught cold in the evening by wearing a damned *habit de printemps*.

"'*Thursday.*—Too ill to go out all day. Unlucky to happen on the ball night. Almost perished with ennui. Went to bed early.

"'*Friday.*—Something better. Went out in the evening. Grew worse and could not sit up at night.

THE PERIODICAL ESSAYS OF GOLDSMITH

"'*Saturday.*—Determined to stay at home all day. New coat came from Paris. Could not resist going to the Opera in it. Monstrously admired. Went home prudently at two o'clock.

"'*Sunday.*—Lay in bed all morning. Dined at the *Dilettanti*. Drank too much. Forced to go home immediately. How different this is from the life of a Dorimant, or a Lovelace! and what a censorious country must this be, where such spotless innocence cannot escape detraction."

The *Spendthrift*, taken on the whole, is superior to the average production of the second half of the period under review. It retains the better features of the others, and as the author justly observes, to have a magazine free from politics is a pleasant relief. There is no subject more interesting at the time, but once the *casus belli* has been removed no subject in retrospect proves more dull and uninspiring—at least from the literary point of view.

CHAPTER VIII

EDINBURGH PUBLICATIONS, INCLUDING THE *MIRROR* AND *LOUNGER*

In many ways the northern capital of Britain, during the eighteenth century, was a most interesting place. And that interest was not least from the side of books. The literary activity of Edinburgh steadily progressed with the century. And several periodicals which call for notice help to justify this assertion.

The *Edinburgh Museum, or North British Magazine* appeared with the New Year (1763), and continued monthly for two years. The motto seems to cast a slur on other magazines, " Sunt bona, sunt quædam mediocria, sunt mala plura." The aim of the projectors is to give " a selection of the most useful and agreeable parts of the arts and sciences and belles-lettres arranged so as to form a pleasing variety "; and to supply " a just and animated picture of the present age taken either in political, literary, or moral points of view." This is a much wider aim than that of the essay periodical, but the features of the latter also appear. Visions are common; essays on *Sleep* and *The Passions;* and the inevitable *Eastern Tale*. This last feature had been overdone. Whenever any moral had to be conveyed, the conventional dress of the East was employed, frequently with small success and no literary taste. Johnson and Hawkesworth wrote such tales well, but with the majority the device remains a lifeless convention.

The *Weekly Magazine, or Edinburgh Amusement*, published in 1768, seems to have been considered a continuation of the earlier *Edinburgh Magazine*. Extracts from other magazines and periodicals are justified by the motto, " Floriferis ut apes in saltibus omnia libant omnia nos."

EDINBURGH PERIODICAL ESSAYS

The magazine existed down to the year 1781. Essays on taste, "characters," criticism of books, and general news are all supplied. In the reviews of books and novels in particular, under date Thursday, 7th July 1768, there is a criticism of Brooke's *Fool of Quality*, where the critic writes: "It will be found greatly superior, notwithstanding its numerous episodes, to most of the numberless novels which have of late years issued from the press." It is not always remembered that, so early as in the decade 1770 to 1780, novels, especially of a sentimental type, were literally poured forth, and even sent in boxes to English families resident abroad. Walter Ruddiman was the editor of the *Weekly Magazine*, and he was successful in getting Fergusson to contribute poems to the periodical, and this, no doubt, helped to make it sell. But in the political section of the paper he came in contact, more than once, with the authorities.

Of a similar nature was the *Edinburgh Magazine and Review*, conducted by a *Society of Gentlemen*. Like the men who gathered round Mackenzie, they were well-known residents of Edinburgh: Creech, Kincaid, Smellie, Dr Stuart, and Kerr. The note of the new magazine was to be variety: "To be generally useful and entertaining," the editors said, "they mean to suit themselves to readers of every denomination. It is not solely their intention to paint the manners and fashions of the times, to interest the passions, and to wander in the regions of fancy. They propose to blend instruction with amusement, to pass from light and gay effusions to severe disquisition, to mingle erudition with wit; and to contrast the wisdom and the folly of men. They wish equally to allure and to please the studious and the grave, the dissipated and the idle." But the variety they offer goes far beyond the variety of the *Spectator* kind. It is a magazine of sorts. Papers of note include essays on the value of a classical education; a criticism of Hawkesworth's *Voyages* (emphasising these features which had involved the author in trouble), and poetry by Smollett. The magazine came to an end in August 1776, owing to the strong feeling aroused by several sarcastic references to Lord Monboddo's recently published books.

THE EIGHTEENTH-CENTURY ESSAYISTS

Another Edinburgh periodical was the *Gentleman and Lady's Weekly Magazine* (1774), which has the old motto: "To hold, as't were, the mirror up to nature; to show virtue her own features, scorn her own image, and the very age and body of time his form and pressure," and the issue for January 1774 opens with an account of the life and writings of Dr Samuel Johnson. The essay is in a very eulogistic strain, and expresses the opinion that " the world are in expectation that he will soon publish an account of the *Tour* made by him and the celebrated Mr Boswell through Scotland and the Western Isles in autumn last; and surely a performance of this kind, executed by a man of his genius and observation, cannot fail in giving the highest satisfaction to every person of curiosity and taste." The world has long had opportunity of judging whether this expectation was rightly founded. The usual features of the Addisonian periodical are reproduced. The tragic story; amusing letters; and the constantly recurring Eastern Tale. In the general news section occurs a far-off echo of the craze for Marathon races:

> "So prevalent is the force of example that since the journey performed by Mr Foster Powell from London to York, several considerable bets have been taken up in this place upon feats of walking: particularly a gentleman, about ten days ago, undertook to walk from Edinburgh to Linlithgow and back again in six hours, but our unfortunate walking hero lost his wager by ten minutes."

The *Gentleman and Lady's Weekly Magazine* had been begun to compete with the *Weekly Magazine*, but it did not manage to oust it, and it came to an end in March 1775.

These magazines, which combined general features with the original Addisonian essay periodical, form the bridge which spans the gulf between the modern magazine and the Queen Anne periodical.

While these four periodicals had all been issued from Edinburgh, the *Batchelor* appeared in Dublin in 1766. It was published twice weekly, on Tuesdays and Saturdays, and there were in all one hundred and thirty-nine numbers. In the customary manner *Mr Wagstaffe* (the editor) relates to us his history. "I am descended from an ancient family of that name in England, and have the honour to be related to the famous *Isaac Bickerstaffe, Esq.*, who so long entertained the world by his tattling. In his lucubrations he makes honourable mention of my uncle, Mr Humphrey Wagstaffe. My father was a citizen of London, where I was born; my cousin Bickerstaff and Nestor Ironside were my godfathers, about the beginning of this century; and I am now past my grand climacteric." He is unmarried, and has a sister *Laetitia* two years his junior, who is also unmarried. The old " characters " are tenaciously retained, and the essays show that *Mr Wagstaffe* has zealously read the earlier periodicals. The usual *dream subjects* and other essay subjects appear. Thus from Dublin there was little fresh at this period by way of essay-periodical writing.

We return to London again with the *Everyman's Magazine* (1771). It is a typical example of the wider range of subject material which these magazines now endeavoured to cover. For example, the September number includes a romantic story; a dialogue " in the shades " between James I. and George II.; a didactic essay; a history of *Alcander and Septimius*; and a number of letters on matrimonial differences.

Another periodical, the *Whisperer* (1770), has a promising title. The *Whisperer* appeared weekly for six months, but the articles prove to be political, and have little purely literary interest. But the *Macaroni and Theatrical Magazine* (1772) is nearer the essay periodical in its nature. It is to be " conducted upon a much more elegant and liberal plan than any other work of the kind hitherto published," we are modestly informed by the author! In the first number the term *Macaroni* is explained. Macaroni, the author tells us, " is a dish known over Italy and France and universally partaken of. It was introduced at *Almack's*, and the subscribers to the dinners came to be distinguished by the title of *Macaronies*. These being the younger and gayer men, it became justly applied as a term of reproach to all ranks of people who fall into absurdity of fashion." The military *macaroni* is then exemplified by a captain in the Army.

In each issue of the *Macaroni* letters, essays, anecdotes,

and poetry and general news are given. A large number of the essays closely resemble the *Spectator* pattern. Many of them display the right style and treatment—they are neither too heavy nor too serious—the great merit in Addison's treatment of the periodical essay. An interesting example is the contrast made between (imaginary) extracts from a county lady's journal in the days of Queen Elizabeth and the diary of a lady of fashion in his own day, the quiet and homely existence of the former being cleverly opposed to the gay, butterfly existence of the latter in town.

Of a more serious kind is the *Templar and Literary Gazette* (1773). The paper opens with a discussion between the author and his publisher: " I hope," says the former, " that we shall fall upon something clever and taking—I heartily wish we may! To be sure Mr Steele was a great man in his day, and so was Mr Addison. They wrote to the manners of their age ; we profess to do no less ; there remains enough unsaid, unsung, for us and as many as shall come after us." The author nevertheless follows the *Spectator* closely. He retains the *Club* idea, and sketches three characters to be associated with him in the venture: *Mr Fairley*, a paterfamilias ; *Sir Walter Wag*, a gentleman of fortune ; and *Mr Miles Saunder*, a man reserved to strangers. The second number discusses methods of getting the paper into circulation ; and the fourth has an interesting discussion on the fate of authors and their works, a favourite subject of Dr Johnson's in the *Rambler* and the *Idler*, and perhaps suggested from him. The fault of the *Templar* is that it is " heavy " and lacks variety. This fault would not seem to lie with the *Convivial Magazine* (1775). The title is suggestive, but in the first number a defence of it is made. " It may be necessary to remark in this place, that the most brilliant effusions of taste and fancy often arise over a cheerful glass, and it is well known that Churchill, Bonnel Thornton, and some others (now living) whose characters have been established for wit and humour, have produced some of their most admired works when in a convivial party. It must be acknowledged that the first idea of this magazine arose in such a meeting, where mirth and good-humour circulated with the glass. But let not our readers imagine all our ideas are confined to mere mirth and jocularity. The more serious parts of the work will be attended to, in those cool moments of reflection and serenity, when philosophy and reason have mounted their throne, and reign without control."

The variety actually given in the *Convivial Magazine* is considerable. There is an article on the theatre; a short essay on politeness; stories; the memoirs of Constance of Brittany; a report of the King's Speech; some anecdotes and general news. But it does not altogether live up to its title.

The *Biographical Magazine*, of the following year (1776), is called " a work replete with instruction and entertainment," by a *Society of Gentlemen*. It opens with a promising introduction: "No magazine solely biographical has hitherto been offered to the public. This work is indeed intended to convey instruction by the channel of amusement." But the magazine turns out to be something of a cross between a modern dictionary of biography and a collection of stories. Some of the anecdotes introduced are of more than doubtful authenticity. Take, for example, the article on Admiral Benbow, which is interesting but sensational. The story is told how Benbow refused to show to the Revenue Officers the heads of fourteen Moors which he had put in a sack as a grim trophy of war, and which a negro servant carried for him. The officers thought it was contraband material which he was carrying, but Benbow declared that it was only " salt provisions for his own use." In the end he is brought before a magistrate, and the heads are tumbled out on the table before the astonished and horrified magnate! As an offshoot, as a specialised biographical department, suggested perhaps by the character-sketches of the earlier periodicals, the *Biographical Magazine* is interesting. Otherwise it possesses little literary interest.

In the same way the *Englishman* (1779) is of too political a character. Steele's paper of the same name had been so violently partisan that he was expelled from the House. The author of the later *Englishman* had no such exciting adventure, but his devotion to politics minimises the literary value of his work for us.

THE EIGHTEENTH-CENTURY ESSAYISTS

There were now at least three different types of periodicals in existence. In the first place, there was still the essay periodical, closely following in nearly every detail the *Tatler* and *Spectator* models. In the second place, there was the periodical, which really undertook the function of a newspaper, and only devoted a small section to letters and essay material. And in the third place, there was the more miscellaneous magazine, which only retained the *Spectator* essay in one of its sections.

It was from the capital of Scotland that two notable periodicals—the *Mirror* and its continuation the *Lounger*—were issued. The undertaking was engaged upon by a number of gentlemen, mostly lawyers by profession, and well known in Edinburgh society; and (perhaps with the same reason as that of Scott later) they took pains to keep their identity secret. Henry Mackenzie, the author of the *Man of Feeling*, conducted the two periodicals; none of the others had had experience in literary work before. They were Messrs Cullen, Bannatyne, Ogilvy, Abercromby, Craig, and Home, but Mackenzie takes the most prominent part.

It will be remembered that in the list of books given as forming the library of Burns, a number of the essayists appear, including the *Mirror* and *Lounger*. The estimation in which they were held at the time is well illustrated by the letter sent by Gilbert Burns (brother to the poet) to Dr Currie, who had objected to the *Mirror* and *Lounger* being included in the library of the *Conversation Club* at Mauchline: " I do not mean to controvert your criticism of my favourite books, the *Mirror* and *Lounger*, although I understand there are people who think themselves judges who do not agree with you. If I am right, the taste which these books are calculated to cultivate (besides the taste for fine writing, which many of the papers tend to improve and to gratify) is what is proper, consistent, and becoming in human character and conduct, as almost every paper relates to these subjects. I am sorry I have not these books by me, that I might point out some instances. I remember two: one, the beautiful story of *La Roche*, where besides the pleasure one derives from a beautiful simple story, told in

EDINBURGH PERIODICAL ESSAYS

Mackenzie's happiest manner, the mind is led to taste, with heartfelt rapture, the consolation to be derived, in deep affliction, from habitual devotion and trust in Almighty God. The other, the story of *General W*——, where the reader is led to have a high relish for that firmness of mind which disregards appearances, the common forms and vanities of life, for the sake of doing justice in a case which was out of the reach of human laws. Allow me, then, to remark, that if the morality of these books is subordinate to the cultivation of taste; that taste, that refinement of mind and delicacy of sentiment which they are intended to give, are the strongest guard, and surest foundation, of morality and virtue. Other moralists guard, as it were, the overt act; these papers, by exalting duty into sentiment, are calculated to make every deviation from rectitude and propriety of conduct painful to the mind,

> " ' Whose temper'd powers
> Refine at length, and every passion wears
> A chaster, milder, more attractive mien.' "

The first number of the *Mirror* was published in January 1779, and the actual circumstances under which it took its rise are explained by Mackenzie in the concluding number: " The idea of publishing a periodical paper in Edinburgh took its rise in a company of gentlemen, whom particular circumstances of connection brought frequently together. Their discourse often turned upon subjects of manners, of taste, and of literature. By one of these accidental resolutions, of which the origin cannot easily be traced, it was determined to put their thoughts into writing, and to read them for the entertainment of each other. These essays assumed this form, and soon after, some one gave them the name of a periodical publication; the writers of it were naturally associated; and their meetings increased the importance as well as the number of their publications. Cultivating letters in the midst of business, composition was to them an amusement only: that amusement was heightened by the criticism which their society afforded: the idea of publication suggested itself as productive of still higher entertainment." Let us examine the *Mirror* as it lies before us. In the first number the writer (Mr Home) states the aim of the periodical. "To hold, as it were, the *mirror* up to nature, to show virtue her own features, vice her own image, and the very age and body of the Time his form and pressure." The motto suggests at once the *Tatler* and *Spectator*, and in the one hundred and ten numbers of the *Mirror* which were issued the Addisonian features are closely reproduced. That the authors understood the true *ethos* of the periodical essay is evidenced by a statement occurring in the preface to the story of *La Roche*: "A work, to be extensively read, must sometimes be ludicrous, and often ironical." Society at the time was in a state of transition. Intercourse was going on between France and England; new Society manners were being introduced; the *nabobs* were coming home rich, from India; it was the age of *pocket boroughs*, and the energetic Pitt the Younger was in power. Thus many interesting pictures are given in these pages of Society, pictures which are nearer actuality than those given in the novels of Fanny Burney, and others of the period. Mackenzie, who had by this time written *The Man of Feeling*, *The Man of the World*, and *Julia de Roubigné*, naturally shows a *nisus* towards the short story, and even towards a lengthened narrative running through several numbers—as *e.g.* the story of *La Roche*, which runs through three numbers, and is specially worthy of note, since it gives an idealised picture of Hume. The *Spectator* of Addison reappears as *Mr Umphraville*. The latter is a man of means, who prefers a retired life of study to the bustle of business or Society, and it is suggested that the peculiarities which he had thus contracted will give sufficient interest to allow of his being brought up again "in order to gratify such of them (his readers) as wish to know somewhat more of his life and opinions": a letter (No. 56) from him is given; his reflections on a *Macaroni* member of Parliament (No. 68), and on modern manners (No. 76). Discussions on æsthetics, manners, advantages of politeness—all the usual subjects are there. A new interest in Nature is seen in the essay on *Spring* (No. 16). The effects of that season are considered with a real appreciation and love of Nature which show a reaction from the conventional " nature schemes " of Addison or Johnson. Literary criticism is not forgotten. Ossian is discussed by Cullen (No. 13). Milton's *L'Allegro* and *Il Penseroso* are considered in relation to Art and Nature; and an interest in contemporary literature is displayed in Craig's paper on the short-lived Michael Bruce. Shakespeare comes in for criticism from more than one writer. Richardson (No. 66) criticises a scene in *Richard III*. He advances the view that, after all, the strange love scene between Richard and Lady Anne " was natural, and attended with that success which it was calculated to obtain."

Mackenzie again (Nos. 99, 100) endeavours to settle the much-debated problem of Hamlet's character. But Craig (No. 83) gives us a glimpse of the position which Scottish men of letters held in relation to the English language, from which it would appear that the majority wrote English as if they were doing a Latin *prose*. Thus Robertson and Hume write English with grammatical clearness and correctness, but with no great freedom of style. Ordinary conversation, even at Edinburgh, was apparently in the Scots dialect.

" The old Scottish dialect is now banished from our books, and the English is substituted in its place. But though our books be written in English, our conversation is in Scotch. The Scottish dialect is our ordinary suit; the English is used only on solemn occasions. When a Scotsman therefore writes, he does it generally in trammels; he expresses himself in a language in some respects foreign to him, and which he has acquired by study and observation."

A good example of Mackenzie's sentimentalism is the forty-ninth number, where he deals with a subject which will be with us for some time to come, the distress of families of soldiers.

" As I walked one evening, about a fortnight ago, through St Andrew's Square, I observed a girl, meanly dressed, coming along the pavement at a slow pace. When I passed her, she turned a little towards me, and made a sort of halt; but said nothing. I am ill at looking anybody full in the face: so I went on a few steps before I turned my eye to observe her. She had, by this time, resumed her former pace. I remarked a certain elegance in her form, which the poorness of her garb could not altogether overcome : her person was thin and genteel, and there was something not ungraceful in the stoop of her head, and the seeming feebleness with which she walked. I could not resist the desire which her appearance gave me, of knowing somewhat of her situation and circumstances ; I therefore walked back, and repassed her with such a look (for I could bring myself to nothing more) as might induce her to speak what she seemed desirous to say at first. This had the effect I wished. 'Pity a poor orphan!' said she, in a voice tremulous and weak. I stopped, and put my hand in my pocket : I had now a better opportunity of observing her. Her face was thin and pale ; part of it was shaded by her hair, of a light brown colour, which was parted, in a disordered manner, at her forehead, and hung loose upon her shoulders ; round them was cast a piece of tattered cloak, which with one hand she held across her bosom, while the other was half out-stretched to receive the bounty I intended for her. Her large blue eyes were cast on the ground : she was drawing back her hand as I put a trifle into it : on receiving which she turned them up to me, muttered something which I could not hear, and then, letting go her cloak, and pressing her hands together, burst into tears.

"It was not the action of an ordinary beggar, and my curiosity was strongly excited by it. I desired her to follow me to the house of a friend hard by, whose beneficence I have often had occasion to know. When she arrived there, she was so fatigued and worn out, that it was not till after some means used to restore her, that she was able to give us an account of her misfortunes.

"Her name, she told us, was Collins ; the place of her birth one of the northern counties of England. Her father, who had died several years ago, left her remaining parent with the charge of her, then a child, and one brother, a lad of seventeen. By his industry, however, joined to that of her mother, they were tolerably supported, their father having died possessed of a small farm, with the right of pasturage on an adjoining common, from which they obtained a decent livelihood : that, last summer, her brother having become acquainted with a recruiting sergeant, who was quartered in a neighbouring village, was by him enticed to enlist as a soldier, and soon after was marched off, along with some other recruits, to join his regiment : that this, she believed, broke her mother's heart ; for that she had never afterwards had a day's health, and, at length, had died about three weeks ago : that, immediately after her death, the steward employed by the 'squire of whom their farm was held, took possession of everything for the arrears of their rent : that, as she had heard her brother's regiment was in Scotland when he enlisted, she had wandered hither in quest of him, as she had no other relation in the world to own her! But she found, on arriving here, that the regiment had been embarked several months before, and was gone a great way off, she could not tell whither.

" 'This news,' said she, 'laid hold of my heart; and I have had something wrong here,' putting her hand to her bosom, 'ever since. I got a bed and some victuals in the house of a woman here in town, to whom I told my story, and who seemed to pity me. I had then a little bundle of things, which I had been allowed to take with me after my mother's death; but the night before last, somebody stole it from me while I slept; and so the woman said she would keep me no longer, and turned me out into the street, where I have since remained, and am almost famished for want.'

" She was now in better hands; but our assistance had come too late. A frame, naturally delicate, had yielded to the fatigues of her journey, and the hardships of her situation. She declined by slow but uninterrupted degrees, and yesterday breathed her last. A short while before she expired, she asked to see me; and taking from her bosom a silver locket, which she told me had been her mother's, and which all her distresses could not make her part with, begged I would keep it for her dear brother, and give it him, if ever he should return home, as a token of her remembrance.

" I felt this poor girl's fate strongly; but I tell not her story merely to indulge my feelings; I would make the reflections it may excite in my readers, useful to others who may suffer from similar causes. There are many, I fear, from whom their country has called brothers, sons, or fathers to bleed in her service forlorn, like poor Nancy Collins, with ' no relation in the world to own them.' Their sufferings are often unknown, when they are such as most demand compassion. The mind that cannot obtrude its distresses on the ear of pity, is formed to feel their poignancy the deepest.

" In our idea of military operations, we are too apt to forget the misfortunes of the people. In defeat, we think of the fall, and in victory, of the glory of Commanders; we seldom allow ourselves to consider how many, in a lower rank, both events make wretched: how many, amidst the acclamations of national triumph, are left to the helpless misery of the widowed and the orphan, and, while victory celebrates her festival, feel, in their distant hovels, the extremities of want and wretchedness."

In the last number Mackenzie calls attention to several factors which had hastened the close of the *Mirror*. The critical juncture of public affairs was the first, " at a period so big with national danger and public solicitude, it was not to be expected that much attention should be paid to speculation or to sentiment, to minute investigations of character or features of private manners." The arraignment of the critics, he imagined, was another drawback. People were very distrustful of authors whose name and position they did not know. But perhaps the greatest disadvantage was the *place* of its publication. Edinburgh, Mackenzie thinks, is rather fastidious of home productions. The author is not without honour, save in his own city, and Edinburgh has not the same fascination for the reader as London. "There is a sort of classic privilege in the very names of places in London, which does not extend to those of Edinburgh. The *Cannongate* is almost as long as the *Strand*, but it will not bear the comparison upon paper; and *Blackfriars-wynd* can never vie with *Drury Lane*, in point of sound, however they may rank in the article of Chastity. In the department of *humour* these circumstances must necessarily have great weight, and, for papers of humour, the bulk of readers will generally call, because the number is much greater of those who can laugh than of those who can think." But the band of writers had no need to be ashamed of their production. One word is sufficient to characterise the *Mirror*: it is a gentlemanly periodical, and the essays are simple yet dignified in style, and the matter above reproach.

It is convenient to group along with the *Mirror* a second essay periodical which was also issued in *Edinburgh*, and which is in almost every respect similar to it. The *Lounger* (1785) was contributed to by the same group of writers, and commenced five years after the close of its predecessor. It was a weekly periodical, and a hundred and one numbers in all were published. The *Mr Umphraville* of the *Mirror* is replaced by *Colonel Caustic*, "a fine gentleman of the last age, somewhat severe in his remarks on the present." He is described as "a gentleman with what is called a fresh look for his age, dressed in a claret coloured coat with gold buttons, of a cut not altogether modern, an embroidered waistcoat with very large flaps, a major wig, long ruffles nicely plaited (that looked, however, as if the fashion had come to them rather than that they had been made for the fashion) : his white silk stockings ornamented with figured clocks, and his shoes with high insteps, buckled with small round gold buckles. His sword with a silver hilt somewhat tarnished, I might have thought only an article of his dress, had not a cockade in his hat marked him for a military man. It was some time before I was able to find out who he was." There is a particularity and a fullness about this description by the author of the *Man of Feeling* which makes it rather notable. It was written about half a century before *Dickens* began to write his wonderful descriptions. In the same essay occurs a phrase which is worthy of note. *Colonel Caustic* is criticising (with the usual sigh for the past) the beauty of the ladies found at the gathering, and he says : " Sir, here are many pretty, very pretty girls. That young lady in blue is a very pretty girl. I remember her grandmother at the same age ; she was a fine woman." An almost exactly similar distinction of phrase occurs in Scott's *Waverley*, but such a fact need not surprise us, when we remember that Scott was a great reader of the eighteenth-century periodicals ; and during his lifetime these essays formed part of the regular reading of youth.

Sir Thomas Lounger is also introduced to our notice, and more is made of these characters than of those in the *Mirror*. A dinner, where *Colonel Caustic* and *Sir Thomas* are in company, is described : also a visit to the former's country house ; an account of the *Colonel's* family ; his occupations in the country ; and his visits to his neighbours. Relatives of the *Colonel's* are also introduced. An effort is obviously being made to accomplish something similar to the *Sir Roger de Coverley* papers of Addison.

The stock subjects of the essay periodical are passed under review : Happiness (No. 86) ; Old Age (No. 72) ; Idleness (No. 59) ; A paper on Novel Writing (No. 20), by Mackenzie, attracts attention, but he disappointingly limits himself to the discussion of the " moral " effect of novels, with special reference to the *sentimental* novel. Drama is reviewed (No. 50), and the criticism of Shakespeare continued by Mackenzie in a discussion on the character of Falstaff (Nos. 68 and 69). But the most interesting paper on the criticism of literature is the ninety-seventh, which forms one of the first studies of Burns' poetry which we possess. It is called an *Extraordinary Account of Robert Burns the Ayrshire Ploughman ; with Extracts from his Poems*, and is written by Mackenzie. Mackenzie opens with a rather grandiloquent disquisition. Genius is often overlooked, and when brought to notice as often over-estimated. Mackenzie's criticism is favourable, but rather hedging in tone. If the swan should turn out an ugly duckling after all, he will not have endangered his own reputation by any rash prophecy. His reference to Burns' diction is notable : " One bar, indeed, his birth and education have opposed to his fame, the language in which most of his poems are written. Even in Scotland, the provincial dialect which Ramsay and he have used, is now read with a difficulty which greatly damps the pleasure of the reader." It would appear that the lapse of a decade had already made a difference ; the state of matters mentioned in the *Mirror* had evidently altered. He quotes from the *Vision*, gives the whole of *To a Mountain Daisy*, and adds a full glossary. He explains, for example, the meaning of *wee, cauld, stane*, and *weet*. But the value of the paper is great. It in a measure forecasts the nineteenth-century review article, and the work of Jeffrey. We give it entire, with the exception of quotations and glossary.

" To the feeling and the susceptible there is something wonderfully pleasing in the contemplation of genius, of that supereminent reach of mind by which some men are distinguished. In the view of highly superior talents, as in that of great and stupendous natural objects, there is a sublimity which fills the soul with wonder and delight, which expands it, as it were, beyond its usual bounds, and which, investing our nature with extraordinary powers, and extraordinary honours, interests our curiosity and flatters our pride.

" This divinity of genius, however, which admiration is fond to worship, is best arrayed in the darkness of distant and remote periods, and is not easily acknowledged in the present time, or in places with which we are perfectly acquainted. Exclusive of all the deductions which envy or jealousy may sometimes be supposed to make, there is a familiarity in the near approach of persons around us, not very consistent with the lofty ideas which we wish to form of him who has led captive our imagination in the triumph of his fancy, overpowered our feelings with the tide of passion, or enlightened our reason with the investigation of hidden truths. It may be true, that 'in the olden time' genius had some advantages which tended to its vigour and its growth: but it is not unlikely that, even in these degenerate days, it rises much oftener than it is observed; that in 'the ignorant present time' our posterity may find names which they will dignify, though we neglected, and pay to their memory those honours which their contemporaries had denied them.

"There is, however, a natural, and indeed a fortunate vanity in trying to redress this wrong, which genius is exposed to suffer. In the discovery of talents generally unknown, men are apt to indulge the same fond partiality as in all other discoveries which themselves have made; and hence we have had repeated instances of painters and of poets, who have been drawn from obscure situations, and held forth to public notice and applause by the extravagant encomiums of their introductors, yet in a short time have sunk again to their former obscurity; whose merit, though perhaps somewhat neglected, did not appear to have been much undervalued by the world, and could not support, by its own intrinsic excellence, that superior place which the enthusiasm of its patrons would have assigned it.

"I know not if I shall be accused of such enthusiasm and partiality, when I introduce to the notice of my readers a poet of our own country, with whose writings I have lately become acquainted; but if I am not greatly deceived, I think I may safely pronounce him a genius of no ordinary rank. The person to whom I allude is *Robert Burns*, an Ayrshire ploughman, whose poems were some time ago published in a country-town in the west of Scotland, with no other ambition, it would seem, than to circulate among the inhabitants of the county where he was born, to obtain a little fame from those who had heard of his talents. I hope I shall not be thought to assume too much, if I endeavour to place him in a higher point of view, to call for a verdict of his country on the merit of his works, and to claim for him those honours which their excellence appears to deserve.

"In mentioning the circumstance of his humble station, I mean not to rest his pretensions solely on that title, or to urge the merits of his poetry when considered in relation to the lowness of his birth, and the little opportunity of improvement which his education could afford. These particulars, indeed, might excite our wonder at his productions; but his poetry, considered abstractedly, and without the apologies arising from his situation, seems to me fully entitled to

THE EIGHTEENTH-CENTURY ESSAYISTS

command our feelings, and to obtain our applause. One bar, indeed, his birth and education have opposed to his fame, the language in which most of his poems are written. Even in Scotland, the provincial dialect which Ramsay and he have used, is now read with a difficulty which greatly damps the pleasure of the reader: in England it cannot be read at all, without such a constant reference to a glossary, as nearly to destroy that pleasure.

"Some of his productions, however, especially those of the grave style, are almost English. From one of those I shall first present my readers with an extract, in which I think they will discover a high tone of feeling, a power and energy of expression, particularly and strongly characteristic of the mind and the voice of a poet. 'Tis from his poem entitled the *Vision*, in which the genius of his native country, *Ayrshire*, is thus supposed to address him. [Six stanzas are here given.]

"Of strains like these, solemn and sublime, with that rapt and inspired melancholy in which the Poet lifts his eye 'above this visible diurnal sphere,' the poems entitled *Despondency*, the *Lament, Winter: A Dirge*, and the Invocation to *Ruin*, afford no less striking examples. Of the tender and the moral, specimens equally advantageous might be drawn from the elegiac verses entitled *Man was made to Mourn*, from *The Cottar's Saturday Night*, the stanzas *To a Mouse*, or those *To a Mountain-Daisy*, on turning it down with the plough in April 1786.

"I have seldom met with an image more truly pastoral than that of the lark, in the second stanza. Such strokes as these mark the pencil of the poet, which delineates Nature with the precision of intimacy, yet with the delicate colouring of beauty and of taste.

"The power of genius is not less admirable in tracing the manners, than in painting the passions, or in drawing the scenery of Nature. That intuitive glance with which a writer like *Shakespeare* discerns the characters of men, with which he catches the many changing hues of life, forms a sort of problem in the science of mind, of which it is easier to see the truth than to assign the cause. Though I am very far from meaning to compare our rustic bard to Shakespeare, yet whoever will read his lighter and more humorous poems, his *Dialogues of the Dogs*, his *Dedication to G—— H——, Esq.*, his *Epistles to a Young Friend*, and *To W. S——n*, will perceive with what uncommon penetration and sagacity this Heaven-taught ploughman, from his humble and unlettered station, has looked upon men and manners.

"Against some passages of those last-mentioned poems it has been objected that they breathe a spirit of libertinism and irreligion.

EDINBURGH PERIODICAL ESSAYS

But if we consider the ignorance and fanaticism of the lower class of people in the country where these poems were written, a fanaticism of that pernicious sort which sets *faith* in opposition to *good-works*, the fallacy and danger of which, a mind so enlightened as our Poet's could not but perceive; we shall not look upon his lighter Muse as the enemy of religion (of which in several places he expresses the justest sentiments), though she has sometimes been a little unguarded in her ridicule of hypocrisy.

"In this, as in other respects, it must be allowed that there are exceptionable parts of the volume he has given to the public, which caution would have suppressed, or correction struck out; but poets are seldom cautious, and our poet had, alas! no friends or companions from whom correction could be obtained. When we reflect on his rank in life, the habits to which he must have been subject, and the society in which he must have mixed, we regret perhaps more than wonder, that delicacy should be so often offended in perusing a volume in which there is so much to interest and to please us.

"*Burns* possesses the spirit as well as the fancy of a poet. That honest pride and independence of soul which are sometimes the Muse's only dower, break forth on every occasion in his works. It may be, then, I shall wrong his feelings, while I indulge my own, in calling the attention of the public to his situation and circumstances. That condition, humble as it was, in which he found content, and wooed the Muse, might not have been deemed uncomfortable; but grief and misfortunes have reached him there; and one or two of his poems hint, what I have learn't from some of his countrymen, that he has been obliged to form the resolution of leaving his native land, to seek under a West Indian clime that shelter and support which Scotland has denied him. But I trust means may be found to prevent this resolution from taking place; and that I do my country no more than justice, when I suppose her ready to stretch out her hand to cherish and retain this native poet, whose 'wood-notes wild' possess so much excellence. To repair the wrongs of suffering or neglected merit; to call forth genius from the obscurity in which it had pined indignant, and place it where it may profit or delight the world; these are exertions which give to wealth an enviable superiority, to greatness and to patronage a laudable pride."

In the concluding issue of the *Lounger* the authors express the feeling that they will be "happy if any of their number, who shall be pointed out as a writer in the *Mirror* or the *Lounger*, need not blush to avow them as works that endeavoured to "list amusement on the side of taste and to win the manners to decency and to goodness."

These concluding remarks suggest how close the connection is from the moral point of view between Mackenzie's work in the periodical essay and his contributions to contemporary fiction. We have already drawn attention to the connection in the case of Defoe and Fielding between the essay and the novel. And Mackenzie's *Man of Feeling*, *Man of the World*, and *Julia Roubigné* (though in this case *prospective* of his essay work) have most of the characteristics of the *Mirror* and *Lounger*. The same moral purpose animates both; the same didactic method of treatment is present; the same somewhat artificial characters and "personified virtues" are to be found. Mackenzie, in his novels, seems to find it difficult to forget that he is not writing an essay; and the merits which secured for him in the *Mirror* and *Lounger* the success of the latter, render the former ineffective and unreal. Mackenzie's essays are better than his fiction. They come later in time and are more mature in every way.

The *moral* method of the periodical essay is seen in the fictional efforts of other of the essay-writers, in Johnson's *Rasselas*, in Goldsmith's *Vicar of Wakefield*, and in Richard Cumberland's novels and plays. It may be said that this obsession for the "moral purpose" prevailed over literary Europe during the greater part of the eighteenth century, and it was one of the results of the Romantic movement to break these rather artificial conventions, to emphasise the importance of giving the writer freedom in his methods of composition, and to justify the maxim "art for art's sake."

In the same year (1785) in which the *Lounger* was issued, the *Edinburgh Magazine* also appeared. It is said that it was intended to be a rival to the *Scots Magazine*, but instead it was amalgamated with it in the year 1804. Sibbald was the first editor, and he explains the scope of the Journal in the first number. He will give extracts: "to such as are in use to look into the *London Magazine*, with any attention, a judicious selection from them must appear a thing desirable"; and original essays, "for even of them in a city and country famed for learning and taste, the publisher has no reason to apprehend any scarcity." Sir Walter Scott makes mention of Sibbald as " a man of rough manners, but of some taste and judgment who cultivated music and poetry, and in his shop I had a distant view of some literary characters." An account of the first number will give an idea of the scope of the *Edinburgh Magazine*. First come an essay on the universality of the French language, an extract from a biographical sketch of Dr Johnson, and observations on the *Sorrows of Werther*; then follow an essay taken from a London paper, giving the description of a fine gentleman, remarks upon some passages of Shakespeare, and an original essay entitled *Thoughts on Crimes and Punishments*. The ubiquitous Eastern Tale appears; reviews of books; and, in the last section, poetry. The poetry given in the eighteenth-century magazines rarely merits republication, but occasionally burlesque pieces or light snatches of song rise above the average. In the latter class are the clever verses by George Coleman, which appear in the March number of the *Edinburgh Magazine*:

> " If life is a bubble that breaks with a glass,
> You must toss off your wine, if you'd wish it to last ;
> For the bubble may well be destroy'd with a puff,
> If 'tis not kept floating in liquor enough.
>
> If life is a flow'r, as philosophers say,
> 'Tis a very good thing understood the right way ;
> For if life is a flow'r, any blockhead can tell
> If you'd have it look fresh, you must *moisten* it well.
>
> This life is a dream, in which many will weep
> Who have strange silly fancies and cry in their sleep ;
> But of us, when we wake from our dream, 'twill be said
> That the tears of the *Tankard* were all that we shed."

An essay which has exceptional interest is a review of Robert Burns' poetry. It appears in the issue for October (1786). It is thus probably the first review of Burns which we possess, because it was published two months before Mackenzie's paper in the *Lounger*. The writer begins by stating that the author he is going to deal with is entirely unknown : " ' Who are you, Mr Burns ? will some surly critic say. At what university have you been educated? What languages do you understand? What authors have you particularly studied? Whether has Aristotle or Horace directed your taste?' . . . To the questions of such a catechism, perhaps honest Robert Burns would make no satisfactory answers. The author is indeed a striking example of native genius, bursting through the obscurity of poverty and the obstructions of laborious life. Some of his subjects are serious, but those of the humorous kind are the best." Sibbald then quotes Burns' *Address to the De'il*, portions of the *Hallow-e'en* piece, and the *Epistle to a Brother-Bard*. The essay is free in its praise of the poet, and it is said that Burns was very grateful to Sibbald for his favourable review, and sent him a warm letter of thanks. Two months later, in the December issue, Sibbald has the following note:—" Burns' fame is spreading rapidly. We hope, therefore, that few will be displeased with us for giving a place to the following elegant critical essay from the *Lounger* of 9th December 1786 "—and he forthwith reprints Mackenzie's paper on Burns which we have already analysed.

Sibbald retired from the management of the *Edinburgh Magazine* in 1791, the new editor being Dr Robert Anderson, a man of some literary talent. Sir David Brewster was also editor for a year, and then the magazine was amalgamated with the older *Scots Magazine*.

The *Edinburgh Magazine* combined new elements with the old. It was a paper in the old manner, but it gave in addition extracts and more general material. In this way it catered for new and expanding tastes, and forms an excellent contrast to the more clearly defined and limited aims of the *Lounger*, its literary contemporary.

All the periodical essays issued at this time did not attain to the same high literary standard reached by the *Mirror* and *Lounger*. For it is not too much to say that a selection of papers from these two Edinburgh periodicals compares favourably with all but the very best essays of Addison and Steele. But if the quality was awanting in most of the others, there was little or no falling off in the number of periodicals issued. Drake in his work gives a long list of those issued. Many of these had the very

EDINBURGH PERIODICAL ESSAYS

shortest of "lives," and have now dropped absolutely out of knowledge; others are survived by single copies in the British Museum or the Bodleian. We shall give an account of the best of them.

Periodical Essays, the title given to a weekly paper published in 1780, is interesting from the manner in which the author proposes to conduct it. "'In the manner of the *Spectators*' is," he writes, "a definition by custom, annexed to every publication of didactic essays, which come forth at weekly or shorter periods; but exact imitation, even of that which is itself faultless and delightful, must become, by frequent repetition, tedious and disgustful (*sic*)." Here is a statement notable not only for the history of the essay periodical, but for literary criticism at large. There is a restlessness evident, a discontent against the eighteenth-century standards and conventions which herald the approaching Romanticism of the nineteenth. But in his practice the writer is not quite so fortunate in his efforts to avoid the Addisonian manner and *régime*. He hopes to give variety first of all by "greater excursions into the regions of pure philosophy and religion"; in the second place he will "solicit no favours from correspondents"; and in the third instance he will not confine himself "to the custom of prefixing a motto to every paper." His list of variations is a meagre one, and he confesses that it will be no easy task to prevent mortifying comparison with Addison, Steele, or Johnson. His actual literary production is indeed small and unimportant, but the periodical has interest because it shows that the sameness and monotony of the periodicals were going by reaction from them to produce changes in the scope of the essay periodical.

The *Scourge* is another periodical published weekly in the same year. As the title serves to indicate, the author does not spare the lash; and attacks even individual members of Parliament. For example, the Lord Advocate for Scotland is virulently abused (No. 16), and in the following number he widens his attack to include everything Scottish:

"Scotish wars, Scotish Generals,
    Scots butchers, Scotify'd councils,
    Scotian usurpations, evils accursed."

THE EIGHTEENTH-CENTURY ESSAYISTS

Though the essays are written in a vigorous manner, they are purely political in tone, and apart from their directness of style they possess little literary interest.

Of more account is the *New Spectator, with the sage opinions of John Bull* (1784). The motto is a beautiful extract from one of Pliny's *Epistles*: " As in a man's life, so in his literary pursuits, I think it the most beautiful and humane thing in the world so to mingle gravity with pleasantry, that the one may not sink into melancholy, nor the other rise up to wantonness," and in the first number the author, discussing his aims and objects, refers to the *Spectator*. He has named his periodical the *New Spectator* because he laments the present degradation of the essay periodical, and hopes to raise it again to something akin to the perfection to which Addison had brought it. The *eidola* are retained in the shape of his friend *John Bull*, whose opinions he will publish, and *John Bull's* sister, *Ann Maria Bull*. The second number includes an essay on the " divine madness " of poets and heroes, while the section under *John Bull* gives news of the theatre and general news of the town. The variety of subjects recalls the *Spectator* also—prejudice and passion (No. 3), fashion in literature (No. 4), duelling (No. 5), life and conduct (No. 6), temperance in diet (No. 14), and the art of puffing (No. 16), while the prevalence of sentimentalism in the novels of the period are strongly satirised in two well-written papers.

As an example of the style of the *New Spectator*, take the following extract from the essay in the third number, where the subject under discussion is female dress :—

" The most provoking circumstance attending the life of a lady of taste is the impudence of the vulgar in presuming to adopt her dress, and render it common before she has shown it to half the town. I have sometimes been amazed that these patronesses of taste and fashion in female dress, the Duchesses of Devonshire and Rutland, never procured his Majesty's ' Royal Letters Patent,' for the exclusive privilege of wearing, appearing in, and exposing to admiration certain dresses, by them the said Duchesses first invented, formed, fashioned, and worn—for in such words, or in words similar to those, doubtless said Patent would run.

" Ladies of distinction have, at last, procured a dress, which cannot easily be adopted by their inferiors; it is too expensive, and indeed too stately for daily exhibition. The body consists of black velvet, the train of white crape, and the petticoat of pink satin. The head is adorned not only with feathers, but with crimp feathers, and it is a happy circumstance, in these times of scarcity, that a lady of fashion may procure a cap fit to be seen in, at the reasonable price of four guineas.

"Balloon hats now adorn the heads of such of the parading impures as can afford them, whilst the more inferior tribe have invented a hat which is not improperly called the bastard balloon—being a humble imitation of the green box balloon, and destitute of feathers. These balloon fashions, I believe, are about their zenith, and must soon burst, and be forgotten!

"I am sorry to observe that the sash has its retainers, even in the depth of winter; but some ladies think they never can appear too airy, and perhaps deem the sash a necessary appendage to the balloon hat. Be that as it may, I cannot but look on the sash, now, as no bad resemblance of a label to a phial of physic, containing directions how to take it. Indeed, if anything were to be inscribed on the sashes of those ladies who *now* wear them, surely nothing could be more apposite than the words—'To be let to the best bidder.' But I believe the sign is pretty generally understood, without the inscription."

The imitation in manner and style of the *Tatler* and *Spectator* essays is obvious, but considerable success in that "sincerest form of flattery" has been attained by the writer.

The *New Spectator* came to an end with the twenty-fifth number, and in it the author gives his farewell. He refers to the unpopularity of his paper, and gives what he thinks is the reason for it. Like the *Rambler*, in his reaction against the more frivolous periodicals, he has been rather heavy and serious. "I admitted not a single article in these papers that could tend to ridicule religion, or to palliate infamy. For this cause, I have not been so general a favourite with the public as I might have been; as he who reproves, is never so welcome as he who flatters."

The *New Spectator* deserves *honourable mention* as an attempt to stem the current which was carrying so many of those minor periodicals of the second half of the century to oblivion.

CHAPTER IX

THE *OBSERVER*, AND *LOOKER-ON*, AND OTHERS

We include in this chapter a discussion of two essay periodicals which are known to the majority of people, because they have been rescued from the waters of oblivion which have overwhelmed so many others of a similar kind. This has been accomplished because they appear in the well-known series of *British Essayists*. The *Observer* was written entirely by one man, Richard Cumberland, a popular writer of plays; and his collection of over one hundred and fifty essays makes a creditable total.

Cumberland was descended from a "philosophic" stock. He had done a good deal of literary work of various kinds, and obtained the doubtful honour of being caricatured in Sheridan's the *Critic*, but he did not always realise the true spirit of the essay kind in his periodical work. It is surprising he obtained any public to read his papers, especially those towards the close, which are all on subjects concerned with Greek literature. In the first number, Cumberland says that his first wish is to follow in the footsteps of Addison, but with an addition: "I have endeavoured to relieve and chequer these familiar essays in a manner that I hope will be approved of; I allude to these papers in which I treat of the literature of the Greeks, carrying down my history in a chain of anecdotes from the earliest poets to the death of Menander." He claims this plan of an exposition of Greek literature as a new one. It is certainly new, and he executes it with great thoroughness, but it is another question whether the scheme could be carried through with propriety in a paper which professed to follow the *Spectator* standard. His initial papers, however, closely follow the Addisonian scheme. He describes the

THE OBSERVER AND OTHER PERIODICALS

Sect of Dampers (No. 2), common in Society at all times; various instances of love of praise (No. 3); and the characters of *Sir Theodore* and *Lady Thimble* (No. 4). This worthy couple reappear once or twice, as also *Mr Jedediah Fish*, a teacher of the *Art of Hearing* (No. 26). At a dinner given in the house of the Baronet (No. 5), the arguments of an infidel against the miracles Christ performed are given, the same subject being continued later (Nos. 10 and 11). The Addisonian manner is continued on the subject of divorce (No. 13), with rules ironically proposed for the further propagation and encouragement of divorce. Stories are also given, two of the best being the tragic tale of *Abdullah and Quarima* (No. 14), and the story of *Geminus and Gemellus* (No. 37); while a third is continued through four numbers. Cumberland also had considerable skill in character-drawing, as e.g. *Vanessa and Leontine*, and he gives also an impressive diary of a misanthrope. His best attempt at character-drawing is in the one hundred and ninth number, where he sketches the humours and characters of a county town. A portion of this paper will suffice to indicate the satire and humour of Cumberland as an essayist :

"The humours and characters of a populous county town at a distance from the capital, furnish matter of much amusement to a curious observer. I have now been some weeks resident in a place of this description, where I have been continually treated with the private lives and little scandalising anecdotes of almost every person of any note in it. Having passed most of my days in the capital, I could not but remark the striking difference between it and these subordinate capitals in this particular : in London we are in the habit of looking to our own affairs, and caring little about those, with whom we have no dealings : here everybody's business seems to be no less his neighbour's concerns than his own : a set of tattling gossips (including all the idlers in the place, male as well as female) seem to have no other employment for their time or tongue, but to run from house to house, and circulate their silly stories up and down. A few of these contemptible impertinents I shall now describe.

"Miss Penelope Tabby is an antiquated maiden of at least forty years standing, a great observer of decorum, and particularly hurt by the behaviour of two young ladies, who are her next door neighbours, for a custom they have of lolling out of their windows and talking to fellows in the street: the charge cannot be denied, for it is certainly a practice, these young ladies indulge themselves in very freely; but on the other hand it must be owned Miss Pen Tabby is also in the habit of lolling out of her window at the same time to stare at them, and put them to shame for the levity of their conduct: they have also the crime proved upon them of being unpardonably handsome, and this they neither can nor will attempt to contradict. Miss Pen Tabby is extremely regular at morning prayers, but she complains heavily of a young staring fellow in the pew next to her own, who violates the solemnity of the service by ogling her at her devotions: he has a way of leaning over the pew and dangling a white hand ornamented with a flaming paste-ring, which sometimes plays the lights in her eyes, so as to make them water with the reflection, and Miss Pen has this very natural remark ever ready on the occasion, 'Such things, you know, are apt to take off one's attention.'

"Another of this illustrious junto is Billy Bachelor, an old unmarried *petit-maître*: Billy is a courtier of ancient standing; he abounds in anecdotes not of the freshest date, nor altogether of the most interesting sort; for he will tell you how such and such a lady was dressed, when he had the honour of handing her into the drawing-room: he has a Court-Atalantis of his own, from which he can favour you with some hints of sly doings amongst the maids of honour, particularly of a certain dubious duchess now deceased (for he names no names) who appeared at a certain masquerade *in puris naturalibus*, and other valuable discoveries, which all the world has long ago known, and long ago been tired of. Billy has a smattering in the fine arts, for he can net purses, and make admirable coffee, and write sonnets; he has the best receipt in nature for a dentifrice, which he makes up with his own hands, and gives to such ladies as are in his favour, and have an even row of teeth: he can boast some skill in music, for he plays Barberini's minuet to admiration, and accompanies the airs in the *Beggars' Opera* on his flute in their original taste; he is also a playhouse critic of no mean pretensions, for he remembers Mrs Woffington, and Quin, and Mrs Cibber; and when the players come to town, Billy is greatly looked up to, and has been known to lead a clap, where nobody but himself could find a reason for clapping at all. When his vanity is in the cue, Billy Bachelor can talk to you of his amours, and upon occasion stretch the truth to save his credit: particularly in accounting for a certain old lameness in his knee-pan, which some, who are in the secret, know was got by being kicked out of a coffee-house, but which to the world at large he asserts was incurred by leaping

THE OBSERVER AND OTHER PERIODICALS

out of a window to save a lady's reputation, and escape the fury of an enraged husband.

"Dr Pyeball is a dignitary of the church, and a mighty proficient in the *belles-lettres* : he tells you Voltaire was a man of some fancy and had a knack of writing, but he bids you beware of his principles, and doubts if he had any more Christianity than Pontius Pilate : he has wrote an epigram against a certain contemporary historian, which cuts him up at a stroke. By a happy jargon of professional phrases, with a kind of Socratic mode of arguing, he has so bamboozled the dons of the cathedral as to have effected a total revolution in their church music, making Purcell, Crofts, and Handel give place to a quaint, quirkish style, little less capricious than if the organist was to play cotillions, and the dean and chapter dance to them. The doctor is a mighty admirer of those ingenious publications, which are intitled *The Flowers* of the several authors they are selected from : this short cut to Parnassus not only saves him a great deal of roundabout riding, but supplies him with many an apt couplet for off-hand quotations, in which he is very expert, and has besides a clever knack of weaving them into his pulpit essays (for I will not call them sermons) in much the same way as 'Tiddy-Doll stuck *plums* on his short pigs and his long pigs and his pigs with a curley tail.' By a proper sprinkling of these spiritual nosegays, and the recommendation of a soft insinuating address, Doctor Pyeball is universally cried up as a very pretty genteel preacher, one who understands the politeness of the pulpit, and does not surfeit wellbred people with more religion than they have stomachs for. Amiable Miss Pen Tabby is one of the warmest admirers, and declares Doctor Pyeball in his gown and cassock is quite the man of fashion : the ill-natured world will have it she has contemplated him in other situations with equal approbation.

"Elegant Mrs Dainty is another ornament of this charming coterie : she is separated from her husband, but the eye of malice never spied a speck upon her virtue ; his manners were insupportable, she, good lady, never gave him the least provocation, for she was always sick and mostly confined to her chamber in nursing a delicate constitution : noises racked her head, company shook her nerves all to pieces ; in the country she could not live, for country doctors and apothecaries knew nothing of her case : in London she could not sleep, unless the whole street was littered with straw. Her husband was a man of no refinement ; 'all the fine feelings of the human heart' were heathen Greek to him ; he loved his friend, had no quarrel with his bottle, and, coming from his club one night a little flustered, his horrid dalliances threw Mrs Dainty into strong hysterics, and the covenanted truce being now broken, she kept no further terms with him, and they separated. It was a step of absolute necessity, for she declares her life could not otherwise have been saved; his boisterous familiarities would have been her death. She now leads an uncontaminated life, supporting a feeble frame by medicine, sipping her tea with her dear quiet friends, every evening, chatting over the little news of the day, sighing charitably when she hears any evil of her kind neighbours, turning off her *femme de chambre* once a week or thereabouts, fondling her lap-dog, who is a dear sweet pretty creature, and so sensible, and taking the air now and then on a pillion behind faithful John, who is so careful of her and so handy, and at the same time one of the stoutest, handsomest, best-limbed lads in all England."

Gradually, however, Cumberland ceased to draw upon such miscellaneous subjects for his papers, and the last forty numbers are devoted to discussions of the Greek poets from Homer to Æschylus and Menander—discussions of some merit indeed, in their own style, but tending to dullness and not suitable for the pages of an essay periodical. Now and again he shows a sound critical judgment: for example, he does the greatness of Æschylus full justice; and he has a good paper in a lighter vein, giving an account of a critic's criticism of *Othello*. Another drawback to the *Observer* is the single authorship. Only a genius can compose a series of this nature single-handed with entire success, and Cumberland had talent, not genius. Even Addison, who wrote almost the whole of the last volume of the *Spectator*, is not entirely free from this censure. Nor was Johnson's *Rambler* a success from this point of view; though Thackeray's ripe genius made the *Roundabout Papers* carried on by himself in the *Cornhill* the complete success they are.

It is significant of the interest taken in different quarters in the essayists to find an association of five school boys at Eton, in 1786, endeavouring to emulate the achievements of Addison and Steele in a periodical they named the *Microcosm*, as representing their small school-world. The first number was issued on Monday, 6th November, and they sent out copies from the school every Monday till 30th July 1787. These schoolboy essays possess both quality and vigour. The "editor" is *Gregory Griffin, Esq.*, and his aim is enunciated in the opening number : " Thus, then, I, Gregory Griffin, sally forth in this *our* lesser world, to pluck up by the roots the more trifling follies, and cherish the opening buds of rising merit." Forty numbers of the *Microcosm* were issued, the last closing with *Gregory Griffin's* death, last Will and Testament, in which he is made to bequeath all his belongings to the five schoolboys who have run the paper. The *Spectator* plan has been closely followed by the young men, as the subjects show : on *Swearing* (No. 2) ; *A Diary of Narcissus* (No. 3) ; *A Dead Lounger*, closely modelled on a similar paper in the *Spectator* ; and on *The Love of Fame* (No. 4). Even literary criticism " of sorts " appears. Poetry in its position as a universal language is considered ; Blackmore is satirised ; Chaucer, Dryden, and Pope are mentioned ; and novel and romance writing are discussed. *Tom Jones* and *Sir Charles Grandison*, for example, are compared and contrasted, and Newbery's *Little Books* are recommended as preferable to novels. It would scarcely be just to judge this periodical by the standard of the best work of *Addison* and *Steele*, but it has an interest besides the purely literary one. Everyone knows the saying of the Duke of Wellington, that " the battle of Waterloo was won on the playing-fields of Eton," and in the literary sphere it cannot be doubted that the *Microcosm*, also from Eton, stimulated the intellect and powers of expression of the youthful writers. That this was actually the case is sufficiently evident from the fact that Canning was one of the contributors to this boys' magazine. If Eton can still publish a magazine equal to the *Microcosm*, it has nothing to be ashamed of. And the idea in the schoolboy world had apparently caught on, because a second periodical of a similar nature was published two years later at Westminster School. This was the *Trifler* (1788). A note by a former owner of the copy examined is as follows :—" The *Trifler* was written at Westminster School by Mr Aston (now Lord Aston), Mr Upton, Mr Slade, and Mr Taunton (now Justice Taunton)." Like the contributors to the Eton *Microcosm*, apparently more than one of the writers rose to place and position in later life. The *Trifler* is called " a new periodical miscellany by *Timothy Touchstone* of St Peter's College, Westminster." A line from Persius is quoted as the motto: " Scribimus inclusi numeros ille, hic pede liber," which is cleverly rendered into English :

> " Pent in our lonely college, we compose
> *Some* measured numbers, *some* unfettered prose."

In the introductory essay the " editor," *Timothy Touchstone*, says he is only a schoolboy, but wishes to follow in the footsteps of the *Connoisseur* : " In order that my essays may be more likely to please the variegated geniuses of my readers, I shall endeavour to catch ' the flying Cynthia of the moment '—essays and elegies, prose and poetry, will alternately succeed each other, through all the mazes of periodical confusion." Forty-three numbers of the *Trifler* appeared. The subjects discussed are the familiar ones: A Vision of the Temple of Judgment (No. 4), into which the author passes and presents with trembling hands his first *Trifler* (which is well received); on Happiness (No. 15); on Prejudice (No. 17); on the Influence of Fashion on Hair-dressing (No. 20); on the Art of Life (No. 41); on Debating Societies (No. 28); and on the Beauties of Homer (No. 29). The essay on Homer presents some sound criticism. Take this passage, for example : " There is, perhaps, no prettier character in the whole of Homer's works than that of Nausicaa in the *Odyssey*; she is beautiful, courteous, and kind in her behaviour to the wretched Ulysses as ever man could desire. The character of Nausicaa, like that of Sarpedon in the *Iliad*, has but one fault, and that is, it is too short." The *Trifler* closes with an appropriate touch of humour. If

> " The cloud-capt towers, the gorgeous palaces,
> The solemn temples, the great globe itself,
> Yea, all which it inherits, shall dissolve,"

" how can the *Trifler* hope to escape a fate common to all the labours of human industry ? Time which subdues all things has, at length, put a period to the efforts of *Timothy Touchstone*." The *Trifler* is a most successful attempt,

THE OBSERVER AND OTHER PERIODICALS

and compares favourably with the *Microcosm*. But the latter has the credit of being the first in point of time.

The *Pharos* (1786) has special interest, because the essays are from the pen of a lady, the authoress of a little-known novel, *Constance*. Fifty papers in all were published, and they were afterwards issued in book form in a two-volume edition. The opening essay follows the manner which had now become fixed and traditional, but several fresh features are introduced:

" The writer of a periodical paper is officially a censor of public manners, and as such, is frequently more the object of dread than of love; he is considered as incessantly purveying for his work, sagacious in discovery and industrious in noting obliquities of character, and when once known, is shunned as a spy and informer. For this reason, and that he may not defeat his purpose of observation by freezing his beholders into petrifaction, concealment is necessary to an author of this class; he must envelop himself in eternal shades, unless his labours effect that stupendous change in the human heart which shall incline it to love what is painful to suffer. The *Pharos*, everyone knows, is nothing more nor less than a lighthouse, whose benefits are chiefly calculated for the service of the sailor; its flame is intended to warn him from the shoal and the rock; and thus, with his super-added knowledge, it proves a guide to safe anchorage, or contributes to the safety of his voyage. In life, a friendly monitor of this kind is no less useful; few, who compare the world to a sea, feign it a pacific ocean, it is by its best friends acknowledged not only exposed to the storm, but likewise to every danger of the deep; whirlpools, quicksands, promontories, and shallows, perpetually oppose the voyager's way; and miserable indeed is he if deprived of light and warning. In one particular I confess my work resembles not a *Pharos*. It is not placed in a conspicuous situation; consequently, the orbit of its rays will be much confined. But let this be no discouragement; it pretends to illuminate no boundless ocean, but its light may be seen timely enough, to avoid every danger it intimates. It will instruct all who, in a steady endeavour after safety, appeal to its power; for however partially it may direct its flame, or however dimly it may burn, still shall be visible to the mariner this important monition, that he can no longer hope for security than while he sails by the chart of Scripture, and the compass of reason. towards that new undiscovered country, where all his labours shall end, and a final remuneration awaits him. But as in one particular, I own my *Pharos* deficient,

THE EIGHTEENTH-CENTURY ESSAYISTS

so in another I hope it will excel its archetype; its light shall be to none terrific. I cannot promise it will ever blaze into admirable brightness, nor that I can always observe more than a lambent flame; but a friend of mine, a very ingenious artist, has promised occasionally to amuse the beholders with a few coruscations, which, if well-timed and applied, may obliterate, or obtain toleration for, any natural defects in my edifice.

"The method by which I shall endeavour to serve those who resort to my light for counsel, will not be always the same. In some cases it may be most useful to render the dangerous body luminous; in others, I may do more good by directing a few rays to the shipwrecked vessel or mariner. To him or his vessel will always be found attached a scroll containing a history of his fate, an attentive perusal of which is all the impost I exact. Sometimes I shall warn, by pointing out the errors of other voyagers, who still vainly beat the waves; and sometimes shall endeavour to make manifest to those I guide, that no nautical skill, nor the best applied exertion, can aid them if they steer towards an uninhabited port."

The way in which these intentions are carried out is creditable to the writer. The subjects are varied, and special attention is paid (naturally enough) to pictures of female life and manners. Considerable life animates the descriptions, and the style throughout, as the extract given above illustrates, is clear, simple, and direct. The *Pharos* is above the average in merit. By the last quarter of the century another difficulty presented itself to authors. So many titles had been employed that it was not easy to find a new one. This difficulty is exemplified in the whimsical title used for a periodical published in 1786—the *Devil*— by a *Society of Gentlemen*. The introductory essay is most amusing. The author represents himself as having sunk into a fit of dejection inducing despair so deep that he was on the point of hanging himself: "When through the medium of a dim taper, that cast a doubtful glimmer round me, I saw, or fancied I saw, a decent-looking gentleman in black approaching me; nor had I the power of recalling my scattered recollections to my assistance, ere he relieved me from my consternation, by saying, in a tone of great sweetness and complacency, 'I am the Devil.'" In an interesting conversation they settle down to a discussion of all subjects, literature and the periodical press! "I told

THE OBSERVER AND OTHER PERIODICALS

him I had some thoughts, in conjunction with a set of literary gentlemen, to carry into execution my design of a weekly paper, in the manner of the *Spectator*. 'The *Spectator*!' exclaimed the devil, 'if you could have the assistance of Addison and all his friends, with the united abilities of all the ancients and moderns, you would not sell a hundred in a year. The *Spectator* in this age! No; if you would sell your work otherwise than by weight, take care to have enough in it of the *Devil*.' So saying, he departed, but in what manner I was too much in a state of deep reflection to notice."

In the essays which are thus strangely introduced the members of the Club are described, and letters of advice from the *Devil* himself given. Poetry is not forgotten. Political essays (usually brought forward as *visions*) by Mr Torpedo, one of the members of the Club, also occur. Stories of the sentimental kind, of which the best are *Heraclitus* and the *Fountain of Tears*, are not infrequent; also letters and dramatic criticisms. An example of the humour of this paper may be instanced in the advertisement for a wife by a young man rather bare of cash. At the end of the advertisement the following postscript is added: "*P.S.*—There is one trifling circumstance which was very nearly forgotten, but very proper to be mentioned here, which is, that it will be necessary that the lady should have a fortune of at least £10,000. The Advertiser will explain his present bareness of cash the day after marriage."

The *Devil*, paradoxical as it seems, is both bright and amusing. Of a more miscellaneous nature than either the *Tatler* or the *Spectator*, it was very popular at the time of its issue, though now completely forgotten.

The *Devil's Pocket Book*, published in the same year, was in all probability by the same author. The issues are smaller, and possess more unity.

The aim of the *Devil's Pocket Book* is given: "To delineate men and manners with the pencil of impartiality." The stories are usually translations from the French, and are of a sentimental kind, as the titles indicate: *The Loves of Ademar and Marianne* and *The Blind Man and his Daughter*. The answers to correspondents are sometimes of interest, but the paper is of a slighter nature, and less remarkable for its vigour than the *Devil*.

The *Busybody* (1787) did not display so much originality as the *Devil*, with regard to its title, for the name *Busybody* had already been made use of. The author, Mr Oulton, in his opening essay, defends the freedom which periodical essayists have hitherto been privileged to employ. Only people " who may justly apprehend the exposition of their own frailties " take exception to this freedom, and he expands into doubtful verse:

> " My pen's my own, my will is pure,
> And so shall be my thoughts;
> No mortal man shall hide from me,
> I'll find out all his faults."

The various branches of the family of busybodies are passed under review; the silly busybody, the mischievous busybody, the impertinent busybody, and the harmless busybody—while the author is the *good Busybody*, holding (in the old phrase) the mirror up to nature. Oulton's wit is often very keen. This is exemplified in the second paper on *The Art of Puffing*, and in the following essay, where he discusses slips in grammar, mentioning such solecisms as: " Says I," and " you was "; and mispronunciations, e.g. *tower* for *tour*. " A gentleman informed me that he had made a ' tower ' all over Italy. ' Indeed,' added I, ' your building must have been very extensive.' " Oulton continues the attempts of Swift, made more than fifty years before, to correct and dignify the language. A feature of these papers is that Oulton concludes a number of them with a little piece of verse (usually octosyllabic), in this way recalling Cowley's practice in the century previous.

An interesting essay is one on critics and criticism (No. 11). Oulton quotes Churchill's lines beginning:

> " A critic was of old a glorious name,"

and proceeds to describe the varieties of critics—first the severe critic who is never pleased at anything, an English *Pococurante*; then the learned critic, the ignorant critic, the officious critic, and lastly the *honest* critic. Of the *honest* critic he makes the sound and sensible statements that: "He should always lean to the merciful side, and instead of looking out for faults, examine the beauties of a work. He should also read a work *twice* before he gives his opinion, for there are things will escape his notice on the first perusal, that will strike the reader in the second."

In an amusing article on female education (No. 15) he relates how a gentleman in search of a girls' school found one with the following inscription:—" Laydies tought to reed and rite"; and going into the building, he interviewed the old lady, who told him, " Oh, yes, sir, I *educates* young ladies, and *teaches* English, French, and all *that their* most grammatically, I assure you, sir!" The essay implies a poor standard of education in the boarding-schools of Oulton's day.

Witty illustrations (No. 22) are given on how to write a comedy, a tragedy, an opera, and a novel. Take the instructions for writing *an elegant novel*:

"Letters are very pretty, and though we are to suppose this comes from *Eliza* to *Harriet*, that from *Lord B.* to *Captain F.*, there is no occasion for a variegated style, for anyone knows they are written by the same author. But as letters are so very hackneyed, let chapters now and then be introduced, especially those with comical heads, Chapter I. being the introduction, Chapter II. *very necessary to be read*, and Chapter III. *may or may not be*, etc. I know several novels of this sort, and vow and protest the heads had more merit than either the *body* or the *tail*. In about the middle of the first volume, let a duel commence; the lover must get a wound, and be given over at the conclusion; the reader is then left in suspense; when the lover has wonderfully recovered, if you wish to make a volume extraordinary, he may relapse. Let the poor young lady in the work defend her virtue two or three times, not with a dagger or knife—they are too common—a pair of *scissors* or a *corkscrew*. As to the language, you may either adopt simple or sublime, the latter preferably—*joyful bliss* or *blissful joy*, *kind benevolence* or *benevolent kindness*, etc., and similar epithets constituting modern sublimity."

These remarks seemed to be aimed against the author of *Pamela*.

In the last number (No. 25) Oulton gives a reason for

concluding so abruptly. He tells the story of a young minister who preached his first sermon upon the text, *Be ye therefore perfect*, and spoke as follows :—" I have two things to put before you, brethren : firstly, to be perfect is to be good ; and, secondly, to be good is to be happy. Be ye therefore perfect that ye may be happy in heaven." The young clergyman repeated this short discourse two or three Sundays. At last he was rebuked for the brevity and repetition of his sermon. " Sir " (says he), " a few words are easier remembered than a great many, and till I see that this discourse has in some measure *perfected* my flock, I do not mean to give another." And Oulton draws the conclusion that he has given enough in *his* essays for the public to ruminate over. The essays were afterwards published in two neat little volumes, and had a fair circulation.

Oulton's *Busybody* is much superior to the average periodical of the decade under review, and the author has command of a vigorous style which helped to animate the familiar subjects with which he dealt.

Olla Podrida, of the same year as the *Busybody* (1787), is not quite so good. Its author, a Mr Munro, Master of Arts of Oxford University, supplies the usual introductory statements in the first number. Like Steele, he will devote papers to the ladies, and other subjects will not be forgotten. Munro obtained help from friends, mostly in Oxford, and the essays offer considerable variety. In the second number Munro supports the view of Warton in the *Adventurer*, and prefers the *Odyssey* to the *Iliad* as a reading book in Greek for boys at school. The inglorious fate of books and authors is lamented in terms which recall some of Martial's epigrams and Horace's *Satires* and *Epistles*. Rules for conversation are given ; while laughter, dress, newspapers, and drunkenness are amongst the subjects of the essayists. A paper on *The dangerous tendency of Modern Novels* condemns novels as " utterly subversive of common sense, and not very warm friends to common honesty." One story is attempted, called the *Vicar's Tale*, which runs through three numbers. It is a rather sentimental domestic narrative. *Olla Podrida* concluded with the forty-fourth number, and it is a rather commonplace attempt to infuse life into a form which was rapidly outliving its use and popularity.

Three essay periodicals published in the year 1790 call for notice, because each presents a special feature of interest. The first of the trio bears a familiar title. The *Bee* is a name which Goldsmith had made famous in the literary history of the eighteenth century, and the title was used again for an Edinburgh periodical. The author was Mr James Anderson, LL.D. In the first number Anderson discusses the advantages of periodical essays, their variety and their aim. But this ground had already been well covered by earlier writers, and he has little new to say. An interesting essay is that on *Poetry*, because he introduces *The Flowers of the Forest*. In rather grandiloquent style he writes: "Poetry is indeed so congenial to the human mind that it has been, among all nations, the first species of composition that has attracted the universal attention of the people; and it is in the language of poetry that a spirit of devotion has naturally been expressed." He then gives *The Flowers of the Forest*:

> "I've heard a lilting at the ewes milking
> Lasses a' lilting before the break o' day," etc.

In doing so he prints the lines widely apart and inserts explanatory words: *have* under I've, a note to explain the word *lilting*, *all* under a', *of* under o', and so on. This evidently was for the benefit of his English readers, and he hoped in this way to popularise the poetry of Scotland in the South. In addition to stories of the *Spectator* type, articles of a more miscellaneous type appear, and the interest of the *Bee* lies in the fact that it is another example of the periodicals which were gradually preparing the way for the modern nineteenth-century magazine.

The second of the three periodicals referred to is the *Speculator*, and its special interest lies in the fact that it was mainly produced by Nathan Drake, with the assistance of another gentleman. Drake made in his lifetime a special study of the periodical essays of the eighteenth century, and published lives of Addison and Steele and essays

THE EIGHTEENTH-CENTURY ESSAYISTS

illustrative of the *Tatler* and *Spectator* and *Rambler* and others. His work, published more than a century ago, though it requires modification and addition and correction, remains still the only extensive critical material we possess on the subject under review. What shape therefore did he himself make at the periodical essay? The first number of the *Speculator* appeared on 27th March 1790, and the twenty-sixth and last on 22nd June of the same year. Drake afterwards republished these *Speculator* essays in an enlarged edition in *Literary Hours*. The introductory number presents the reader with a sketch of the habits and frame of mind of the *Speculator*: " Life and letters will be the objects of his attention. To those who, amidst the bustle of the world, can watch the fleeting influence of fashion on the ever-changing scene of manners, the task is left to catch the shifting colours as they appear, and instruct the world, by faithful pictures of the nicer features of the times. Lineaments of life more broad and general, an outlook more free and comprehensive of these motives which influence the characters of men, are more adapted to the pencil of a retired *Speculator*. Variety will not be wanting; the precept, which is tedious in a formal way, may acquire attractions in a tale, and the sober shades of truth be divested of their austerity by the graces of innocent fiction." It will be seen that Drake follows closely the aim and method of the periodicals which he knew so well. The papers are on the whole good, but rather heavy and formal in style, and as a rule longer than the average *Spectator* essays. Mention may be made of a group of papers on literary criticism, with special reference to the state of belles-lettres in Germany. Schiller is styled the Æschylus of the German drama, and Klopstock and Wieland are brought to the notice of his readers. This group of critical essays is the outstanding feature of the *Speculator*. In other respects Drake does nothing to break the sequence of the tradition for these essay periodicals.

The third periodical of this group has special interest because of the picture it draws of the state of the periodical essay at the forefront of the last decade of the century. These are the *Winter Evenings, or Lucubrations on Life and*

THE OBSERVER AND OTHER PERIODICALS

Letters of Vicesimus Knox. To be perfectly accurate, these are not periodical essays in the sense that each one was published separately at stated intervals; they were issued together, but the forty essays which they comprise are exactly of the same type and character as the periodical essays, and Knox evidently regards them as such. The first essay attractively presents the advantages of the ingle-nook in winter, and the transporting power of a good book, and the succeeding papers discuss wit and humour, the dress of ladies, friendship and avarice. These are still the usual subjects for the essayist. But the eleventh number on the *Character of Dr Johnson* makes interesting reference to the abuse of biography and laments the *searchlight* method which panders to "the mere gratification of an impertinent, not to say, a malignant curiosity." In a later essay Knox criticises Dr Johnson's style and compares it with Sir Thomas Browne's, and gives extracts from the *Vulgar Errors* in support of his views. But in the third essay, in which he discusses the common features of periodical essays, he reflects a view which we have already noted had been becoming increasingly common. He says that everything has been tried to sugar the moral—Allegories, Diaries, Eastern Tales, Little Novels, Letters from Correspondents, Humour, Irony, Argument, and Declamation, but all have been repeated *ad nauseam* and have become threadbare and ineffective. He wishes a miscellany without these *useless ornaments*, which have lost their effectiveness by reason of constant repetition. They can no longer surprise and amuse the reader, who instantly recognises and is bored by the familiar subjects, and is tempted to throw the essay aside as yielding him no entertainment. Knox in his own essays does not, however, despise these *useless ornaments* —but this by the way. The importance of his statement is that the essay periodical with its stubborn conservatism was outliving its attractiveness and use; it was losing its vital power, and a fresh start was soon to be found necessary. The literary devices employed, the rather artificial framework, the visions and allegories had to give place to the fresh, new, varied, and vigorous modern magazine. It was only a combination of men of talent, or some lucky chance

THE EIGHTEENTH-CENTURY ESSAYISTS

or circumstance which made the periodical essay successful in its later career.

Perhaps it was due to the operation of the latter factor which has preserved for us the *Looker-on* of Roberts. It is the last on the list of the *British Essayists*, and fills four neat little volumes. Roberts, who was a Fellow of Christ Church College, Oxford, writes under the pseudonym of the *Rev. Simon Olive-branch*, and in the general introduction which he wrote to the essays in collected form he gives an interesting if pessimistic picture of the state of the country, plunged as it was in the wars of that restless period. " Of the effects of war very different accounts may be given. In former times, ere funding systems were thought of, war brought only its immediate evils. Quarrels between states were the means of a circulation of treasure which peace had accumulated, and supplied, in some measure, the want of commerce; in modern times it proceeds by an anticipation of resource and contrives that future generations, though no sharers in its iniquity, shall yet be visited with its worst effects. There cannot be imagined an era more destructive than the present, of the arts and polite literature. In the midst of times that are but too much calculated to repress the growth of genius, by the spirit of profligacy that prevails and by a distraction of mean pursuits in social life, that enervates the force of every generous sentiment, there has sprung up a wasting war, founded in an irreconcilable strife of opinion, and interwoven with so many domestic wrongs and animosities, as to disclose no prospects of permanent peace to Europe, till the pride of ancestry and the ties of blood are forgotten. Yet in the midst of these national sorrows, luxury and debauchery are nowhere checked in their career; but are become, by the crooked chicane of modern policy, a great and standing source of revenue. The English go sullenly on in their wasteful pleasures, and gild their despondency with unremitted profusion. Almost converted, by the recurrence of public loans, into a nation of annuitants, they all rush to the capital whence their incomes arise, which, by its present injurious plan of extension, promises to become the universal mart of vicious profusion." How true some of these remarks read in the light of the great European War of 1914, how gloriously untrue some of the others. But Roberts feels that at such a time essays such as his will not gain a large audience.

The first number of the *Looker-on* opens in the accustomed manner with an account of the writer, *Sir Simon Olive-branch* : " I am an old man, whose best years have been employed less in the service than the survey of my fellow-creatures. It has been with me as it fares with most of us ; the season of action was spent in speculation, and in harbouring up wise resolutions to be executed by-and-by. The by and by is a sort of phantom which seduces us on till we drop into old age ; and upon the first serious attack of the gout it vanishes for ever, and carries along with it all our gay projects and cherishing hopes. Thus a youth of expectation is sure to prepare an old age of regret : especially if, under favour of these holiday resolutions and speculative atonements, we think we may fairly contract a few debts to virtue, and intrust a little upon our future stock by the rule of anticipation." He was sent to Oxford in 1740, became a fellow eleven years later, and continued reading quietly. At the age of forty-five he entered holy orders on the earnest persuasion of his mother, who is still with him. He, himself, has a pretty good character, but the youngest of his ancestors, who died at the age of seventy-one, was called a giddy fellow and met his death in the act of putting on a tight pair of boots after eating a basin of broth with cayenne pepper—" it has ever since been looked upon in our family as an unpardonable debauch, to swallow anything that can raise the smallest combustion within us." It will be perceived that there is a striving towards a certain mild humour, but the prominent feature of the ninety-two essays of the *Looker-on* is their ethical quality. Roberts is very much in earnest in his endeavour to reform, and the literary quality of the essays sometimes suffers by that prepossession. They lack the sparkle of the *Spectator* essays, and at times are actually dull. But when Roberts points the moral with the aid of irony and satire he is most successful. The letter of *Belinda Daub* (No. 14) is excellent, as also the satire on certain divines (No. 57) : " It is my plan in general to preach comfortable and cheerful doctrines to my congregation; not that I spare them either, when I see grounds for severity and reprehension. But I find that the minister of the new parish has drawn off a part of my audience by the very winning manner of his denouncing them to perdition; he tosses about his damns with such a grace (as Addison says Virgil, in his *Georgics*, did his dung) that his church is crowded with voluntary victims who repair to the sacred edifice to be launched into a dreadful eternity with as much cheerfulness as to a christening." His attempts at a tale (Nos. 43–46) are not so successful, and of literary criticism he has nothing. He succeeds better in his *Sheet omitted in B——'s Life of Johnson*, given in the seventy-ninth number. The mannerisms of Johnson and the method of Boswell are well presented, and the paper is an excellent example of Roberts's style as an essayist:

"*April the* 20*th.*—I dined with him at Sir J. R——'s. I regret that I have preserved but few minutes of his conversation on that day, though he was less talkative, and fuller of capriciousness and contradictions than usual; as the following dialogue may show— whilst at the same time it proves that there is no question so entirely barren of matter or argument, which could not furnish him an occasion of displaying the powers of his mighty mind. We talked of public places; and one gentleman spoke warmly in praise of Sadler's Wells. Mr C——, who had been so unfortunate as to displease Dr Johnson, and wished to reinstate himself in his good opinion, thought he could not do it more effectually than by decrying such light amusements as those of tumbling and rope-dancing; in particular, he asserted that 'a rope-dancer was in his opinion the most despicable of human beings.' Johnson (awfully rolling himself as he prepared to speak, and bursting out into a thundering tone), 'Sir, you might as well say that St Paul was the most despicable of human beings. Let us beware how we petulantly and ignorantly traduce a character which puts all other characters to shame. Sir, a rope-dancer concentrates in himself all the cardinal virtues.'

"Well as I was by this time acquainted with the sophistical talents of my illustrious friend, and often as I had listened to him in wonder, while he 'made the worse appear the better reason,' I could not but suppose that, for once, he had been betrayed by his violence into an assertion which he could not support. Urged by my curiosity, and perhaps rather wickedly desirous of leading him into a contest, I ventured, leaning briskly towards him across my friend the Duke of ——'s chair, to say, in a sportive, familiar manner, which he sometimes indulgently permitted me to use: 'Indeed, Dr Johnson! did I hear you right? a rope-dancer concentre in himself all the cardinal virtues!' The answer was ready. Johnson, 'Why, yes, sir; deny it who dare. I say, in a rope-dancer there is Temperance, and Faith, and Hope, and Charity, and Justice, and Prudence, and Fortitude.' Still I was not satisfied; and was desirous to hear his proofs at full length. Boswell, 'Why, to be sure, sir, Fortitude I can easily conceive.' Johnson (interrupting me), 'Sir, if you cannot conceive the rest, it is to no purpose that you conceive the seventh. But to those who cannot comprehend, it is necessary to explain. Why, then, sir, we will begin with Temperance. Sir, if the joys of the bottle entice him one inch beyond the line of sobriety, his life or his limbs must pay the forfeit of his excess. Then, sir, there is Faith. Without unshaken confidence in his own powers, and full assurance that the rope is firm, his temperance will be of but little advantage; the unsteadiness of his nerves would soon prove as fatal as the intoxication of his brain. Next, sir, we have Hope. A dance so dangerous, who ever exhibited, unless lured by the hope of fortune or of fame? Charity next follows: and what instance of charity shall be opposed to that of him, who, in the hope of administering to the gratification of others, braves the hiss of multitudes, and derides the dread of death? Then, sir, what man will withhold from the funambulist the praise of Justice, who considers his inflexible *uprightness*, and that he holds his *balance* with so steady a hand, as never to incline, in the minutest degree, to one side or the other? Nor, in the next place, is his Prudence more disputable than his Justice. He has chosen, indeed, a perilous accomplishment; but, while it is remembered that he is temerarious in the maturity of his art, let it not be forgotten that he was cautious in its commencement; and that, while he was yet in the rudiments of rope-dancing, he might securely fail in his footing, while his instructors stood ready on either side to prevent or to alleviate his fall. Lastly, sir, those who from dullness or obduracy shall refuse to the rope-dancer the applauses due to Temperance, Faith, Hope, Charity, Justice, and Prudence, will yet scarcely be so desperate in falsehood or in folly, as to deny him the laurels of Fortitude. He that is content to vacillate on a cord, while his fellow-mortals tread securely on the broad basis of *terra firma*; who performs the jocund evolutions of the dance on a superficies, compared to which, the verge of a precipice is a stable station;

may rightfully snatch the wreath from the conqueror and the martyr; may boast that he exposes himself to hazards, from which he might fly to the cannon's mouth as to a refuge or a relaxation! Sir, let us now be told no more of the infamy of the rope-dancer.' When he had ended, I could not help whispering Sir J. Boswell, 'How wonderfully does our friend extricate himself out of difficulties! He is like quicksilver: try to grasp him in your hand, and he makes his escape between every finger.' This image I afterwards ventured to mention to our great Moralist and Lexicographer, saying, 'May not I flatter myself, sir, that it was a passable metaphor?' Johnson, 'Why, yes, sir.'"

In the final number, Roberts makes acknowledgment of help with several of his papers from two or three friends, but claims that he has written with these exceptions all the others himself. He contemplates his work with something like complacency, for his aim has been "to oppose something like a barrier to that usurping march of nonsense," and to lead men "unawares to their better interest, unconscious of the path they are pursuing till they lose the wish to retreat." And he succeeded best in that laudable endeavour when he mixed humour with his moral. Yet it is hard to tell sometimes the mood in which he wrote some of his papers. In the closing number he gives a most moving picture of the death of his old mother; but what exactly was the mood in which these words were penned, when the dying mother proceeds, "Simon, my voice begins to fail me, but not too soon, for I have little more to say; yet one thing at this moment comes into my mind: might not you signify through that paper of yours that you want a notable and youngish woman for your wife? Doubtless, they cannot choose but offer themselves in crowds, to one so pious and discreet. In the top drawer of my great bureau, thou wilt find that tobacco-stopper of thy great-grandfather which thou thoughtest to have been long ago lost to thee and thy family. It seemed good to me, Simon, to conceal it there till the day of my death, that, when I should be removed out of thy sight, still thou mightest have something by thee, to put thee strongly in mind of thy ancestors; and I thought it might the more impress thee if the recovery of it should bear the date of thy mother's dissolution. There are human beings that are worse companions for thee than thy great-grandfather's tobacco-stopper."

It had been a predominant characteristic of the periodical essay from the commencement in the hands of Steele and Addison to deal almost exclusively with the life of the town and the doings of a rather artificial society. And we have scarcely had to consider any essay periodical work carried on outside of one or other of the capitals of the three kingdoms. Occasionally in some local centre where people of leisure and education gathered some literary attempt might be made along the lines of the periodical essay, but this was exceptional. One example is the *Bath Miscellany* (1740), which is made up of verse and prose contributions sent in by writers to that famous watering-place. The tone of the paper is light and rather frivolous. A much more serious attempt to supply the omission of the urban periodicals was the *Country Spectator* (1792), published at Gainsborough. The motto is from Horace, *Ego rure viventem*, and in the opening essay the author says: "Of the numerous class of writers, who have undertaken to furnish instruction or amusement in periodical essays, no one has, hitherto, I believe, made the *Country* the subject of his speculations. Their talents seem to have been uniformly directed to the delineation of such scenes as the *Town* exhibits; the diversions, the fashions, or the follies most prevalent in the Capital, having been the almost unvaried scheme of every essayist." Neither the *Spectator* nor the *Adventurer*, the *World* nor the *Connoisseur*, have taken any interest in the country or country life. But he will endeavour to supply the deficiency. His criticisms and poetry, tales and allegories, will of necessity be the same, but when he is led into "disquisitions which derive their complexions from the place in which they are written," he promises his country readers that *they* shall have the preference. A characteristic note at the end of the first number advises that—" If the *Country Spectator* should be thought too grave, let it be remembered that he is anxious for the fate of this, his first number."

In the thirty-three numbers of the *Country Spectator*

there are several interesting features. While the author continues the older features, *allegory* (*e.g.* allegory *on the head and the heart*), *story* (No. 27 is a domestic and sentimental tale), *satire* (*e.g.* an account given of the *thermometer of popularity*), and letters (*e.g.* from *Querulous Moody*), the country element is fresh. Descriptions of a country news-room (No. 5), of morning calls in the country (No. 14), and of quiet, uneventful country life (No. 17) are all good. But the author admits it is difficult for him to escape identification: " In a small town every minute event forms a kind of era among its inhabitants; the news of the day, which everywhere constitutes a great part of the conversation, is there necessarily confined to a very few topics." It was exactly this quiet life which, a few years later, Jane Austen described in her novels; and contrived to make interesting the deadly dullness of the reality.

The author's attempts to develop pictures of country life soon became too much for him: " It will be confessed that whoever has encountered the task of writing at stated periods, will readily testify that the burthen is heavier than is generally believed." But the writer deserves credit for a praiseworthy attempt to infuse new life into the older forms. And that he clearly realised the aims of such literary work, if unable for long to execute them, is seen from his closing remarks: " I have sometimes endeavoured to lead the reader into abstract speculation, and sometimes I have prattled about the nonsense of the day, at other times I have been colloquial and have been negligent from design."

The last half-dozen periodicals which call for notice before the close of the century are mainly of interest because they show that while the life was gradually leaving this literary kind and being transferred to the new, the outward form and features remained to the end. The *Whisperer* (1795), *or Tales and Speculations*, by *Gabriel Silvertongue*, are essays which first appeared in a weekly provincial paper, and were bound up together in volume form in 1798. The copy in the British Museum Library has the following note written at the forefront: " Only one other copy of this periodical is suffered to be in existence, the author having carefully destroyed the issue." No reason for this action on the part of the author is given. His opening essay continues the tradition of the essay periodicals: " It has been an ancient periodical memory, to dedicate their first essay to themselves, and therein discover just so much concerning their birth, parentage, and education, as cannot fail to awaken in the breast of the curious reader an earnest desire of better acquaintance." An account of the *Silvertongues* follows.

In the second number, on *Hints Concerning Title-pages, and a Whisper about Whispering*, the author confesses his failure to find a new title (*cf.* the *Whisperer* of 1770). " It requires the toil and patience of Sisyphus himself in rolling back the stone, to invent a new and flaring title-page." In his character as a *Whisperer* he has whispered his way through " a noisy, bustling, bawling, world; has peeped into business and sported through pleasures, mingled with company and conversed with solitude." The earlier periodicals are also imitated by the introduction of characters, *Sir Solomon Sombre* and *Dr Alexander Lapwing*. They serve as purveyors of moral maxims. The former has passed from a gay youth to a quiet old age; the latter is the Rector, a brisk little man " who has so many titles after his name that he often merrily observes that he should write his name—*Alex. Lapwing, A.B.C., etc.*! The twenty-four numbers of the *Whisperer* are strongly moral and didactic in tone, and in this respect draw more closely to the *Rambler* than the *Spectator* type.

The *Sylph* (1795) is a similar production. A slight touch of freshness is given in the introductory paper. The *Sylph* Ariel communicates to Mr Longman in a vision the intention of periodically warning and admonishing the world, " By the *Sylph*—A proclamation, Ariel of his own authority and grace, to the inhabitants of the earth, greeting." In the forty numbers of the *Sylph* which follow the follies, frailties, crimes, and passions of mankind are subjected to the jurisdiction of Courts established on the authority of Ariel. There is a considerable variety of subject-matter. Including Eastern Tales, there are papers on self-love, humility, poverty, love of fame, and filial piety. Thus

THE EIGHTEENTH-CENTURY ESSAYISTS

in a somewhat novel setting the old features and subjects reappear.

The *Trifler* of the same year is an Edinburgh periodical. The "editor," *Richard Maw-worm, Esq.*, discusses the difficulty of finding a new title, and thinks he has invented one. But there had been a *Trifler* before 1795. He promises pictures of both town and country life.

"My principal papers will be furnished with observations on the inhabitants of this city; but I will occasionally convey my readers into the country, and either give them a delineation of the innocent manners of rural life, or of the beauties of nature." He will eschew politics, and hopes to have as extensive a reading public as *Mr Town* of the *Connoisseur*. A vision (No. 2) of Bruntsfield Links, over which passes an army of females, bearing the badge *A.F.O.R.* (Association for our Rights), has some startlingly modern statements on the rights of women. A Russian love-story (No. 3) is good. The seventh is satiric, and suggests that since swearing is now so universal, a *professorship* in that art might be started.

His aim (No. 8) is "to convey amusement as well as instruction, and not to fatigue the attention by trite observations, or by examining subjects of little use to mankind." After an Eastern Tale (No. 10) of the usual type, he refers to the *Spectator*, sketches characters (as that of *Fulvia* in No. 23), and gives a letter (No. 21) from a *ghost* who warns the *Trifler* that a committee of ghosts under *Mr Phantom* will publish a paper presently. This was the *Ghost* of 1796.

In the thirty-third number he draws a conclusion: "Who can expect," he says, "to find in a *Trifler* the beauties of Addison or the learning and ingenuity of Johnson, but if ever my papers have had the effect of innocently beguiling a few hours I will be happy." There is some excellent work in this periodical.

The *Ghost* (1796), a companion periodical, also published in Edinburgh, is dated from Fairyland. It appeared twice a week, and was sold by Mudie & Son, South Bridge, Edinburgh, and also at Glasgow. The author is said to have been Mr Constantia, a Portuguese, who was then a student at Edinburgh University. Twenty-five numbers

THE OBSERVER AND OTHER PERIODICALS

were published. The pseudonym adopted is *Felix Phantom, Esq.*, and the *Ghost* opens thus: "It has been a constant practice with authors who have published periodical lucubrations, to follow the manner of their predecessors. The *Tatler* and *Spectator* have been closely imitated by a multitude of writers, who had not the courage to open themselves new roads to fame; and the weakness of human nature sufficiently accounts for such timidity. But the originality of my person, my superior knowledge, and my being the first spirit that ever declared himself an author, gives me the right to invent, as well as to conduct these essays in my own way, without regard to any precedent of mortals. I am a departed Spirit. During my abode on earth, I made the views of mankind my chief study; but the hand of death snatched me away from the world just as I was about to relieve its distresses." But he will write in the manner of men; and "if he fails to please and delight mankind, he will *give up* the *Ghost*!"

These introductory remarks raise expectations which are not altogether fulfilled; the essays are only of average merit. The fourth essay is interesting. It is a criticism of *The Fortunate Shepherdess*, a poem in the Scottish dialect, by Alex. Ross, A.M., published in the year 1778. The writer gives a number of extracts from it, and retells the story. A letter from a Frenchman who has come to Edinburgh (Nos. 5 and 11) revives in an interesting way the idea first presented by Tom Brown. In the twenty-fifth number an Italian's impressions are similarly given. A remark in his description of *Edinburgh University* helps to fix the date of his essays: "The College naturally attracted my attention, and I easily conceived what a massy building it would be, if it should ever be completed."

The rivalry between the *Ghost* and the *Trifler* seemed to be acute. The *Ghost* (No. 15) writes: "On Saturday last, arrived in these regions, Richard Maw-worm, Esq., commonly known in Edinburgh, by the name of *Dicky the Trifler*. This unfortunate youth, naturally of a weak constitution, and without sufficient stamina to support longevity, had long been in a declining state. He died on Saturday morning, much regretted." An amusing description follows of his arrival "amongst us." But the *other side* replied by publishing a spurious copy of the *Ghost*, the twenty-fourth and last, dated July 1796, and containing scurrilous remarks. The writer is supposed to have been Robert Heron, a rather disreputable but unfortunate journalist of the period.

These two Edinburgh periodicals tend to burlesque this literary kind, but make amusing reading.

The *Gleaner* (1795) was a third Edinburgh periodical which promised well, but only one number appeared. The opening essay says: "Readers (for I trust I shall have more than one), judge not of this production by its name. The very word (*Commentator*, No. 1, was at the forefront of the paper) may prepossess you with an opinion that I shall resemble some of my *illustrious* German and Dutch brethren, in dullness as well as in title. But if I should prove dull, the fault will not lie with my choice of subjects, but with my manner of treating them. The conversation, the dress, the amusements of the place will all be treated. Political subjects are the only ones which I mean scrupulously to avoid."

In the number are included a miscellaneous set of papers: an essay on *The Pronunciation of the Latin language*; a second *On the Ruins of Edinburgh*; a third on *Cheap Pleasures*; and extracts and poetry complete the issue.

On the Ruins of Edinburgh is an essay which takes the form of a vision or dream: "On the summit of one of those high hills which overlook the city, I lay musing on the confused scene that was spread under my eye. I fell into a deep sleep and dreamed." A picture of Edinburgh in ruins, as it would appear to some person in the future coming to visit the deserted city, is then given. It is an early example of those *anticipations* which Lytton was one of the first to execute on an extensive scale in the novel, and which have been repeatedly done by recent writers of romance.

In the two last essay periodicals which fall to be discussed the chief feature to note is their close resemblance to the *Spectator*. Until the very end the influence of the earlier form is maintained. The *Loiterer* (1796) *or Universal*

THE OBSERVER AND OTHER PERIODICALS

Essayist actually mentions his adherence to Steele and Addison in the opening number in so many words, " That I may not appear before the public altogether a stranger, and agreeing with my predecessor the *Spectator* that readers like to know who authors are, I shall employ this number in an introductory manner, by giving some account of myself and the nature and origin of my present undertaking." Brought up as a lawyer, the *Loiterer* has now received an annuity and is therefore at leisure. He is a member of several clubs, and will introduce various characters, including *Jack Volatile*, *Mr Quadrangle* (a metaphysical genius), *Mr Fyfe* (a painter), and *Arthur O'Neil*, an Irishman by birth. The essays which follow are not outstanding, and the various individuals with the *ticket names* are not developed into full-bodied personalities. They seem to be mentioned simply because it is the manner and custom so to do.

This endeavour to emulate the Queen Anne essayists is seen even more clearly in the *Friend* (1796), a weekly paper by Mr W. Fox. In the first number Fox gives his aim : " To mingle delight with instruction, to preserve the morals and improve the manners of the age in which he lives, is the *Friend's* design in the work he proposes to submit to the public." The second number discusses the most popular of all subjects with the periodical essayists— happiness. The motto is, " Be happy, and make others so "; and the moral, " Happiness is the constant effect of virtue, and unhappiness the inseparable attendant on vice." An enumeration of the subjects treated of in the succeeding eight numbers—order, friendship, religion, industry, marriage, prudence, temperance, and justice—shows how closely the scheme follows the *Spectator*. Even the outward form is maintained, each issue consisting of a short essay on a single sheet in the manner of the Queen Anne periodicals. Fox himself in these essays shows that he has acquired to a considerable degree the style of Addison. His style is clear ; he has applied in his own work his advice (No. 12) on writing, " think well, and you cannot speak or write ill."

It must not be supposed that the periodical essay as a literary kind came absolutely to an end with the close of the century. There was no magic in the year 1800, nothing to prevent the essay periodical " crossing the bar " of the new century, and many indeed thought they saw Steele *redivivus* in Leigh Hunt. But in general the essay periodical as a literary kind lived and died within the eighteenth century. An endeavour will be made in the next chapter to indicate the stages by which the old gave way to the new.

CHAPTER X

THE PASSING OF THE EIGHTEENTH-CENTURY PERIODICAL ESSAY

WHEN we look back over the eighteenth century and pass once again in review the long list of essay periodicals, the lasting impression left upon the mind is the predominating influence of the *Tatler* and *Spectator* throughout. Addison and Steele in their writings had proved complementary to each other. Each supplied what the other lacked. They had not collaborated together in the way in which Colman and Thornton had written; for the work of the latter pair was so blended together that the one could not be distinguished from the other. But the essays of Steele and Addison, grouped together as they were in the *Tatler* and *Spectator*, combined to produce an effect which lasted for the best part of the century. The more free and less laboured compositions of Steele were supplemented by the carefully finished productions of Addison. Addison, in particular, is the characteristic genius of his age; and the periodical essayists followed, almost without exception, the features and method and manner provided by the *Tatler* and the *Spectator*. Every writer on the age of Queen Anne has remarked on this outstanding feature, and made special mention of Addison's influence. " His refined scholarship," says one, " his delicate humour, his simple piety, and his unwillingness to give pain, make up the characteristics of a Christian gentleman. The absence of enthusiasm and the predominance of reason fix a type which was not superseded as an object of imitation for seventy years after his death." Can any reason be found which will explain this unbroken influence extended over so many years? Attention has already been directed to that " psychological moment," that conjunction of circumstances which helped to make the essay periodical the success it was in the reign of Queen Anne; but there is another factor which is important. In our modern magazines the majority of the articles are of purely topical interest. They amuse at the moment, but their value is also only for the moment. But with Addison it is different. His work is not merely topical; it is notable for the absence of features which possess a merely topical interest. Thus its value remained. The essays deal largely with subjects which are of an ethical nature or have their substructure grounded on moral considerations. It is as if Addison had endeavoured to fulfil those functions of the pulpit which were but faultily performed in his day by ministers of religion. Macaulay indicates the low social position of the clergy at the time. Other writers have stated the same. For example, Paul in his *Queen Anne* makes a strong point of this. "There was not much spiritual fervour in the Church of Anne, and the drinking habits of the period were not confined to the laity. The level of the sermon, always written, was not high, and the best sermons of the day have been not ill-described as essays from the *Spectator* without the Addisonian elegance." Thus one of the causes of the continual success of the *Spectator* was that it had not merely a topical interest, but dealt with subjects which had importance for each succeeding generation.

Gradually, however, as the century progressed and new influences began to be felt, a restlessness became evident, a desire here and there to break from the Queen Anne *régime* so rigorously followed by the majority. The essayists began to realise that they were being restricted and hampered by this adherence to a plan and design which, however successful in Addison's day, might not altogether agree with their own. They sought for variety of subject, yet they did not always know how to attain it. Undoubtedly the most successful attempt to create a new atmosphere for the periodical essay is found in the *World* periodical. A group of brilliant writers made the *World* a success in a lighter vein, and an admirable contrast to the heavier type of Johnson's *Rambler*. The somewhat cumbrous method of the *Club* was never completely satisfactory, and the various

THE PASSING OF THE PERIODICAL ESSAY

members of the Club are often simply mentioned and then forgotten; they do not become *live* personalities such as the characters Addison successfully developed, *Sir Andrew Freeport*, *Will Wimble*, and the inimitable *Sir Roger* himself. The moral allegories (sometimes of a highly complex nature) inevitably grew stale as time went on. Above all, the majority of the essayists failed to infuse into their writings a sufficiently personal tone, despite their attempt to do so by the device of an *eidolon* or editor (if we may call him so) who was supposed to be responsible for the production of the whole paper. The "short-faced silent" man was never reproduced in the later periodicals with entire success—the *Spectator* died with Addison. We have noted from time to time these signs of dissatisfaction with the Addisonian *régime*, until they became strongly articulate in the *Winter Evenings* of Vicesimus Knox, who spoke of the "little arts which have lost their grace and power by being so frequently read already as to be anticipated, and even loathed by the reader, who is apt to yawn over them and exclaim, 'I'm sick of this dull dose of daily trash.'" One other example of this *rebellion*, if we may call it so, may be given. In the *Monthly Mirror* (1795) the author says: "Periodical publications are daily coming into disgrace. The moral and intellectual world were never so enlightened and improved as when Addison, Steele, and others gave their lucubrations to the public. The form, the method, the system remained, but the animation, the genius, the soul were fled." Addison and Steele had, in fact, done their work too well! Steele, with his admirable knowledge of the fair sex, had covered the wide circle of their activities with so perfect a grace that no new subject could be found; and Addison in the part of *Spectator* thrust his head into a group of the Politicians at *Wills'*, smoked a pipe at *Child's*, listened while others conversed at the *Postman*, appeared on Sundays at *St James*, and knew the *Grecian* and *Cocoa Tree* and the theatres of Drury Lane and the Haymarket so well that he transferred the whole life of the society of the time to paper with complete literary success. It was left for their followers simply to imitate them. This invariable practice was, in reality, a mistake, because the

THE EIGHTEENTH-CENTURY ESSAYISTS

essay periodical need not have been limited in this way. It was capable of almost infinite extension and variety. It cannot be said, however, that with the close of the eighteenth century the influence of Addison and Steele came entirely to an end. More than one nineteenth-century essayist in his work reveals a close acquaintance with the *Tatler* and *Spectator*. In the *Examiner* (1800) Leigh Hunt intended to issue a series of essays similar to those of the eighteenth-century writers under the title of the *Round Table*. This plan, for various reasons, was departed from and never finished by Hunt, but the design is suggestive. And in his spirit of restless energy Hunt resembles Steele. He started numerous periodicals, several of which bear strong resemblance to the *Spectator*—notably the *Indicator* (1819) and the *Companion* (1828). Still later he revived Steele's first title in the *Tatler* (1830), and in the *Travellers Mr Town, Jr.*, supplied a direct reminiscence of *Mr Town* of the *Connoisseur*. A second writer who reveals the earlier influence is Praed. In the *Etonian*, which he published along with others, many essays appear which recall the eighteenth-century periodicals. And not to mention Hazlitt, whose stronger personality makes his work more complete, fresh, and individual, nor Lamb, who is unique in his own line; Thackeray himself in his *Roundabout Papers*, published in *Cornhill*, seems for a little to revive the older method and with the happiest results. But having noted these lines of influence persisting into the nineteenth century, we are still justified in saying that as a distinct kind the essay periodical is practically confined to the limits of the eighteenth century.

What, then, were the factors which operated to bring about the change in magazine form from the eighteenth to the nineteenth centuries? This is an interesting question to ask. Dr Saintsbury has said that it would be interesting to trace out the process by which the eighteenth-century periodicals merged into the *Reviews* and *Magazines* of the opening years of the nineteenth: " One of the things which have not yet been sufficiently done in the criticism of English literary history is a careful review of the successive steps by which the periodical essay of Addison

THE PASSING OF THE PERIODICAL ESSAY

and his followers during the eighteenth century passed into the magazine papers of our own days. The later examples of the eighteenth century, the *Observers* and *Connoisseurs*, the *Loungers* and *Mirrors* and *Lookers-on*, have a considerable gap between them and the productions of Hunt, Lamb, *Blackwood*, with Praed's attempts not left out." At least three or four factors were present assisting this change.

And, first of all, let us consider the newspaper. At the very outset periodical essays had appeared in newspapers. Defoe's *Review* was, practically speaking, a newspaper, and it was for his own paper that he wrote his series of *Scandal Club* essays. This section of Defoe's paper was isolated by Steele and elevated into a new literary kind, the essay periodical in the shape of the *Tatler*. But from time to time newspapers continued the practice which Defoe had adopted. Defoe's later essay work appeared in this way in Nathaniel Mist's papers. Fielding contributed to newspapers in a similar fashion, and the great names of Johnson and Goldsmith will not be forgotten. Both published some of their best essay work in this way. This practice, only irregularly carried out, it is true, must have done something to suggest the absorption of the main features of the essay periodical into a paper or magazine of a more varied type, and help to merge its identity with the larger whole. But as events were to prove, it was not the newspaper, pure and simple, that proved the chief rival to the success of the periodical essay, it was a magazine of another kind.

Nor can it be said that the second great achievement of the century in prose—the novel—proved a friend to the periodical essay. It was the opposite way about. We have indicated that the novel really sucked the essay dry. It need not have been so. If Dickens had lived a century earlier all might have been well. Novels in serial form might have first seen the light in the essay periodical. For Dickens was strongly in favour of the serial system. In his *Postscript* to one of his last novels, *Our Mutual Friend*, referring to the difficulty of grasping the plot when the book is published serially, he says : " Yet that I hold the advantage of the mode of publication to outweigh its disadvantages, may be easily believed of one who revived it in the

Pickwick Papers after long disuse, and has pursued it ever since." Taking the hint from the *Sir Roger de Coverley* series, Fielding might first have published *Tom Jones* in a *True Patriot* or *Covent Garden Journal*. But he did not do so. On the other hand, *Tom Jones* seemed to have absorbed the periodical essay into its bulk—for the inter-chapters are little else than such essays. The *Sentimental Journey* of Sterne could excellently have appeared first in the essay periodical. In thus keeping apart from the essay periodical the novel proved a strong rival and absorbed the most promising fictional features which the essay periodical possessed.

In the third place, another feature of the periodical essay which was taken up and developed separately was criticism. It cannot be said that the essay periodical produced many great critical essays. It was critical work, as a rule, of a very modest kind. Yet it made a good commencement in the hands of Addison, as we have seen, and when it is selected out of the multitude of essayists its bulk is not small. But there is the absence in it, as a whole, of a real critical spirit. Two reasons may be given for this. The critics were hampered by the *rules*, some self-imposed, and no doubt willingly obeyed; and, secondly, the artificial nature of the society of the time hindered its free development. Feeling was repressed in obedience again to the self-imposed restrictions of the time. The true *man of feeling* was Goldsmith, not Mackenzie. Mackenzie in actual life was shrewd; in his legal business cold and hard; and in his sport fond of a " grand evening's " cock-fighting. But gradually the true critical spirit emerged and developed. We have noted the new *Memoirs of Literature* (1722) and others which displayed only this lower order of criticism, but before the close of the century progress was made.

For example, in the *British Critic* (1793) we have something which approaches the style of the critical magazines and reviews of the following century. It was a monthly review, and in the preface it is stated that the object is to give a critical account of all publications which call for consideration—Divinity, History, Travels, Biographies, and Antiquities. In addition to mere extracts, which the earlier magazines—the *Gentleman's Magazine*, the *London Magazine*,

THE PASSING OF THE PERIODICAL ESSAY

and the *Scots Magazine*—had been in the habit of giving, there is a genuine if amateurish attempt really to *criticise*. A single sentence in the opening review of a book may serve, even if only verbal criticism, to indicate this: "Mr Maurice's apology for his style does not to us seem necessary. It is generally nervous and good; there appears, however, throughout somewhat of a predilection for words of less than usual occurrence." The *British Critic* led the way for the *Edinburgh Review* and the others, and that it satisfied a felt want is evident from the fact that it had a life of twenty years.

The *Edinburgh Quarterly Magazine* (1798) does not help us in this direction, because it was a paper purely religious in tone, save as a guide to the city where the new departure was made, which gathers completely to itself this critical element in the earlier periodicals. The *Edinburgh Review*, a *Critical Journal*, was founded by Jeffrey and his friends in 1802. It was not the first of its name. As we have already mentioned, there was an *Edinburgh Review* published in the year 1755. Jeffrey himself had been contributing to the *Monthly Review* for a number of years before. The *Edinburgh*, together with the *Quarterly*, begun seven years later, maintains a strictly review character, and does not attempt to imitate the distinctive nature of the *Spectator*; but papers like Mackenzie's article on *Burns*, in the *Lounger*, distinctly foreshadowed the discussions on politics, literature, and religion with which these new reviews are occupied. It would be absurd, however, to deny that the *Edinburgh Review* appeared to the public to be something entirely fresh and original. Cockburn, in his *Life of Jeffrey*, who gives a reliable account of the state of Edinburgh life and letters at the time, distinctly states: "It is impossible for those who did not live at the time, and in the heart of the scene, to feel, or almost to understand, the impression made by the new luminary, or the anxieties with which its motions were observed. It was an entire and instant change of everything that the public had been accustomed to in that sort of composition. The old periodical opiates were extinguished at once."

But the influence of the earlier periodicals was to die

THE EIGHTEENTH-CENTURY ESSAYISTS

hard. Both the *London Magazine* and *Blackwood's Magazine*, founded in 1817, have reminiscences of the old method ; Christopher North's *Noctes Ambrosianæ*, contributed to *Maga*, have characters, like *Tickler* and the *Shepherd*, which are full-bodied representatives of the earlier and rather lifeless characters of the eighteenth-century periodicals. And *Mr Punch* we have still with us ! But in the main they had got rid of the cumbrous machinery which had prevented free action in the eighteenth century, and these really *critical* magazines and reviews of the early nineteenth century left far behind the (by comparison) puny critical efforts of the eighteenth.

But the fourth factor proved by far the most formidable in bringing about the change from the essay periodical of the eighteenth century. This was the magazine of a more general and varied nature, greater in bulk and size than the more limited and compact periodical of the *Tatler* and *Spectator* pattern. These more general magazines began to appear as early as the thirties, and we have noted a number of them in what has gone before. The earliest, as it was the longest lived (it occupies seventy volumes in the British Museum Library), was the *Gentleman's Magazine*, and others were the *London* (1732), the *Scots* (1737), the *British* (1747), the *Ladies'* (1749), the *New Universal* (1754), the *Edinburgh* (1757), and the *Town and Country* (1787) magazines. Let us pause for a moment to examine the nature of one of these magazines. The last-named, the *Town and Country Magazine*, was produced by a society of gentlemen. The introductory address emphasises the fact that these magazines were becoming increasingly popular. " In the course of twenty or thirty years past, the great demand for magazines has given rise to an incredible number of such publications ; and nothing can be better calculated for general instruction and amusement than a properly conducted magazine." The first issue of the *Town and Country Magazine* is divided into several sections. The first is called the *Monthly Mirror*, and supplies general reflections on the state of the times and a story : the second section is named *Levities*, and includes lighter paragraphs, small talk, and a discussion about the fashions. Paragraphs of a

THE PASSING OF THE PERIODICAL ESSAY

didactic complexion succeed—the subjects of them comprising happiness, temperance, and virtue; poetry is not forgotten; and the issue closes with a number of items of general intelligence. The outline is almost exactly similar to that which might be drawn up for any of the magazines mentioned. It will be seen that it is of a fairly general nature, and supplies items of interest for others not interested in didactic essays or little paragraphs on fashion: it appeals also to the man interested in politics and in general news. This appeal to a wider public inevitably reacted upon the periodical essay, which, during the whole century, had its circulation confined to a more or less select circle of society. This magazine class undoubtedly affected the fortunes of the essay periodical, and the ultimate result was the modern magazine with its infinitely varied dietary of story and article informative and amusing. And the illustrations must not be forgotten. Illustrations in magazines in the eighteenth century were almost totally non-existent. For a time *Hogarth* seemed to absorb the very cream of the periodical essay into his great didactic series of pictures, and the influence of them was long continued. In the *Comic Magazine* (1796), for example, a print of Hogarth's appeared in each number; and an *Edinburgh* periodical entitled the *Bee or Literary Weekly Intelligencer*, published in 1792, also has illustrations. The author terms his *Bee* "a work calculated to disseminate useful knowledge among all ranks of people at a small expense," but its importance lies in the fact that, in giving a sketch of the life of Andrew Fletcher of Saltoun, he includes a portrait: in his description of Inchcolm he adds an illustration of the island, and gives a woodcut along with an account of a tiger; as well as the usual moral reflections, grammatical disquisitions, and poetry. Though the *Bee* resembles at times nothing so much as a child's school-book, it undoubtedly, in a faint and far-off way, heralds the advent of the illustrated magazines. That this power of the picture was soon realised will be admitted when it is recalled that Dickens was requested to "write round" some sketches of Cruickshank the *Posthumous Papers* of the Pickwick Club. The new features of the nineteenth century were thus present (even

THE EIGHTEENTH-CENTURY ESSAYISTS

in germ) in the older periodicals, but with a difference. In many cases the novelist did not run in direct rivalry with the newer magazine. He rather aided its circulation by contributing his tale in serial form, week by week, or month by month. It was in this way that Dickens and Thackeray (to mention only two outstanding names) first published the majority of their novels. Not only so, the nineteenth-century magazines became channels for more general contributions. The eighteenth-century periodicals had been run in the main by a select few. The numerous "letters from correspondents" were in the majority of cases written "at the office," but the newer periodicals encouraged the literary aspirant and excited more general interest in the magazines.

But the eighteenth-century essay periodical, defective no doubt in the directions indicated, accomplished a valuable work in the long term of its existence. Early in the century, in the reign of Queen Anne, the summit of variety and excellence had been reached in the *Tatler*, *Spectator*, and *Guardian*. This trio (and more particularly the *Spectator*) had in volume form been accepted as standards, and dominated that field of literature for wellnigh a century. Johnson in the *Rambler* and *Idler* had illustrated more especially the moral and didactic side; the contributors to the *World* and *Connoisseur* had sought to depict passing fashions and seize the humorous incidents of life and set them forth to amuse, without any prominent didactic purpose. But the outward form had been religiously preserved; the weekly or bi-weekly issue on small sheets; the retention of the *eidolon*, though little made use of; and *visions*, *allegories*, and *stories*. The disappearance of the form coincides with the close of the century, when so many of the old things were passing away, when new standards for the novel, for the essay, and for poetry were being introduced. But the services which had been rendered by the essay periodical had been great. Addison and Steele have left us a body of work which not only fulfilled a special purpose at the time, but which remains the most delightful and successful attempt in this special literary form. Johnson, in the *Rambler*, has written a set of moral

THE PASSING OF THE PERIODICAL ESSAY

essays full of thoughts and reflections which can never quite grow stale. And Goldsmith's periodical-essay work included papers which are amongst the happiest examples we possess. He has created characters which come *sub specie æternitatis*, which rival Addison's *Sir Roger de Coverley* papers and approach the level of the characterisations of Fielding himself. Contributors, again, to the *Adventurer* and *World*, *Connoisseur*, *Mirror*, *Lounger*, and other periodicals have written single papers of outstanding merit, not only valuable as regards style, but for the contemporary pictures they give of morals and manners. The essays on literary criticism pointed the way to the *Edinburgh Review* and the *Quarterly*, and the more general articles suggested miscellaneous subjects to the magazines of the nineteenth century. If the essay periodical retained features which were needless and machinery which was cumbrous, not distinguishing the essential from the non-essential, it was only because the Queen Anne periodical had so dominated the field that later writers seldom altered the early type to suit new conditions. It was left to the nineteenth-century periodical to discard all useless encumbrances, and to develop into an important adjunct of the literary life of the day. Yet in the eighteenth century the essay periodical maintained a wonderful popularity amidst the vogue of the sermon, the drama, and the novel. The essay had not been a purely English growth, but it found congenial soil for development in our land. England had indeed followed France when Bacon (and later Cowley) refashioned the Montaigne type, but in the periodical essay in particular the manner of Addison was so distinctive that it was France which followed England when Marivaux began a second development of the essay in France. The work of the periodical essayists in the eighteenth century must remain one of the chief contributions which that often misunderstood period of English literature has handed down to posterity.

CHRONOLOGICAL LIST OF EIGHTEENTH-CENTURY PERIODICALS

Title of Periodical.	Year of Issue.	Reference Page.
A Review (by Defoe)	1704	15
The Monthly Miscellany	1707	19
The British Apollo	1708	20
The Tatler	1709	20
The Female Tatler	1709	30
The Examiner	1710	49
The Whig Examiner	1710	55
The Spectator	1711	32
Delights for the Ingenious	1711	51
The Guardian	1713	39
The Englishman	1713	46
Applebee's Journal	1714	65
The Lover	1714	52
The Reader	1714	54
The Censor (in Mist's Journal)	1715	65
The Freeholder	1715	55
Towntalk	1715	54
Flying Post	1715	64
Post Bag	1715	65
Daily Courant	1715	65
Dublin Gazette and Courant	1715	65
St James' Evening Post	1715	65
Mist's Weekly Journal	1715	65
Occasional Papers	1716	71
Chitchat and Tea-Table	1716	55
The Entertainer	1717	71
The Wanderer	1717	71
The Mercury, or The Northern Tatler	1717	73
The Freethinker	1718	57
The Old Whig	1719	61
The Plebeian	1719	61
The Delphick Oracle	1719	61
The Theatre	1720	61
The Anti-Theatre	1720	62

CHRONOLOGICAL LIST OF PERIODICALS

Title of Periodical.	Year of Issue.	Reference Page.
Terræ Filius	1721	74
New Memoirs of Literature	1722	83
Pasquin	1723	62
The True Briton	1723	62
The Tea-Table	1724	74
The Plain Dealer	1724	76
Mist's Weekly Journal	1725	79
The Humorist	1725	81
The Craftsman	1726	87
The Occasional Writer	1727	88, 104
The Senator	1728	89
The Intelligencer	1728	92
The Echo, or Edinburgh Weekly Journal	1729	92
The Free Briton	1730	95
Memoirs of the Society of Grub Street	1730	94
The Gentleman's Magazine	1731	83
The Universal Spectator and the Auditor	1731	97
The London Magazine	1732	84
The Comedian	1732	95
Fog's Weekly Journal	1732	80
The Bee	1733	96
The Weekly Amusement	1734	99
The Conjurer	1736	102
Commonsense	1737	99
The Reveur	1737	101
The Occasional Writer	1738	104
Letters of the Critical Club	1738	102
The Scots Magazine	1739	85
The Citizen	1739	104
The Champion	1739	108
The Universal Spy	1739	105
Bath Miscellany	1740	237
The Patriot	1740	104
The Female Spectator	1744	106
The Agreeable Companion	1745	107
The True Patriot	1745	108, 112
The Penny Medley	1746	107
The Parrot	1746	107
The Jacobite's Journal	1748	112
The Ladies' Magazine	1749	86
The Rambler	1750	116
The Student	1750	156
The Inspector	1751	156
The Scourge	1752	158
The Covent Garden Journal	1752	113

THE EIGHTEENTH-CENTURY ESSAYISTS

Title of Periodical.	Year of Issue.	Reference Page.
The Adventurer	1752	132
Gray's Inn Journal	1752	157
The World	1753	141
The Connoisseur	1754	149
The New Universal Magazine	1754	161
The Monitor	1755	162
The Old Maid	1755	162
The Edinburgh Review	1755	163, 169
The Critical Review	1756	163
The Prater	1756	164
The Universal Visiter	1756	164
The Test	1756	164
The Centinel	1757	165
The Crab-tree	1757	168
The Monitor	1757	169
The Edinburgh Magazine	1757	170
The Annual Register	1758	171
The Idler	1758	125
The Bee	1759	172
The Busybody	1759	172, 184
The Public Ledger	1760	185
The Court Magazine	1761	185
The Auditor	1762	185
The Weekly Amusement	1763	187
The Schemer (date of volume form)	1763	186
The Plain Dealer	1763	187
The Edinburgh Museum	1763	192
The Spendthrift	1766	188
The Batchelor	1766	194
The Weekly Magazine	1768	192
The Whisperer	1770	195
Everyman's Magazine	1771	195
The Macaroni and Theatrical Magazine	1772	195
The Templar and Literary Gazette	1773	196
The Edinburgh Magazine and Review	1773	193
The Gentleman and Lady's Weekly Magazine	1774	194
The Convivial Magazine	1775	197
The Biographical Magazine	1776	197
The Englishman	1779	197
The Mirror	1779	198
Periodical Essays	1780	213
The Scourge	1780	213
The New Spectator	1784	214
The Lounger	1785	204
The Observer	1785	216

CHRONOLOGICAL LIST OF PERIODICALS

Title of Periodical.	Year of Issue.	Reference Page.
The Edinburgh Magazine	1785	210
The Devil	1786	224
The Devil's Pocket Book	1786	225
The Microcosm	1786	220
The Pharos	1786	223
The Busybody	1787	226
The New Town and Country Magazine	1787	252
Olla Podrida	1787	228
The Trifler	1788	221
The Bee	1790	253
The Speculator	1790	229
Winter Evenings	1790	230
The Country Spectator	1792	237
The Looker-on	1792	232
The British Critic	1793	250
The Monthly Mirror	1795	257
The Whisperer	1795	238
The Sylph	1795	239
The Trifler	1795	240
The Gleaner	1795	242
The Loiterer	1796	242
The Friend	1796	243
The Comic Magazine	1796	253
The Ghost	1796	240

ALPHABETICAL LIST OF EIGHTEENTH-CENTURY PERIODICALS

Title of Periodical.	Year of Issue.	Reference Page.
Adventurer, The	1752	132
Agreeable Companion, The	1745	107
Amusement, The Weekly	1734	99
Annual Register, The	1758	171
Anti-Theatre, The	1720	62
Apollo, The British	1708	20
Applebee's Journal	1714	65
Auditor, The	1731	97
Auditor, The	1762	185
Batchelor, The	1766	194
Bath Miscellany, The	1740	237
Bee, The	1733	96
Bee, The	1759	172
Bee, The	1790	253
Biographical Magazine, The	1776	197
British Apollo, The	1708	20
Briton, The Free	1730	95
Briton, The True	1723	62
Busybody, The	1759	172, 184
Busybody, The	1787	226
Censor, The	1715	65
Centinel, The	1757	165
Champion, The	1739	108
Chitchat	1716	55
Citizen, The	1739	104
Comedian, The	1732	95
Comic Magazine, The	1796	253
Commonsense	1737	99
Companion, The Agreeable	1745	107
Conjurer, The	1736	102
Connoisseur, The	1754	149
Convivial Magazine, The	1775	197

ALPHABETICAL LIST OF PERIODICALS

Title of Periodical.	Year of Issue.	Reference Page.
Country Spectator, The	1792	237
Court Magazine, The	1761	185
Covent Garden Journal, The	1752	113
Crab-tree, The	1757	168
Craftsman, The	1726	87
Critical Club, Letters of the	1738	102
Critical Review, The	1756	163
Daily Courant	1715	65
Defoe's Review	1704	15
Delights for the Ingenious	1711	51
Delphick Oracle, The	1719	61
Devil's Pocket Book, The	1786	225
Devil, The	1786	224
Dublin Gazette and Courant	1715	65
Echo, The, or Edinburgh Weekly Journal	1729	92
Edinburgh Magazine and Review	1773	193
Edinburgh Magazine, The	1757	170
Edinburgh Magazine, The	1785	210
Edinburgh Museum, The	1763	192
Edinburgh Review, The	1755	163
Englishman, The	1713	46
Englishman, The	1779	197
Entertainer, The	1717	71
Everyman's Magazine	1771	195
Examiner, The	1710	49
Examiner, The Whig	1710	55
Female Spectator, The	1744	106
Female Tatler, The	1709	30
Flying Post, The	1715	64
Fog's Weekly Journal	1732	80
Free Briton, The	1730	95
Freeholder, The	1715	55
Freethinker, The	1718	57
Friend, The	1796	243
Gentleman's and Lady's Weekly Magazine	1774	194
Gentleman's Magazine, The	1731	83
Ghost, The	1796	240
Gleaner, The	1795	242
Gray's Inn Journal	1752	157
Guardian, The	1713	39

THE EIGHTEENTH-CENTURY ESSAYISTS

Title of Periodical.	Year of Issue.	Reference Page.
Humorist, The	1725	81
Idler, The	1758	125
Ingenious, Delights for the	1711	51
Inspector, The	1751	156
Intelligencer, The	1728	92
Jacobite's Journal, The	1748	112
Ladies' Magazine, The	1749	86
Letters of the Critical Club	1738	102
Loiterer, The	1796	242
London Magazine, The	1732	84
Looker-on, The	1792	232
Lounger, The	1785	204
Lover, The	1714	52
Macaroni and Theatrical Magazine, The	1772	195
Memoirs of the Society of Grub Street	1730	94
Mercury, or The Northern Tatler	1717	73
Microcosm, The	1786	220
Mirror, The	1779	198
Mist's Weekly Journal	1715	65
Monitor, The	1755	162
Monitor, The	1757	169
Monthly Mirror, The	1795	257
Monthly Miscellany, The	1707	19
New Memoirs of Literature	1722	83
New Spectator	1784	214
New Town and Country Magazine, The	1787	252
New Universal Magazine, The	1754	161
Observer, The	1785	216
Occasional Papers	1716	71
Occasional Writer, The	1727	88
Occasional Writer, The	1738	104
Old Maid, The	1755	162
Old Whig, The	1719	61
Olla Podrida, The	1787	228
Parrot, The	1746	107
Pasquin	1723	62
Patriot, The	1740	104
Penny Medley, The	1746	107

ALPHABETICAL LIST OF PERIODICALS

Title of Periodical.	Year of Issue.	Reference Page.
Periodical Essays	1780	213
Pharos, The	1786	223
Plain Dealer, The	1724	76
Plain Dealer, The	1763	187
Plebeian, The	1719	61
Post Bag	1715	65
Post, The Flying	1715	64
Prater, The	1756	164
Public Ledger	1760	185
Rambler, The	1750	116
Reader, The	1714	54
Reveur, The	1737	101
Review, A (Defoe's)	1704	15
St James' Evening Post	1715	65
Scots Magazine, The	1739	85
Scourge, The	1752	158
Scourge, The	1780	213
Senator, The	1728	89
Spectator, The	1711	32
Spectator, The Country	1792	237
Spectator, The New	1784	214
Spectator, The Universal	1731	97
Speculator, The	1790	229
Spendthrift, The	1766	188
Student, The	1750	156
Sylph, The	1795	239
Tatler, The	1709	20
Tatler, The Female	1709	30
Tatler, The Northern, or The Mercury	1717	73
Tea-Table	1716	55
Tea-Table	1724	74
Templar and Literary Gazette, The	1773	196
Terræ Filius	1721	74
Test, The	1756	164
Theatre, The	1720	61
Town Talk	1715	54
Trifler, The	1788	221
Trifler, The	1795	240
True Briton, The	1723	62
True Patriot, The	1745	108, 112

THE EIGHTEENTH-CENTURY ESSAYISTS

Title of Periodical.	Year of Issue.	Reference Page.
Universal Spectator, The	1731	97
Universal Spy, The	1739	105
Universal Visiter, The	1756	164
Wanderer, The	1717	71
Weekly Amusement, The	1734	99
Weekly Amusement, The	1763	187
Weekly Magazine, The	1768	192
Whig Examiner, The	1710	55
Whisperer, The	1770	195
Whisperer, The	1795	238
Winter Evenings	1790	230
World, The	1753	141

Lightning Source UK Ltd.
Milton Keynes UK
UKHW011015210820
368606UK00002B/405